The Ultimate SAP® Pricing Guide

By Matthias Liebich

The Ultimate SAP® Pricing Guide

Published by eCruiting Alternatives, Inc. (JonERP.com)
Web site: JonERP.com
Author's Web site: mli-solutions.com
Editor's Web site: JonERP.com

ISBN: 978-0-9725988-6-6
Available retail from Amazon.com
Available wholesale from Ingram and Baker &Taylor

Copy Edit by Jennifer Gabrielle
Content Edit by Jennifer Gabrielle
Cover Design by Jon Reed and Rachel Meyers
Interior Book Design by Jennifer Gabrielle

Dedications

I'd like to dedicate this book to my wife Jennifer, and my children Jessica and Christopher, who gave me the time and support to fulfill my lifelong dream.

Acknowledgements

The author would like to thank the following people for their contributions to this book. Jon Reed for all his support, encouragement and advice in the publishing process. Thanks to Jennifer Gabrielle for editing the book. Thanks also to Rachel Meyers for assisting with the design of the book cover. Thanks to Andy Klee of ERPtips, who provided the initial publishing opportunity for my work on SAP Pricing, some of which turned into the foundation for this book. And finally, thank you to all my customers and to my fellow consultants, without whom I would never have had the experiences that contributed to this book.

Contents

Introduction

Pricing. Whenever this word is uttered during an SAP implementation, people start to clam up and want to crawl under a desk.

The Ultimate SAP Pricing Guide was written to alleviate this discomfort and fear, and to help you get a better understanding of how pricing works in SAP. Its goal is to explain in easy to understand terms and with plenty of examples how to set up pricing calculations, how they apply in daily business processes and how the standard settings can be manipulated to fit your business processes.

This book is written for business users and consultants alike.

As you will see, pricing in SAP is extremely flexible and can accommodate even the most complex pricing scenarios. The flip side of this flexibility? For the scope of this book, it is impossible to get into every possible permutation of pricing logic (and, of course, I would like to be able to sell you my consulting services at a later date).

This book aims to provide a solid understanding of how pricing works so you, the readers, will be able to apply it to your business requirements.

There are a few pre-requisites you should have, which will make the understanding of this *Pricing Guide* easier. You should have basic knowledge of how to navigate throughout the SAP system. Another pre-requisite is a basic understanding of how the organizational structure in the Sales and Distribution Module is set up and how the standard flow of documents from quote to cash works. Terms like transaction codes, Sales Area, customer and material, Sales Order, Delivery Note or Billing Document should not raise any eyebrows.

The Ultimate SAP Pricing Guide will not go into any Industry Solution applications such as IS-OIL or IS-Retail.

This *Pricing Guide* is structured in five main chapters.

Chapter 1 explains the Condition Technique, which is the basis of all pricing logic in SAP. All parts of the Condition Technique and their inter-connectivity are explained. With that knowledge you will be able to configure your own pricing design.

Chapter 2 describes several different ways to create, change and display pricing Condition Records, which are the master data of pricing. This chapter will also describe how to execute a mass price increase.

Chapter 3 explores the application of this master data on Sales Documents and Billing Documents in the SAP system.

Chapter 4 provides details on special pricing scenarios like Free Goods and Rebates, which also use the Condition Technique but reside outside the regular pricing setup.

Lastly, Chapter 5 gives insight into some custom modifications that can enhance the standard SAP pricing functionality.

The examples and screen captures in this Guide were done in an SAP ECC 6.0 system. However, the basic pricing functionality hardly changed since the SAP R/3 4.6 releases, so most explanations are valid for SAP systems from release 4.6C forward. Any specific changes between releases will be indicated when applicable.

Some of the fields described have check tables behind them with a number of possible entries; we will explore the values that fit with the explanation of a chapter.

Throughout the book I refer to previous configuration steps and chapters which, you will see, show how the pricing design comes full circle throughout the system.

Chapter 1: The Condition Technique

To understand how pricing works in SAP, it is important to be familiar with the SAP terminology used in this context. Pricing is one application of SAP's Condition Technique. Other applications such as Output or Text Determination also use the Condition Technique to flexibly apply Master Records based on specific criteria.

In this chapter, the following terms will be explained in great detail: Condition Table, Access Sequence, Condition Type, Pricing Procedure and Pricing Procedure Determination.

Before we go in depth into these terms, the following illustration in Figure 1.1 gives a visual overview of how pricing is configured in the SAP system versus how it applies on a Sales Document.

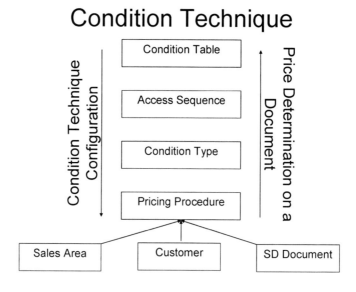

Figure 1.1: Flow of Condition Technique

If you review SAP's online documentation, you will find that the Condition Technique is explained in a different sequence as shown here. However, based on long years of experience, I am confident that the sequence of steps explained in this book makes it easier to understand how pricing works in the SAP system.

The Condition Table defines a combination of key fields by which valid pricing Master Records are identified.

The Access Sequence is the search strategy by which prices and discounts for a particular Condition Type are looked for in the system. It determines the sequence of Condition Tables in which the system searches for Condition Records.

The Condition Type defines the characteristic of a pricing element; for example, if it is a price or a discount.

The Pricing Procedure groups a number of Condition Types in a particular sequence that represents the total calculation of a pricing design.

The term "Condition Record" was already mentioned several times, although it does not appear in the graphic in Figure 1.1. A Condition Record is the master data record in which prices and discounts are stored. The combination of Condition Table, Access Sequence and Condition Type creates a unique Condition Record. Chapter 2 explains the creation of these Condition Records in great detail, and I will refer back to the Condition Technique configuration in that chapter.

Before trying to configure your SAP system to match your business pricing processes, the following questions need to be answered in order to ensure a sound design and an easy implementation of that pricing design:

- Which characteristics/fields are necessary to determine prices, discounts and surcharges?
- What type of prices, discounts and surcharges are there and in which order do they apply?
- Which prices, discounts and surcharges are stored in the system as Master Records and which ones are applied manually?

- Is the price calculation different by type of customer or Sales Order Type?
- What are the subtotals, like the gross and net value in the pricing schema, and which Condition Types do they consist of?

This chapter will show you how to set up your own pricing design.

Although I will indicate all IMG menu paths and transaction codes, I want to mention that transaction "VOKo" provides an overview menu for all the pricing relevant configuration tasks mentioned next.

Let's dive right into the first step of the pricing configuration to set up your own pricing design.

1.1 Condition Table

The Condition Table should be the first step in a pricing configuration. It defines the combination of key fields by which a pricing element, like a list price, is set up. These key fields can be a combination of organizational, customer master and material master fields.

Example:	Prices in our example company are set up by business group, price list type and material. The key combination, or Condition Table, in this case would be Sales Organization/ Distribution Channel/ Division/ Customer Price List Type/ Material Number.

In the standard version of the SAP R/3 system, a list of available fields with which a Condition Table can be built is stored in a "Field Catalog." This "Field Catalog" can be found in the IMG under menu path *SPRO-> Sales and Distribution-> Basic Functions-> Pricing-> Pricing Control-> Define Condition Tables.* From the following pop-up window, select "Conditions Allowed Fields." You will see a list of technical field names from the Data Dictionary (DDIC) with their respective descriptions (see Figure 1.1.1).

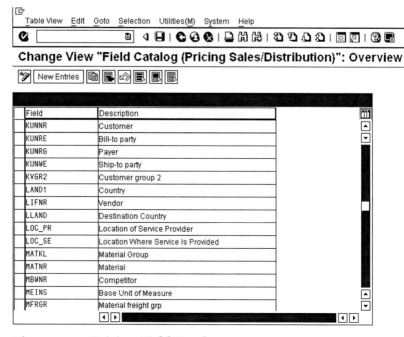

Figure 1.1.1: Pricing Field Catalog

This list is not a complete representation of all the organizational, customer or material master fields that are available in the SAP system. Scroll through the list to see which fields are available in the standard Field Catalog. If there is a field you would like to price on, but it is not in this list, click on the "New Entries" button and select the pull-down for field "Field." All available DDIC fields in the pricing communication structures "KOMG", "KOMK" (Header) and "KOMP" (item) will be displayed. Select the one you are looking for and save it to be included in the Field Catalog.

If a field name is added that already exists in the Field Catalogue, an appropriate error message is given. In case you attempt to add a field name that is not in the current DDIC structure for the pricing Field Catalog, such as the Sales Area specific "Customer Group 1" field, the error message "Field KVGR1 does not exist in table KOMG, KOMK, or KOMP" is displayed. Chapter 5.1 explains how any field you would like to price on can be added to the pricing Field Catalog.

Once you are confident that all the fields you want to price on are available, you need to identify an existing Condition Table or create a new one that fits your business needs. To do that, select IMG path *SPRO-> Sales and Distribution-> Basic Functions-> Pricing-> Pricing Control-> Define Condition Tables*. To display existing Condition Tables, select "Display Condition Tables" from the following pop-up screen. Select the pull-down of field "Table" and a list of available pricing Condition Tables will be displayed.

In case the desired key combination is not yet created, a new Condition Table can be created with the same IMG path as for the display function. Just select "Create Condition Tables" in the resulting pop-up. In the "Table" field in Figure 1.1.2, enter a three-digit number between 501 and 999. This is the available number range for SAP customer created Condition Tables, which is protected during SAP release upgrades. If a number was selected that already exists, the system will issue an appropriate error message. To avoid that, select the pull-down to see which table numbers are already taken.

To save time, an existing Condition Table can be copied by entering the existing Condition Table number in field "Table" in the "Copy from Condition" box in Figure 1.1.2. However, for the following example, let's walk through the creation of a Condition Table without referencing an existing Condition Table going forth.

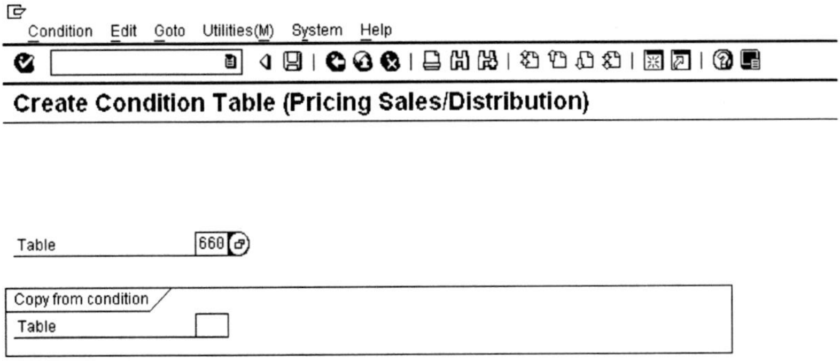

Figure 1.1.2: Creating a New Condition Table

After the new Condition Table number is entered (in our example "660" is entered), press enter. The following screen shows two columns in Figure 1.1.3.

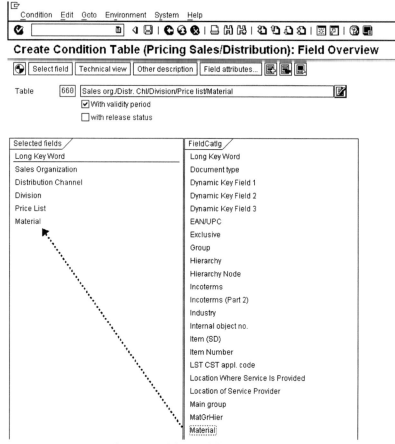

Figure 1.1.3: Condition Table Fields

The left column, labeled "Selected Fields," displays any selected fields of the Condition Table. The right column, labeled "FieldCatlg," displays the available fields from the Field Catalogue that was just discussed. Clicking on the "Other Description" button on the top of the screen toggles between the following different descriptions of the Field Catalog fields: "Long Keyword," "Short Description," "Technical and Medium,"

"Medium and Technical," "Short Keyword" or "Medium Keyword." To select a field from the right column, either double-click it or select it and press the "Select Field" button.

For our example, select these fields in the following order: "Sales Organization," "Distribution Channel," "Division," "Customer" and "Material Number."

As a general rule when creating custom Condition Tables, select document Header fields first, like "Sales Area" and "Customer." Then add line item fields such as "Material Number."

When creating your own Condition Tables, be aware that there is a maximum of 200 bytes for the length of the Condition Table. If you don't attempt to create a table with a crazy number of fields, this should be sufficient space. But if you want to see how long a field is before you select it from the Field Catalog, click on it once and press the "Field Attributes" button. This also works for fields that are already selected in the left column.

You should also be aware that the same field can't be selected twice.

If a field was selected by mistake, it can easily be deleted by selecting it in the "Selected Fields" column and pressing the "Delete Line" 🖰 button. Confirm that you want to delete the field in the resulting pop-up window.

If instead a field should be inserted in the Condition Table, select the field in front of which you would like to add the new field and press the "Insert Row" 🖰 button. Then select the field to be inserted from the Field Catalog. This is useful when an existing Condition Table is referenced and additional fields need to be added.

The description of the Condition Table changes on the top of the screen as fields are added. This defaulted description can be changed at any time by clicking on the "Propose/ Maintain Text" 🖰 button next to it.

Below the text field are two selection boxes. The "With Validity Period" option indicates that when Condition Records are created later, a beginning and an end date for when the price or discount should be valid will be assigned. Always select this box.

The second box, "With Release Status," is turned on by default. You should only turn this option on if you want to work with price releases. This functionality is explained in detail in Chapter 2.9 during Condition Record creation. For now, leave this field unchecked.

Once all required fields are selected, click on the "Technical View" button.

Figure 1.1.4: Technical View of Condition Table

The "Key" column in Figure 1.1.4 indicates which fields of the Condition Table define its key. Leave these defaults unchanged. The "Footer Fld" field indicates which fields of the Condition Table will appear on line item level of the "Fast Entry" screen when a Condition Record is created. Finally, the "Text" field defines which line item level field on the "Fast Entry" screen during Condition Record creation shows its field description. Only one of the fields can be selected to show this text. In addition, the DDIC fields of the selected table fields with their individual length are displayed on this screen.

After making all the necessary selections, the newly created Condition Table needs to be generated. To do that, click on the "Generate" 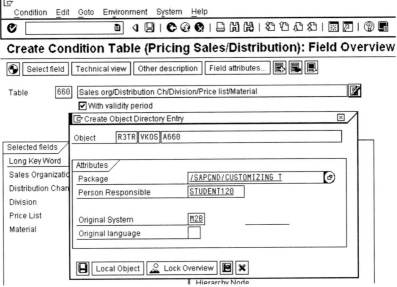 button. Confirm that you want to generate the Condition Table. On the resulting screen (see Figure 1.1.5), confirm that you want to generate the Condition Table and enter a development package from the available options. Since a Data Dictionary table is being created, the development area to which it should belong is identified in this development package.

Figure 1.1.5: Assignment of a Development Package

A message will confirm that the new Condition Table AXXX has been saved, where XXX=new Condition Table number

(660 in our example). The "A" identifies the generated Condition Table as a pricing table (see Figure 1.1.6).

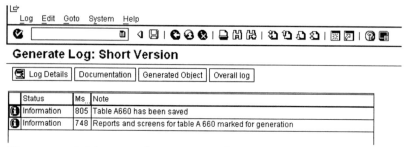

Figure 1.1.6: Message for Generated Condition Table

You can change a Condition Table by selecting IMG path *SPRO-> Sales and Distribution-> Basic Functions-> Pricing-> Pricing Control-> Define Condition Tables* and selecting "Change Condition Tables" from the resulting pop-up screen. The only thing that can be changed is the description of the Condition Table or the assignment of footer or text fields on the "Technical View" screen.

In Appendix A, you will find a list of Condition Technique-related Data Dictionary tables in which the Field Catalog resides.

1.2   Access Sequence

The Access Sequence represents a search strategy for finding a valid Condition Table. In Chapter 1.1 we defined the key combinations by which prices, discounts or surcharges are set up. A price can be set up by a number of different key combinations.

Example:	A list price can be created by either Sales Area/ Price List Type/ Material Number or by Sales Area/ Sold-to Customer Number/ Material Number

The Access Sequence determines the order in which the pricing Condition Technique looks up valid pricing Condition Tables.

In order to review existing Access Sequences, access IMG path *SPRO-> Sales and Distribution-> Basic Functions-> Pricing-> Pricing Control-> Define Access Sequences*. In the following pop-up, select "Maintain Access Sequences." On the next screen (see Figure 1.2.1), all available Access Sequences in the standard SAP system are displayed with their description.

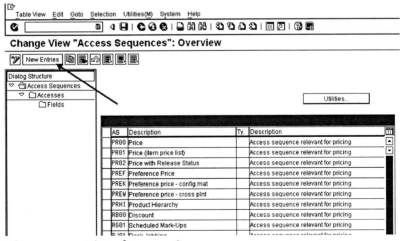

Figure 1.2.1: List of Access Sequences

To create a new Access Sequence, click on the "New Entries" button and enter a new four-character Access Sequence name. The first letter of the Access Sequence should be a "Z" to protect it from being overwritten during system upgrades. Enter "ZR01" for the Access Sequence and a description in field "Description." The "Ty" field should be left blank for pricing Access Sequences (see Figure 1.2.2).

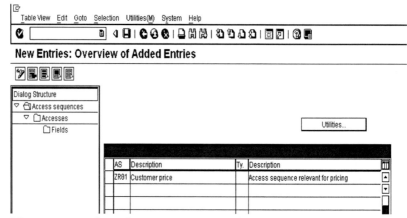

Figure 1.2.2: Creating a New Access Sequence

Select the line for "ZR01" and double-click on the "Accesses" folder in the left window pane. Since we are creating a new Access Sequence, no Condition Tables will be displayed initially in Figure 1.2.3. Click on the "New Entries" button on that screen and enter the Condition Tables for this newly created Access Sequence.

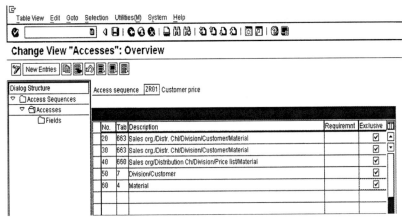

Figure 1.2.3: Condition Tables in an Access Sequence

Column "No." (called "AcNo" in prior SAP release ECC 6.0) indicates the sequential number of the Condition Table in the Access Sequence. The most specific Condition Table key should always be listed first, going from the most specific to the most generic one. In case of the "ZR01" Access Sequence (see Figure 1.2.3), the Condition Table including customer and material determines a more specific price than the last Condition Table in the sequence, which is material.

Enter the Condition Table number in the "Tab" column. By entering the number here, all fields of the Condition Table will be pulled into the Access Sequence. The description of the Condition Table is automatically displayed in column "Description." The same Condition Table can be listed more than once. This is useful when a Condition Type can be priced by different partner types, like Sold-to, Ship-to or Payer. There is no need to create separate Condition Tables for that. Different partner types can be assigned in the next configuration step.

The "Requirement" column allows the addition of pieces of ABAP code that controls whether a Condition Table can apply under certain circumstances or not. I will go into more detail about requirements in Chapter 1.4.

The use of the "Exclusions" column improves system performance by selecting it for each Condition Table in the Access Sequence. The system will stop looking for valid Condition

Records after finding a valid one in its Access Sequence search, if this field is selected.

For our example, enter the Condition Tables as indicated in Figure 1.2.3.

To see which fields are populating the Condition Table in the Access Sequence, select one Condition Table (for our example, table "663") and double-click the "Fields" folder in the left window pane.

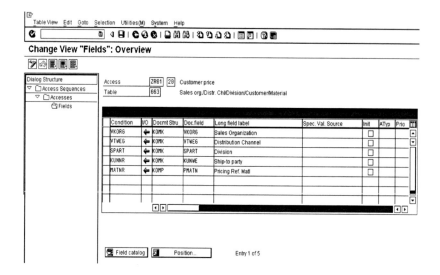

Figure 1.2.4: Fields View of an Access Sequence Table

The DDIC field names of the source fields of the Condition Table are displayed in Figure 1.2.4. DDIC table "KOMK" indicates fields from the document Header, "KOMP" from the document line item. If you would like to change the source of a field, select the respective line of the field you want to change and click on the "Field Catalog" button. The Field Catalog, as discussed in Chapter 1.1, is displayed in Figure 1.2.5 where you can select the desired field.

For example, the field in the Condition Table is "Customer." The default source field is "Sold-to." If you want to change the source to be the "Ship-to" number, select field "KOMK-KUNWE" (see the framed fields in Figure 1.2.5). Of course, the selection of the source field has to make sense: you don't want to select material number as the source for the customer number.

If a value is entered in column "Spec. Val. Source" (see Figure 1.2.4), it becomes the default value for this Condition Table field during pricing on a document. This default value overwrites the value that would normally originate from the source field.

Table Name Field Name	Short Description Short Description			Short	Medium Field Label	Long field label
KUNNR	Sold-to party			Sold-to pt	Sold-to party	Sold-to party
KUNRE	Bill-to party			Bill to	Bill-to party	Bill-to party
KUNWE	Ship-to party			Ship-to	Ship-to party	Ship-to party
LAND1	Country of Destination			Dest. Ctry	Dest. Country	Destination Country
LIFNR	Vendor Account Number			Vendor	Vendor	Vendor
MVGR1	Material group 1			Matl grp 1	Material Group 1	Material group 1
MWSKZ	Sales Tax Code			Tax Code	Tax Code	Tax Code
PLTYP	Price list type			Price list	Price List	Price List
VKBUR	Sales Office			Sales Off.	Sales Office	Sales Office
VKGRP	Sales Group			Sales Grp	Sales Group	Sales Group
VKORG	Sales Organization			Sales org.	Sales Org.	Sales Organization
VKORGAU	Sales organization of sales order			SOrg-order	SOrg of order	Sales org. of order
VSBED	Shipping Conditions			Shpg Cond.	Shipping Cond.	Shipping Conditions
VTWEG	Distribution Channel			Distr. Chl	Distr. Channel	Distribution Channel
WAERK	SD Document Currency			Currency	Doc. Currency	Document Currency
WERKS	Plant			Plant	Plant	Plant
KOMP	Determination item					
ADDNR	Material number for additional			Additional	Additional	Additional
AKTNR	Promotion			Promotion	Promotion	Promotion
AUBEL	Sales Document			Sales Doc.	Sales Document	Sales Document
AUPOS	Sales Document Item			Item	Item	Sales Document Item
BEMOT	Accounting Indicator			AcctIndic	Acctg Indicator	Accounting Indicator
BONUS	Volume rebate group			Rebate grp	Vol. rebate grp	Volume rebate group

Figure 1.2.5: Source Fields for an Access Sequence Table

It is important to get to the field level for every single Condition Table in the Access Sequence, even if no source fields are being changed. The Access Sequence will not work if this step is missed.

After going through the field level step for all Condition Tables, save the Access Sequence.

1.3 Condition Type

The Condition Type is the heart of the pricing configuration. The most important settings are made in this configuration step. The Condition Type defines what type of pricing element it is. It can be a price, a discount or surcharge, a tax or an expense (Rebate) item. The Condition Type defines if the amount of the pricing condition is positive, negative or if it can be both. It defines if changes to the Condition Type are allowed on a Sales Document and much more. The most important fields in the configuration of the Condition Type are explained below.

To display an existing Condition Type, select IMG path *SPRO-> Sales and Distribution-> Basic Functions-> Pricing -> Pricing Control-> Define Condition Types.* In the following pop-up, select "Maintain Condition Types." The following Figure 1.3.1 shows the "Condition Type Overview" screen.

CTyp	Condition Type	Condition class	Calculation type
PR00	Price	Prices	Quantity
PR01	Price incl.Sales Tax	Prices	Quantity
PR02	Price Increased	Prices	Quantity
PR0T	Price for Transfer	Prices	Quantity
PR10	Price for base scale	Prices	Quantity
PR11	Price for to-scale	Prices	Quantity
PR12	Price Interval Scale	Prices	Quantity
PRA0	Promo SP wholesale 1	Prices	Quantity
PRA1	Promo SP wholesale 2	Prices	Quantity
PREF	Preference	Prices	Quantity
PRRP	Repair Price	Prices	Quantity
PSPM	Margin	Discount or surcharge	Percentage (travel expense
PSPR	Profit	Discount or surcharge	Percentage
PSVB	Sales price basis	Prices	Quantity
PTAM	American Express	Discount or surcharge	Fixed amount
PTBL	Invoice amount	Discount or surcharge	Fixed amount
PTCH	Payment Type - Check	Discount or surcharge	Fixed amount
PTCS	Payment Type - Cash	Discount or surcharge	Fixed amount

Figure 1.3.1 Overview of Condition Types

For an example of a Condition Type, select the SAP standard price condition "PR00" and click on the "Details" 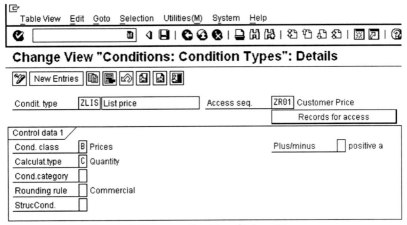 button.

Figure 1.3.2: Control Data 1 of a Condition Type

On the top of the screen in Figure 1.3.2, the Condition Type and its description are displayed. This description will print on an Invoice or order acknowledgment. In field "Access seq." the previously created Access Sequence "ZR01" from Chapter 1.2 is assigned. During document processing the system then knows for which Condition Tables in the Access Sequence to find Condition Records of this Condition Type. If the Condition Type should not be using Condition Records, but only be applied manually on a document, no Access Sequence needs to be assigned here. Certain fields in the Condition Type configuration will become unavailable in this instance (for example: "Condition Index," "Reference Condition Type" and "Reference Application").

The "Records for Access" button will let you branch out to transaction "VK13" to display Condition Records of this Condition Type.

In the "Control Data 1" box of Figure 1.3.2, the following functions can be defined (for a full list of possible entries of any of the fields, select the pull-down menu for each respective field):

Cond. Class: The Condition Class identifies the Condition Type as a price, a discount or surcharge, or a tax or Rebate (expense item). This identification is important since it defines later, during document processing, how the Condition Type behaves. For example, there can only be one active price Condition Type, but multiple valid discounts can apply at the same time on a Sales Order line item.

Calculat.type: The Calculation Type indicates how the Condition Type is being calculated. A quantity Calculation Type will calculate a price per unit. A gross weight condition, on the other hand, would calculate a price per the gross weight of the product you are selling. The Calculation Type also controls the allowable field inputs during pricing. For example, when you try to create a Condition Record for a Condition Type that has a percentage Calculation Type, the pricing Unit of Measure automatically defaults to "%".

Cond.Category: With the Condition Category it is possible to group multiple Condition Types together. For example, all freight-related Condition Types could be assigned to Condition Category "F" for freight. This becomes important when I discuss Pricing Rules in Chapter 3.4. Certain Pricing Rules re-price all freight conditions, which will be identified by the "F" in the "Condition Category" field. Another example is to assign all tax Condition Types to the same Condition Category. As you can see when you select the pull-down for this field, there are several categories labeled as "Customer Reserve." This allows the creation of your own groupings that can later be used in a custom Pricing Rule.

Rounding Rule: This field defines how a Condition Value is rounded. A blank entry in this field rounds based on common business rules (i.e., 20.355 rounds up to 20.36 and 25.544 rounds down to 25.54). Different rounding rules for entries in this field are value "A," which will always round up (i.e., 20.351 rounds to 20.36) or value "B," which will always round down (i.e., 21.459 rounds to 21.45).

StrucCond.: This field is only necessary if you are pricing materials with a sale Bill of Material (BOM), such as configurable materials. For all other pricing scenarios, this field will remain blank. If configurable materials are used, set an "A" if the value of the higher level item should be duplicated to all lower level items of your Bill of Material. With a "B" setting in this field, the values of all the respective sub-item conditions would be accumulated into the higher level item.

Plus/Minus: If you want to allow only positive values for the specified Condition Type, mark this field with an "A." This setting is valid for entries in Condition Records as well as manual entries on any kind of Sales Document. Even if the entry of a negative value is attempted, the system will revert back to a positive value. I highly recommend setting the positive value for any price Condition Types you might use. In contrast, the value of "X" in this field will only allow negative values. This should be the setting for all discount-related Condition Types. A blank value in this field will allow both.

The "Group Condition" box in Figure 1.3.3 enables Condition Types to be used as Group Conditions:

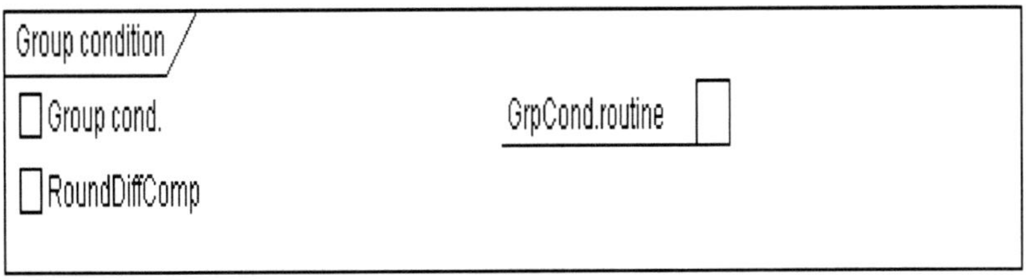

Figure 1.3.3: Group Condition Settings of a Condition Type

Group cond.: Checking this field indicates that the Condition Type is a Group Condition. For the Scale Basis in a Sales Document, this means the system takes the sum of multiple items into account to determine the Scale level. More about Group Conditions in Chapter 3.9.

GrpCond.routine: This field goes along with the Group Condition setting. Here it is defined which items will be valid to be included in a Group Condition calculation. The following options are available in the standard SAP system:

- Blank = Order quantities of line items with the same Condition Type and Condition Table key are added to the Scale Base Value. Example: Both line items need to have Condition Type "ZG03" apply with a key combination of Sales Area/ Customer/ Material. If one line item had the "ZG03" with a different key combination, the quantities would not be added.

- 1 = The same as the blank rule with the exception that the applied Condition Table keys can be different. One line item can have a "ZG03" apply by Sales Area/ Customer/ Material and another a "ZG03" by Sales Area/Material, and both line item quantities would be added to the Scale Base Value.

- 2 = A combination of the blank and "1" rule. Line item quantities are combined to the Scale Base Value if they have the same Condition Type or a different Group Condition Type with the same Group Condition Routine "2" and the same or different Condition Table key.

- 3 = Only line item quantities of items that have the same Condition Type and the same Material Pricing Group and the same or different Condition Table key are added to the Scale Base Value.

If none of these routines satisfies your business needs, you can certainly define your own Group Condition routine. Go to transaction "VOFM" and select *Formulas-> Structure of grp. Key,* to add a routine in the customer reserved area, starting with number 500.

RoundDiffComp: The "Rounding Difference Comparison" field is used if a Group Condition amount is distributed across multiple line items. For example, if the Group Condition amount is $100 and this amount should get distributed across the three line items on the Sales Document, $33.33 would be allocated to each line item. The sum of the line items ($99.99) is then compared with the amount from the Header ($100). Checking the rounding field will allocate the difference between these amounts to the item with the largest net value, making it therefore $33.34. If all line items are the same, the difference is allocated to the last line item. If no Group Condition Rounding is specified, the system automatically assigns the rounding difference to the last line item, regardless of its value. If the defined Condition Type is a Fixed Amount (Calculation Type "B"), the setting of the Rounding Difference Comparison flag is mandatory.

Group Conditions also work in unison with the Alternate Condition Base Value in the Pricing Procedure (see Chapter 1.4).

The "Changes which can be made" box summarizes changes that you do or do not allow for pricing:

Changes which can be made			
Manual entries	C Manual entry has priority		
☐ Header condit.		☑ Amount/percent	☐ Qty relation
☑ Item condition	☐ Delete	☐ Value	☐ Calculat.type

Figure 1.3.4: Possible Changes Within a Condition Type

Manual Entries: This field determines if values of Condition Records or manual entries for the same Condition Type in a Sales Document take priority. No entry or an entry of "A" in this field will allow any kind of changes.

Blank and "A" = No limitations.

B = The value of the Condition Record takes precedence over any manual entry. This means if a Condition Record exists, no manual entry is possible. If no Condition Record could be determined, a manual entry would be possible.

C = The manual entry has priority. If a value for this Condition Type is entered manually, the system does not check for a Condition Record.

D = No manual entry is possible.

Header Condition: This field indicates if the Condition Type can be entered on the "Header Condition" screen of a Sales Document. The amounts that are entered on the Header are either applied with the same amount to all line items or are distributed across the line items by a pre-defined key (Chapter 1.4 about Pricing Procedures has more details about that). If a Condition Type is flagged as a Header Condition only (meaning not also as an Item Condition), no Access Sequence can be assigned to it. This is because pricing determination occurs at line item level; therefore, the "Manual Entries" settings explained before are not applicable for a Header Condition.

Item Condition: This setting means the Condition Type can be entered at the line item level of a document. A Condition Type can be marked as Header and as Item Condition. This setting also allows the assignment of an Access Sequence to the Condition Type and therefore the creation of Condition Records.

Delete: Indicates whether the Condition Type can be deleted from a Sales Document. Checking this field allows a price that applied based on a Condition Record to be deleted. For Condition Types that are determined automatically, I suggest you do not check this field for much better audit control. If a price would be incorrect, change the Condition Record and re-price the Sales Document line item instead. The correct price will then apply the next time this item is sold. Conditions that are entered manually on a Sales Document can always be deleted, even if the "Delete" field is not checked.

Amount/percent: Checking this field allows the manual change of the amount or the percentage value of the Condition Type in a document.

Value: Turning on this field allows the manual change of the total value of a Condition Type.

Qty Relation: This setting allows the change of the conversion factors of the pricing Unit of Measure (UoM). For example, instead of $10 per 1 piece you could change the quantity relation to $10 per 10 pieces.

Calculation type: Checking this field allows the change of the Calculation Type of the Condition Type. Instead of a quantity-related condition, you could change it to a gross weight-related Condition Type.

The "Master Data" box in Figure 1.3.5 includes settings that relate to the creation of Condition Records:

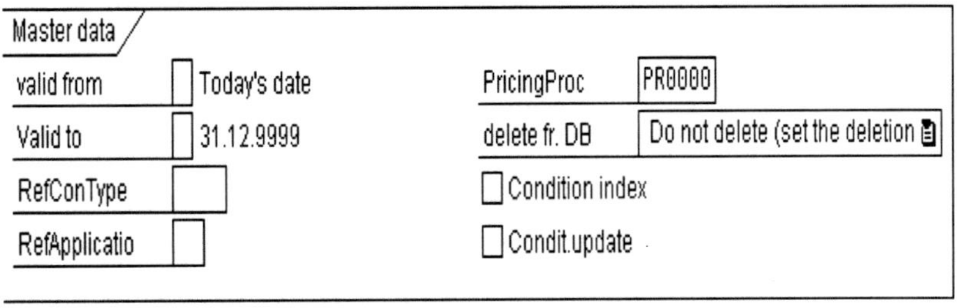

Figure 1.3.5: Master Data Fields of a Condition Type

Valid From: Whenever a Condition Record is created, a date from which the record should be valid needs to be entered. The "Valid From" field determines the default in the Condition Record. Leaving it blank will default the date on which the Condition Record is entered as the "Valid From" date. A value of "2" in this field would instead default the first day of the current month. Select the pull-down next to this field for more options.

Valid To: Each Condition Record also has a date on which the validity ends. This "Valid To" date is defaulted based on this setting. A blank value will default the date of 12/31/9999, or the "End of Time," as I call it. A value of "1" in this field would default the end of the current month. I suggest using the "End of Time" setting. I will explain the reason behind this when I discuss Condition Record creation and maintenance.

RefConType: You can reference Condition Records of another Condition Type with the "Reference Condition Type" field. This eliminates dual maintenance.

RefApplicatio: This field represents the system application from which the Reference Condition Type is referenced. Within Sales and Distribution, "V" is the correct entry. More about this use in Chapter 2.12 regarding Condition Record maintenance.

PricingProc: If Condition Supplements are being used, the Supplement Pricing Procedure is entered in this field. Supplements are being used when a Condition Type should be applied based on the existence of another Condition Type (which is explained in Chapter 1.4.2).

Delete fr. DB: This setting defines how Condition Records are deleted. Prior to SAP R/3 release 4.6, a Condition Record was "Marked for Deletion" when it was deleted. The Condition Record then still existed in the SAP system but was ignored during pricing in a Sales Document. This allowed the option to "un-delete" the Condition Record in case it was unintentionally deleted. Archiving of pricing Condition Records also takes this "Marked for Deletion" indicator into account. Another option for this field is to delete the Condition Record from the database entirely. In that case, you have the option to define if a pop-up window with a warning is issued before finally deleting the record, or to delete it right away.

Condition update: Turning on this field tracks how often a Condition Record for this Condition Type is used and allows you to set limits on it as well (for example, how many times it can be used). Chapter 3.7 explains this in detail.

The "Scales" box in Figure 1.3.6 addresses the use of Scales within a Condition Record:

Scales			
Scale basis	C Quantity scale	Scale formula	
Check value	A Descending	Unit of meas.	PC
Scale type	can be maintained in con		

Figure 1.3.6: Scales Settings of a Condition Type

Scale Basis: Defines the values on which the Scale is based. A quantity Scale, for example, uses the number of units to determine which level of the Scale is reached. A volume Scale would use the volume of the item. For a complete list of possible Scale Basis Types, click on the pull-down for this field.

Check Value: This field determines if the Scale values for the respective Condition Type should be ascending or descending. A descending Scale might look like this:

From 1 PC	$ 10
From 10 PC	$ 8
From 100 PC	$ 5

The "Descending" term is related to the price, not the quantity levels of the Scale. This means that the quantity of units is ascending with each level of the Scale and the price for each level is actually being reduced. The more you buy of an item, the less you pay for it. If the dollar amounts were set to increase with each level in a descending Scale Condition Record, the system would issue an information message and will not let you save the Condition Record. A descending Scale is most common for a "Base-Scale."

Scale Type: The Scales functionality is discussed in detail in Chapter 3.8. This configuration field determines what type of Scale should be used. The Scale Types available in the standard SAP system are "Base-Scale," "To-Scale," and "Graduated-to Interval Scale." No entry in this field lets you determine the type of Scale in the actual Condition Record.

Scale Formula: The SAP system allows adding custom code via the "Scale Formula" field to determine a different Scale Basis for the Condition Type than what the standard system calculates. This will be discussed in more detail in Chapter 3.8 about Scales.

Unit of Meas.: Depending on the Scale Basis, a default Unit of Measure (UoM) can be entered in this configuration field, which will automatically apply in the Condition Record. For example, for a weight-related Scale, "LBS" or "KG" can be defaulted. The Scale UoM can be different than the actual pricing UoM. For example, the Condition Type may be quantity dependent, but the Scale is volume based. The price would apply per unit, but the Scale would be determined by the number of cubic feet (CFT).

An exception to the default UoM is if a Condition Record has the material number as part of its key. In this case, the base UoM of that material would apply as the Scale UoM, regardless of what the configured default UoM indicates. Any Condition Record without a material number in its key will take the configuration UoM as its default. If no configuration UoM exists, the system will prompt for the input of a valid UoM at Condition Record maintenance time.

The "Control Data 2" section in Figure 1.3.7 defines additional settings that allow a Condition Type to behave in different ways:

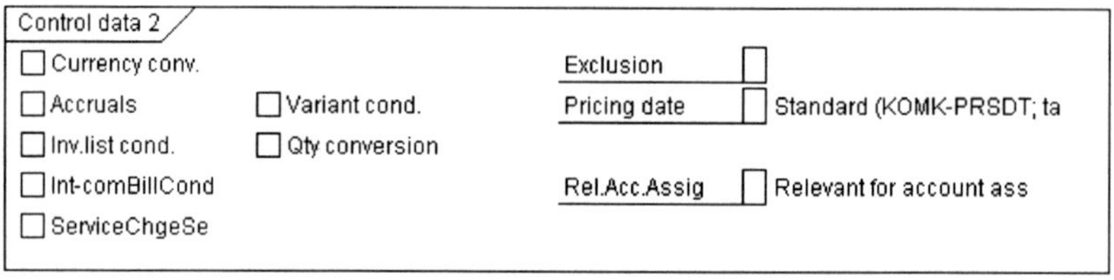

Control data 2		
☐ Currency conv.		Exclusion ☐
☐ Accruals	☐ Variant cond.	Pricing date ☐ Standard (KOMK-PRSDT; ta
☐ Inv.list cond.	☐ Qty conversion	
☐ Int-comBillCond		Rel.Acc.Assig ☐ Relevant for account ass
☐ ServiceChgeSe		

Figure 1.3.7: Control Data 2 Settings of a Condition Type

Currency conv.: The system calculates the Condition Value of an item by multiplying the rate amount from the Condition Record with the item quantity (or any other measure depending on the Calculation Type of the Condition Type). The "Currency Conversion" field comes into play when the currency of the Condition Record differs from the currency of the Sales Document that is being created. The field determines when the currency conversion takes place in that scenario. If this field is turned on, the conversion takes place after the multiplication of rate times units. If it is left blank, the Condition Record rate is converted first before it is multiplied to the Condition Value.

Accruals: Turning this field on will post the amounts of this Condition Type to financial accounting as accruals. The Condition Type will show on the document as "Statistical," which means the amount will not be added to the net value of the item and the customer will not be charged for it.

Int-comBillCond: In SAP releases prior to 4.0, it was not possible to define an inter-company Condition Type as a freight Condition at the same time. Checking this field identifies the Condition Type as an inter-company condition and allows the assignment of a freight Condition Category in addition. If this field is not checked, the Condition Type will not apply on the "IV" inter-company Invoice.

Variant cond.: In SAP releases prior to 4.0, it was not possible to define a variant Condition Type as freight or for inter-company billing at the same time. This flag identifies the Condition Type as a variant condition so it can be used in addition for inter-company billing or freight. For this and the "Inter-company" field, read OSS note 93426 for additional information.

Qty conversion: The pricing UoM, the sales UoM and the base UoM of an item can all be different. The "Quantity Conversion" flag determines which quantities are used when the Condition Value of an item is determined. If the field is checked, and the sales and pricing UoM are the same, the quantity of the Sales Document item is used for the calculation. If the field is left blank, the sales quantity is converted to the quantity in base UoM of the material, which, however, can cause rounding errors.

Exclusion: This indicator lets you exclude Condition Records from applying on a document in concert with a pricing requirement. This was the old way of doing exclusions prior to SAP release 4.0A. Examples of how this old exclusion worked and the new exclusion functionality are described in Chapter 3.6.

Pricing Date: Each Sales Document line item has a Pricing Date. This date is used to determine if a Condition Record Validity date range is within this date in order to apply on the document. That line item Pricing Date is valid for all Condition Types. The Pricing Date on the Condition Type, however, will supersede the line item Pricing Date if it is set. For example, you might want to price a freight condition based on the goods issue date but price all other items based on the order date. In that example, enter "A" in the "Pricing Date" field of the freight Condition Type.

Finally, the "Text Determination" box in Figure 1.3.8 allows the assignment of a text procedure that includes one or more text types. This will allow you to enter text during Condition Record Maintenance.

Figure 1.3.8: Text Determination of a Condition Type

TextDetPrc: Enter the Text Determination Procedure in this field. Text is being configured with transaction "VOTXN", option "Pricing Conds."

Text ID: Enter the Text ID that should be maintained during Condition Record maintenance.

1.4 Pricing Procedure

So far, you learned what type of prices, surcharges, discounts and taxes comprise the way the final price for a customer is calculated. The sequence in which this calculation is processed is defined in a Pricing Procedure. This pricing schema defines which Condition Types are used, under which circumstances they are allowed or blocked, what subtotals exist and to which G/L accounts each active Condition Type should be posted.

To create, change or display a Pricing Procedure, go to the IMG path *SPRO-> Sales and Distribution-> Basic Functions-> Pricing-> Pricing Control-> Define And Assign Pricing Procedures*. Select "Maintain Pricing Procedures" from the resulting pop-up menu.

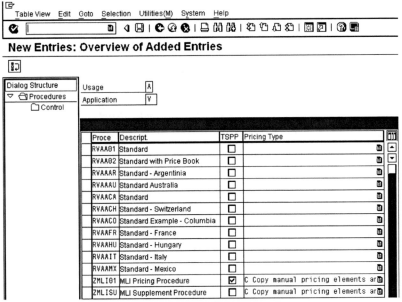

Figure 1.4.1: List of Pricing Procedures

A list of Pricing Procedures with their respective descriptions is displayed in Figure 1.4.1. On top of the screen, the fields "Usage" with value "A" and "Application" with value "V" indicate the listed Pricing Procedures are related to Sales and Distribution pricing. In comparison, in a different configuration task, Shipment Cost Pricing Procedures are shown as Usage "A" (remember, our Condition Tables started with an "A" indicating that it is related to pricing) and Application "F" for "Shipment Cost."

The field "Pricing Type" allows the definition of a Pricing Rule to be used when manually updating Sales Orders with *Edit->New Pricing Document* (see Chapter 3.4). Leaving the "Pricing Type" field blank will apply Price Type "B" as a default rule during re-pricing.

To create a new Pricing Procedure, click on the "New Entries" button. Enter a six-character alphanumeric Pricing Procedure name starting with a "Z" in field "Procedure" and its description in field "Descript.." For the examples in this book, Pricing Procedure "ZMLI01" was created. Select that line and double-click the "Control Data" folder in the left window pane.

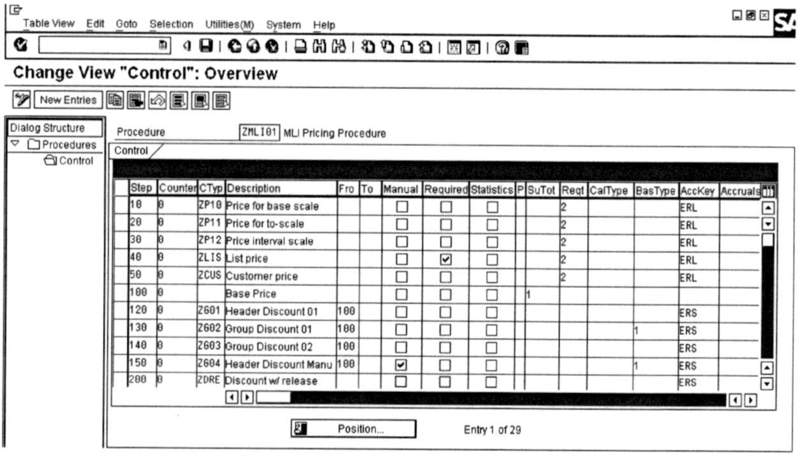

Figure 1.4.2: Pricing Procedure Details

Figure 1.4.2 displays custom Pricing Procedure "ZMLI01". Besides the Condition Type created in Chapter 1.3, several other custom Condition Types were created for the examples in this book. These are displayed in the Pricing Procedure above. For your purposes, either use standard SAP Condition Types or create more custom Condition Types to create your own Pricing Procedure. The fields in the Pricing Procedure and their meaning are explained in this chapter.

Step: This is a three-digit numeric field that identifies the sequence of Condition Types and subtotals in the Pricing Procedure. I recommend reserving adequate space for each logical group of Condition Types. For example, price Condition Types could be in a range from 0-100, discounts from 200-300 and so on. I also recommend starting with steps in increments of 10, which will make it much easier to insert Condition Types or subtotals at a later time. Pricing Procedures with steps like 1, 3, 5 will require the re-numbering of the whole Pricing Procedure if additional steps need to be inserted later.

Counter: This two-digit numeric field defines the sequence of Condition Types within a Step number. This field is rarely used.

Ctyp: Enter the applicable Condition Type in the "Condition Type" field. Leaving this field blank defines a subtotal in the Pricing Procedure.

Description: Description of the Condition Type from Condition Type configuration. This field is automatically filled.

Fro: This field indicates the Step number from which the current line in the Pricing Procedure is referencing its Condition Base Value. This is used for percentage-based Condition Types or subtotals.

To: This field indicates the Step number up to which the current line in the Pricing Procedure is referencing its Condition Base Value. This is used for percentage-based Condition Types or subtotals. Together with the "Fro" field, it defines a range of Condition Type values as reference. For example, you might want to base your cash discount on the gross value of a line item that is calculated from line 10 to 50. However, there are several Condition Types between line 50 and let's say 600 where the cash discount Condition Type is listed. Enter "From" line 10 and "To" line 50 for the cash discount Condition Type, and the percentage is calculated from that Base Value. Another option is to create a subtotal line after step 50 and reference this subtotal line for the cash discount.

Manual: The "Manual" indicator defines if a Condition Type can be applied manually in the Pricing Procedure.

Required: This field indicates if the respective Condition Type is mandatory. In SAP releases prior to ECC 6.0, this column was labeled "Mandatory." If the Condition Type has no valid Condition Record or is not entered manually, the line item on the Sales Document becomes incomplete due to incomplete pricing. It is common to make your base price mandatory. That's how you catch missing pricing Condition Records for new items or new customers that were created.

Statistics: Setting a Condition Type as statistical will not include its value in the calculated net value of the line item that is being charged to the customer. Accrual Condition Types are automatically statistical and don't have to be flagged as such in the Pricing Procedure.

Print: This field indicates if the Condition Type should be printed on a Sales Order confirmation or an Invoice. Leaving this field blank will not print the Condition Type and its value. A value of "a" (note this is lowercase) will print the Condition Type with its value at line item level. A value of "A" (now uppercase) prints the Condition Type sum of all line items at the end of the Sales Document in the "Totals" section.

SuTot: The "Subtotal" field allows you to store the value of a Condition Type or a subtotal line in one of the pre-defined fields that are available in the pull-down list. For example, in order for credit checking to work, the value of the credit amount has to be stored in subtotal "A." Rebate processing (see Chapter 4.3) will only work if the amounts that the Rebate conditions refer to are stored in subtotals. These fields are available for SIS reporting as well. If the same subtotal value is indicated for multiple Condition Types in the same Pricing Procedure, the system accumulates the values.

Reqt: The "Requirement" field controls if and when a Condition Type is taken into account in the calculation of the total value of an item. The Requirement number refers to a piece of ABAP code that describes these requirements. There are several standard requirements to choose from, but you can create your own requirement to suit your business needs (see Chapter 5.3 on how to do that). Requirement "2," for example, checks if the item category of the line item is relevant for pricing and that the Exclusion Indicator (see configuration of Condition Types in Chapter 1.3) is not turned on for the Condition Type. Only if these conditions are met will the system look for valid Condition Records.

CalType: The "Alternate Calculation Type" is also a piece of ABAP code that allows you to calculate the value of a Condition Type differently than the standard system would. We will look into an example in Chapter 3.5 for the Customer Expected Price.

BasType: The "Alternate Condition Base Value" field is also a piece of ABAP code that allows you to set the Condition Calculation Basis to something different than the standard. For example, if a Header Condition is a Group Condition and is supposed to distribute its total value to all line items by volume, the Alternate Condition Base Value would be "1." The system then takes the line item volume in relation to the other line items into account and distributes the Header value accordingly.

Example:	Header Condition $100
	Line item 10: Volume 20 CFT
	Line item 20: Volume 50 CFT
	Line item 30: Volume 30 CFT
	An Alternate Condition Base Value of "1" would therefore allocate $20 to line 10, $50 to line 20 and $30 to line 30.

AccKey: The "Account Key" is used in Account Determination to post the value of a Condition Type to the appropriate G/L account.

Accruals: This Account Key is used in Account Determination to post the value of an accrual Condition Type to the appropriate accrual accounts. Rebate Condition Types, for example, use this field (see Chapter 4.3).

Once all necessary entries are made, save the newly created Pricing Procedure.

1.4.2   Condition Supplements

As mentioned in the Condition Types chapter, it is possible to maintain a Condition Supplement Pricing Procedure for the Condition Type in field "PricingProc" (see Figure 1.3.5). This Condition Supplement Pricing Procedure includes the Condition Type for which Condition Supplements should be maintained, as well as the Supplement Condition Types. The maintenance of the Condition Supplement Pricing Procedure is the same as that of a regular Pricing Procedure. However, a few things are to be considered when using Condition Supplements:

- The Condition Supplement Pricing Procedure needs to include the Condition Type for which a Condition Supplement is maintained.

- The regular Pricing Procedure has to include the Condition Type for which a Condition Supplement is maintained, as well as the Supplement Condition Types.

- The Step numbering of the main Pricing Procedure takes precedence over the numbering in the Supplement Pricing Procedure. This means that if the Supplement Condition Type was in step 20 of the Supplement Pricing Procedure but is in step 300 of the main Pricing Procedure, it will apply as step 300 after all the preceding Condition Types.

- Any Condition Type can serve as a Condition Supplement Condition Type for another Condition Type.

Figure 1.4.2.1 displays the Supplement Pricing Procedure "ZMLISU":

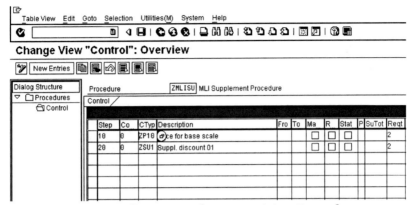

Figure 1.4.2.1: Condition Supplement Pricing Procedure

Chapter 2 explains the Condition Record maintenance and goes into detail on how to maintain the Supplement Condition Types.

1.5 Pricing Procedure Determination

The last configuration step necessary to have pricing apply on a Sales Document is to assign the Pricing Procedure based on certain criteria. This is done by using IMG path *SPRO-> Sales and Distribution-> Basic Functions-> Pricing-> Pricing Control-> Define And Assign Pricing Procedures.* There are several options in the resulting pop-up screen that are required for the determination of the proper Pricing Procedure. They are explained in this chapter.

A unique Pricing Procedure is determined by a combination of the following: Sales Organization, Distribution Channel, Division, Document Pricing Procedure Indicator and Customer Pricing Procedure Indicator.

Document Pricing Procedure Indicator

Select "Define Document Pricing Procedure" in the configuration pop-up. Individual Pricing Procedure Indicators for Sales Documents and Billing Documents are defined here. You can have a different indicator for a regular Sales Order Type "OR" and a different one for a Sample Order (e.g., for which you don't charge the customer). For a sample listing of Sales Document Pricing Procedure Indicators, please see Figure 1.5.1.

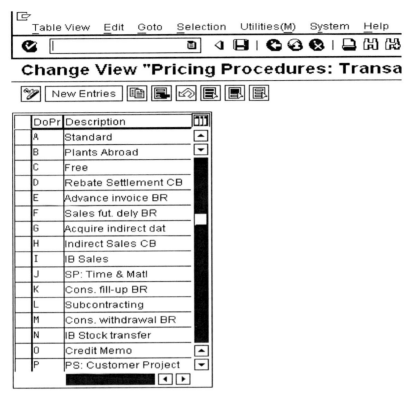

Figure 1.5.1: Document Pricing Procedure Indicators

The assignment to a Sales Document Type (see Figure 1.5.2) occurs in the option "Assign Document Pricing Procedure To Order Types" in the configuration pop-up. The assignment could also be made directly in the configuration setting of the Sales Order Type in configuration step *SPRO-> Sales and Distribution-> Sales-> Sales Documents-> Sales Document Header-> Define Sales Document Types* or transaction "VOV8".

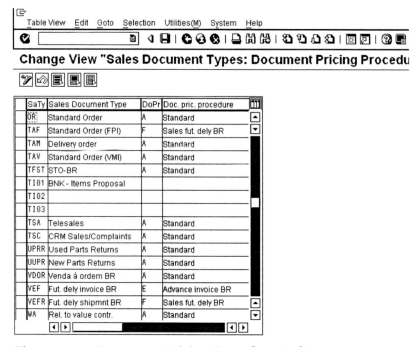

Figure 1.5.2: Document Pricing Procedure Indicator Assignment to Sales Order Types

The assignment of a Pricing Procedure Indicator to a Billing Document (see Figure 1.5.3) occurs in configuration step "Assign Document Pricing Procedure To Billing Types." The reasons for having a potentially different assignment at billing time are explained in Chapter 3.4 when I discuss Pricing Rules.

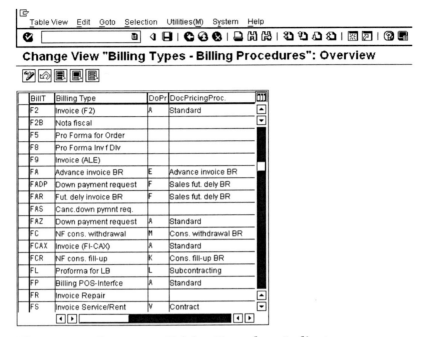

Figure 1.5.3: Document Pricing Procedure Indicator Assignment to Billing Types

Customer Pricing Procedure Indicator

In configuration step "Define Customer Pricing Procedure" on the pop-up screen, individual Customer Pricing Procedure Indicators are defined (see Figure 1.5.4). It is possible to define different indicators based on different groups of customers that would require different pricing within a given Sales Area.

Create a new Customer Pricing Procedure Indicator "M" by clicking on the "New Entries" button.

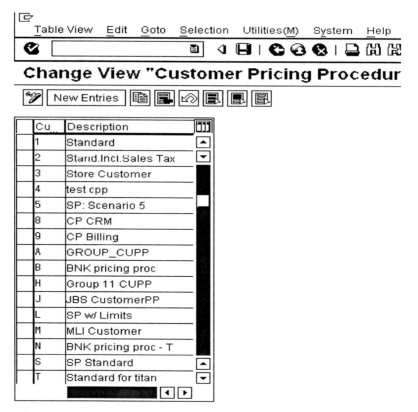

Figure 1.5.4: Customer Pricing Procedure Indicators

The assignment to a customer occurs in the Customer Master Record. During customer maintenance via create transactions "XD01", "VD01" or change transactions "XD02" or "VD02", click on the "Sales Area" button, click on the "Sales" tab and scroll down to the "Pricing/Statistics" section. Assign the appropriate Customer Pricing Indicator in field "Cust.Pric.Proc" (see Figure 1.5.5).

Figure 1.5.5: Assignment of Customer Pricing Procedure Indicator in Customer Master

Finally, after defining and assigning all indicators, it is time to assign a Pricing Procedure. Select the "Define Pricing Procedure Determination" option in the configuration pop-up.

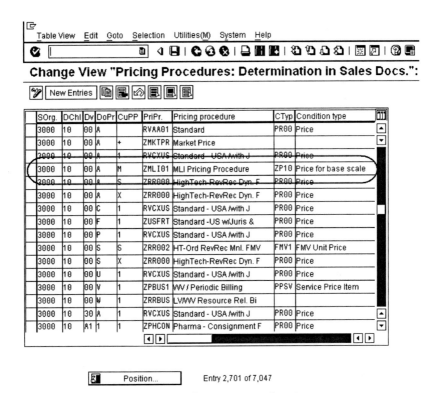

Figure 1.5.6: Pricing Procedure Determination

Figure 1.5.6 displays entries of combinations of existing Sales Areas, Document Pricing Indicators and Customer Pricing Indicators. A Pricing Procedure is listed for each entry. Manually enter a Pricing Procedure or select one from the pull-down list.

In this configuration step, it is also possible to define the default Condition Type that can be entered and edited on the single and double line "Sales Order Entry" screen.

Click on the "New Entries" button. Enter your Sales Area, Document Pricing Procedure Indicator "A" (for standard) in field "DoPr" and "M" for the newly created Customer Pricing Procedure Indicator in field "CuPP." Then assign our custom Pricing Procedure "ZMLI01" in field "PriPr." Save your changes.

Summary of Chapter 1

Chapter 1 had a lot of information, some of it very technical. But understanding the Condition Technique is fundamental to understanding how pricing works in the SAP applications. In the following chapters, I always refer back to the configuration settings made in Chapter 1.

Reviewing the graphic in Figure 1.1 summarizes the configuration steps for the Condition Technique:

First define your key combinations in Condition Tables, then group them as a search strategy in an Access Sequence.

Assign this Access Sequence to one or more Condition Types, which are grouped as a pricing schema in a Pricing Procedure.

Finally, assign this Pricing Procedure to a combination of Sales Area, customer and Sales Document.

In the next chapter, we will use this knowledge to create the pricing master data in Condition Records.

Chapter 2: Condition Record Maintenance

Chapter 1 described how to configure your pricing business rules with the Condition Technique. Before any pricing can apply on a Sales Document, pricing master data will need to be set up in the form of pricing Condition Records.

The Condition Record is a combination of the Condition Type, the Access Sequence that is linked to that Condition Type and the Condition Tables of the Access Sequence. Depending on the settings in a Condition Type, certain fields and features are displayed or suppressed in the Condition Record.

Condition Records cannot be created for Condition Types without an Access Sequence. There are several ways to create Condition Records: using a unique Condition Type (via Transaction "VK11"); for multiple Condition Types at the same time (via Transaction "VK31"); and with a program (via Transaction "VK15").

In the following chapters you will learn about the fields required to create a Condition Record and their meaning. You will also learn how to change and display Condition Records and how to mass update prices for a price increase or decrease. Let's get started.

2.1   Creating Condition Records Using Condition Type

This method of creating Condition Records was one of two ways before SAP R/3 release 4.0. To create a Condition Record, execute either transaction code "VK11" or use the SAP menu *Logistics-> Sales and Distribution-> Master Data-> Conditions-> Select Using Condition Type-> Create*. The resulting screen requires the entry of the Condition Type for which a Condition Record should be created.

Enter our previously created Condition Type "ZLIS." Either hit enter or click on the "Key Combination" button. This will display the Condition Tables from the Access Sequence that are attached to the entered Condition Type (see Figure 2.1.1).

Note that they appear in the same order as in the Access Sequence, from the most specific to the most generic key combination.

Select the key combination for which you would like to enter Condition Records; for example, the "Material" combination. Click the check mark.

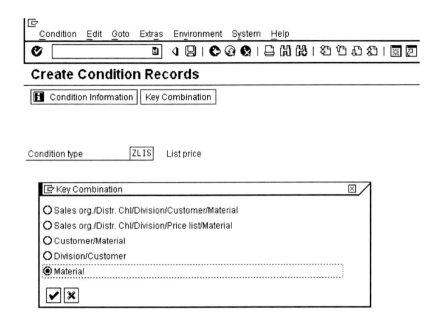

Figure 2.1.1: Possible Key Combinations for a
Condition Record

On the next screen (see Figure 2.1.2), you will see the
"Sales Organization" and "Distribution Channel" fields in the
Header section of the Condition Record. The "Material" field is
on line item level, just as configured on the "Technical View" of
the Condition Table. Enter the material number you want to
create a price for and hit enter.

Although only the material number was entered, the pricing currency, the pricing UoM as well as the Validity Period are
defaulted. The pricing currency, if not manually entered, defaults from the currency of the Company Code to which the
entered Sales Area is linked. If the Condition Type is a percentage, the percentage sign is defaulted. The pricing UoM is defaulted with the base UoM of the entered material. If a key
combination was selected that does not have the material
number in the key, no UoM is defaulted and an error message
requires the entry of a Unit of Measure.

Figure 2.1.2: Condition Record "Fast Entry" Screen

The Valid-From and Valid-To dates are defaulted according to the settings in the Condition Type. I recommend the Valid-To date is always set to "12/31/9999" (which I call the "End of Time"), unless you are creating Condition Records for, say, promotional discounts that should be limited to a certain period of time. The "12/31/9999" date will make price changes easier when they are needed.

The "DeletionID" column "D" indicates if the Condition Record is marked for deletion. A check in this column would indicate this.

The "Suppl.cond" column shows the existence of Condition Supplements for this Condition Type.

The "Scales" column indicates if Scales were maintained for this Condition Record.

The "Texts" column indicates if text was maintained for this Condition Type.

The "Exclusion" column ("Excl") would display an "X" if the Exclusion Indicator was set in the configuration of the Condition Type.

The "Payt Terms," "FixValDate" and "AddValDays" columns on this "Fast Entry" screen reflect the values that have been set in the "Additional Sales Data" screen of the Condition Record.

Select any Condition Record line and select *Goto->Details* to access the Condition Record "Details" screen (see Figure 2.1.3). Alternate ways to get there are pressing the "F6" key or clicking on the "Details" 🔲 icon. Some data from the "Fast Entry" screen is displayed here as well, such as the Validity Period, the amount with currency and UoM. The "Details" screen also shows the Scale Calculation Type and base, if the Condition Type was configured for Scales. The Exclusion and Deletion Indicator is displayed as well. These two fields can be manually maintained.

The "Lower Limit" and "Upper Limit" fields allow the user to maintain a value range between which manual changes would be allowed on a Sales Document. Entering values for this Condition Record manually on the Sales Document outside the specified value range would result in an error message. The maintenance of these two fields is optional. Condition limits are explained in more detail in Chapter 2.13.

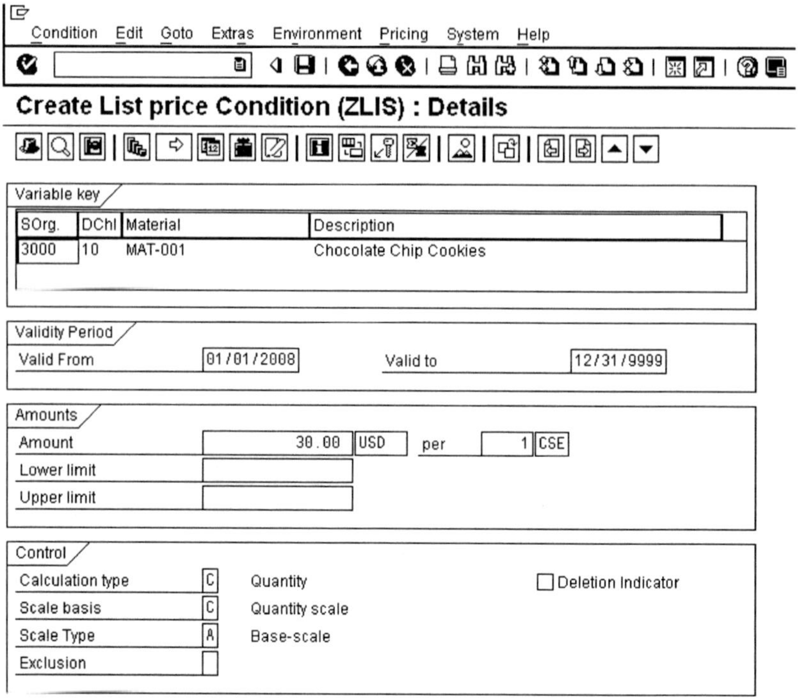

Figure 2.1.3: Condition Record Details Screen

From both the "Fast Entry" screen and the "Details" screen, you can branch over to the "Additional Data" screen. Either select *Goto-> Additional Data*, click on the "Additional Data" button or press "F7."

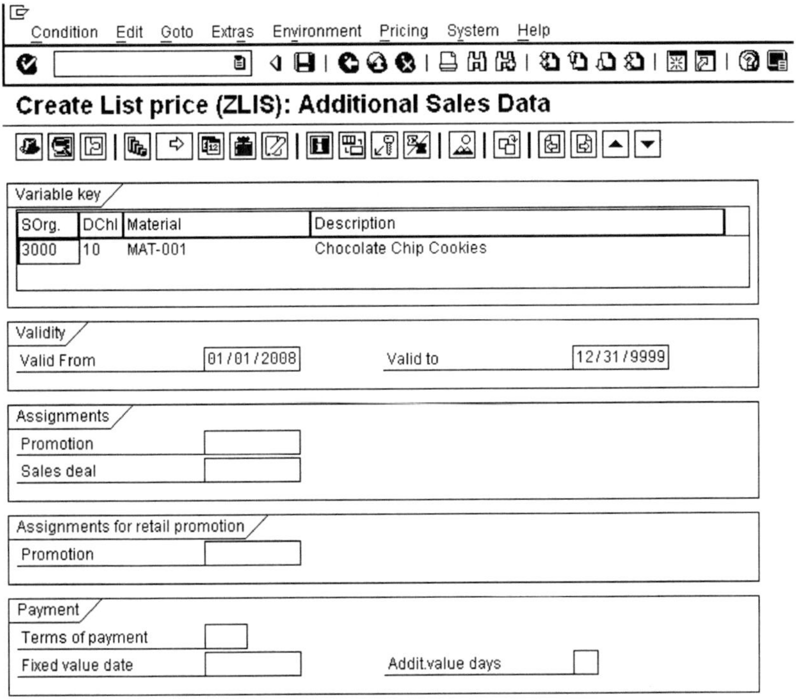
Condition Edit Goto Extras Environment Pricing System Help
Create List price (ZLIS): Additional Sales Data
Variable key
SOrg.
DChl
Material
Description
3000
10
MAT-001
Chocolate Chip Cookies
Validity
Valid From
01/01/2008
Valid to
12/31/9999
Assignments
Promotion
Sales deal
Assignments for retail promotion
Promotion
Payment
Terms of payment
Fixed value date
Addit.value days

Figure 2.1.4: Condition Record "Additional Data" Screen

The Valid-From and -To dates in Figure 2.1.4 are displayed and open to be changed. Be aware that these are the Validity dates for the selected Condition Record only. If you would like to link the selected Condition Record to an existing Sales Deal, you can enter that Sales Deal number in field "Sales Deal." If the Condition Record was maintained from within a Sales Deal (see Chapter 4.2), this number is automatically populated.

The same is true for the field "Promotion," although it is not available for input within the Condition Record. If the entered or applied Sales Deal is linked to a Promotion, the Promotion number is pulled into this field. As mentioned before, the Terms of Payment, Value Days and Additional Value Days can be maintained here. These dates and values will overwrite the defaulted line item data on a Sales Order. An example would be a specific promotion for which you would like to extend the terms of payments for a specific customer or group of customers.

Based on the settings in the Condition Type configuration, there are additional fields displayed on this screen, which we will look at a little later in the book.

If you configured the Condition Type to allow Scales, you can maintain them by either selecting *Goto->Scales*, clicking on the "Scales" 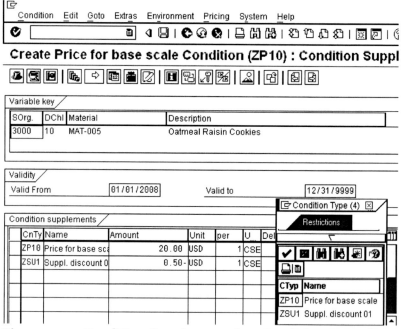 button or pressing the "F2" key. Detailed explanations about Scale maintenance and its application on Sales Documents can be found in Chapter 3.8.

If Condition Supplements were defined for the Condition Type, they can be maintained by selecting *Goto->Condition Supplement*. This option is only available if a Condition Supplement Pricing Procedure was maintained in the Condition Type for which Condition Records are being created.

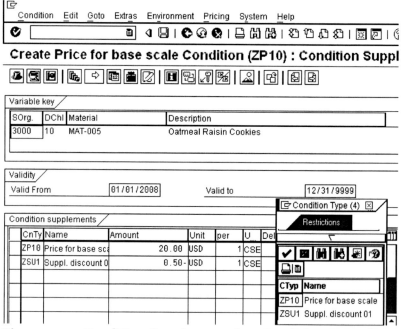

Figure 2.1.5: Condition Supplements in a Condition Record

Figure 2.1.5 displays the "Condition Supplements" screen. The pull-down of the "CnTy" field shows the Supplement Condition Types, in this example "ZSU1". As displayed in the top part of that screen, the Condition Record key and the Validity Period will apply to all Condition Types that are maintained here. This ensures that all Condition Types apply at the same time. Creating these Condition Types with different keys or Validity Periods would not ensure this consistency. In our example, the "ZSU1" discount will always apply when the "ZP10" pricing Condition Type applies.

If any type of notes should be attached to a particular pricing Condition Record, click on the "Condition Texts" 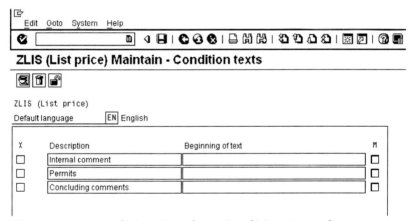 button. This will display the "Maintain Condition Texts" screen (see Figure 2.1.6) on which either internal notes or any comments that should be printed on external notifications to the customers (such as price letters) can be maintained. The configuration that drives what types of texts are available is done with transaction "VOTXN", section "Pricing Conds," but is not covered in this book.

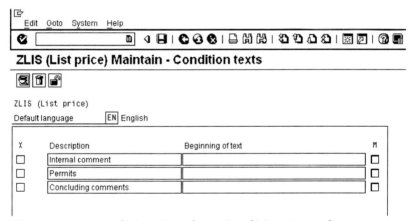

Figure 2.1.6: Condition Text for a Condition Record

Enter any comments in the appropriate text fields. If more space than the one line per text type is needed, double-click the line, which will branch into the SAP text editor.

After all necessary Condition Records are maintained, they can be reviewed either on the "Fast Entry" screen or on the "Create List Price ZLIS: Overview" screen. To get there, either select menu *Goto-> Overview of Condition Records*, click on the "Overview of Condition Records" ▣ button or press the "F5" key.

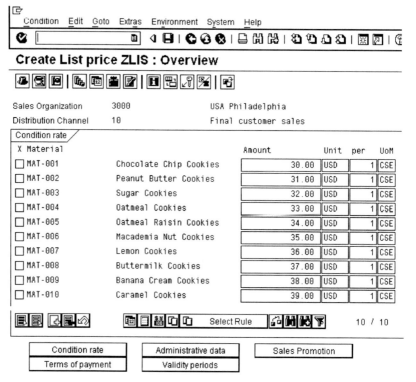

Figure 2.1.7: "Condition Record Overview" Screen

The default view in Figure 2.1.7 is the "Condition Rate" view, which displays the Condition Record rate in the maintained currency and UoM. Try all of the alternate views that will show different data by pressing the respective buttons on the bottom of the screen. All the data can be found in the other screens explained above. It is possible to make changes to all the selected Condition Records on the "Condition Record

Overview" screen, which leads us to the next chapter on how to change Condition Records.

But first, one more note on the creation of Condition Records. It is possible that a Condition Record was previously created for the exact same Condition Record key and Validity Period. The system recognizes that and presents the following screen in Figure 2.1.8 upon save time.

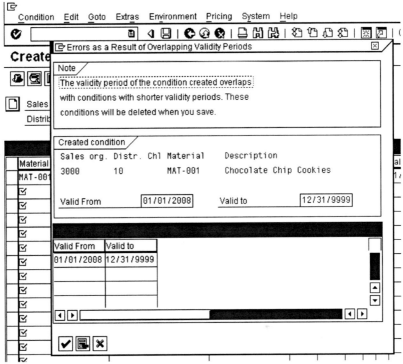

Figure 2.1.8: Overlapping Condition Records

This screen displays the overlapping Condition Record(s). Clicking on the check mark will delete the previous overlapping Condition Record and let the currently entered record take precedence. On the other hand, clicking on the "Delete" button next to the check mark will delete the currently entered Condition Record, and allow the previous Condition Record to remain intact.

2.2 Changing Condition Records Using Condition Type

After Condition Records were created, it might be necessary to make changes to them, such as price, Validity of the record or Scales. To do that, either execute transaction "VK12" or use the SAP menu *Logistics-> Sales and Distribution-> Master Data-> Conditions-> Select Using Condition Type-> Change.* Enter the Condition Type you want to change Condition Records for and either hit enter or click on the "Key Combination" button. As with the creation of Condition Records, the Condition Tables of the Access Sequence attached to the Condition Type are displayed. Select the one you would like to change and click the check mark. On the following screen (see Figure 2.2.1), you will see a number of selection fields according to the selected Condition Table in the previous pop-up window.

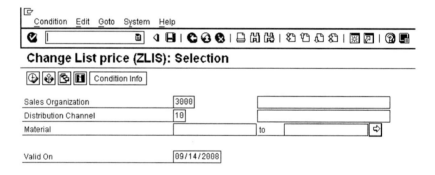

Figure 2.2.1: Selection Screen to Change Condition Records

The Header fields of the Condition Table are mandatory on the selection screen (see the "Technical View" of the Condition Table in Chapter 1.1). The fields marked as line items in the Technical view of the Condition Table are optional. In our example of the "ZLIS" Condition Type with the material-specific key combination, the "Sales Organization" and "Distribution Channel" are the mandatory selection fields and "Material Number" is the optional selection field. The Valid-On date is the selection date that valid Condition Records should be looked for. The Condition Records will have to have the same or an earlier From-date than the selected Valid-On date and the same or a later Valid-To date in order to be selected. Make your selections and click on the "Execute" button.

The Condition Records based on our selections are displayed in Figure 2.2.2. Since no material number was specified, all material-specific list prices are displayed.

Figure 2.2.2: Changing Multiple Condition Records

It is not possible to change the currency or the UoM of an existing Condition Record, but you can change the rate and the Validity Period. These changes can be made manually for each Condition Record or they can be changed all at once. To do it manually, just overwrite the rate or the Validity dates. In order to change multiple Condition Records at once, select all applicable Condition Records either one by one or by clicking on the

"Select All" 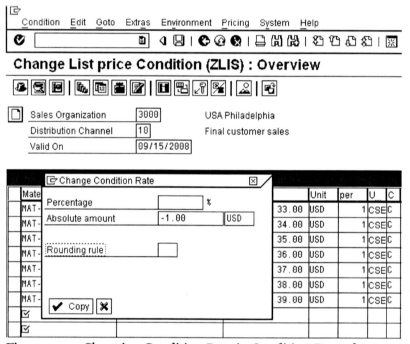 button. To change the Condition Record amount by a specific value or a percentage, select the "Change amount" button that looks like a calculator.

In the resulting pop-up (see Figure 2.2.3) you can then enter either a percentage in field "Percentage" or an amount in field "Absolute Amount."

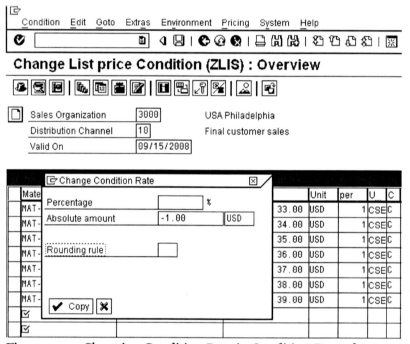

Figure 2.2.3: Changing Condition Rate in Condition Record

To increase the Condition Record value, enter a positive amount. In order to reduce the value, enter the amount with a negative sign, like "-1", as in Figure 2.2.3.

If the Condition Record value should be changed by a percentage, rounding issues may occur. For these instances you can enter a Rounding Rule in the field with the same name. This Rounding Rule is a piece of ABAP code that can, for example, round the changed amount to the nearest nickel. It is possible to create your own rounding rules by using transaction "VOFM", menu *Formulas->Rounding Rules.*

The resulting screen in Figure 2.2.4 shows the old and new values for each selected Condition Record. Use the green back arrow from this screen to return to the "Change Overview" screen which will then display the newly changed Condition Record values.

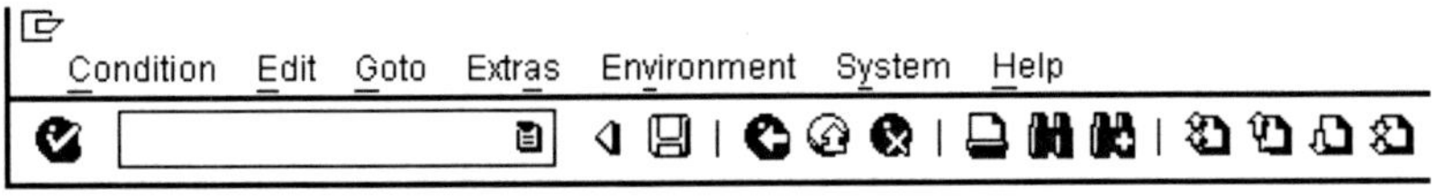

Log for Price Change of 1.00- USD

Price change flow trace (ZLIS) List price

Sales Org. 3000	Distr. Channel 10			
Material	Rate (old)	Rate (new)	Unit	
MAT-001	30.00	29.00	USD	
MAT-002	31.00	30.00	USD	
MAT-003	32.00	31.00	USD	
MAT-004	33.00	32.00	USD	
MAT-005	34.00	33.00	USD	
MAT-006	35.00	34.00	USD	
MAT-007	36.00	35.00	USD	
MAT-008	37.00	36.00	USD	
MAT-009	38.00	37.00	USD	
MAT-010	39.00	38.00	USD	

Figure 2.2.4: Old and New Condition Rate Log

Unfortunately, if you want to change the amount of a Condition Record to a specific value, this "Change Price" function cannot be used; the desired amounts have to be manually entered.

Also, be aware that if you change the value of a Condition Record that has Scales, you either need to use the "Change Amount" function or go to the "Scales" screen to manually adjust each Scale level. If you just manually change the value on the "Change List Price (ZLIS): Overview" screen, it will only change the first Scale level of the Condition Record, leaving the other levels unchanged.

In order to change any of the Validity dates, select the applicable Condition Records and click on the "Change Validity" button on the bottom of the aforementioned "Change List Price" screen. It is important to use this button on the bottom since there is an identical-looking button on the top of the screen, called "Validity Periods." Clicking that button will only change the first Condition Record on the screen, ignoring the rest, although they might all be selected.

On the resulting pop-up screen in Figure 2.2.5, change the Valid-From, the Valid-To or both dates. Click the check mark and the changed Validity dates are reflected on the "Change List Price" screen.

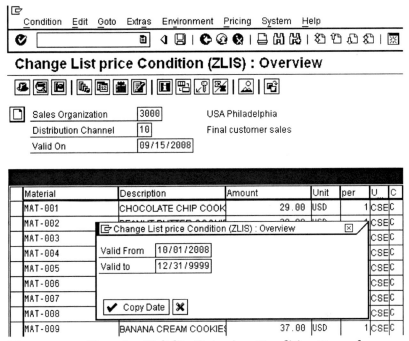

Figure 2.2.5: Changing Validity Dates in a Condition Record

If one or more Condition Records should be deleted, select them on the "Change List Price" screen and click on the "Delete Row" ![button] button. If the Condition Type was not configured to delete the Condition Record from the database, the Condition Record will be marked for deletion. This is indicated with a check mark in the "DeletionID" column. To reverse a deleted record, select it and click the "Undo Deletion" ![button] button. The check mark in the "DeletionID" column is then removed.

Although "VK12" is a change transaction, fields are open to potentially enter new Condition Records. If the same key as an existing Condition Record is entered again, a message is issued, stating that "The Condition is being processed in the current session." The system will then delete the last instance of this Condition Record key. It is possible to add Condition Records of different keys in the change transaction, but I advise against this.

2.3 Creating Condition Records with Template Using Condition Type

This option of creating a Condition Record uses existing Condition Records as a template or reference. It is the ideal tool to execute price increases or decreases. To execute this transaction, also known as "Create Condition Records with Reference," execute either transaction code "VK14" or use the SAP menu *Logistics-> Sales and Distribution-> Master Data-> Conditions-> Select Using Condition Type-> Create with Template.* Enter the Condition Type you would like to create Condition Records for, hit enter or click on the "Key Combination" button and select the appropriate key combination from the resulting pop-up screen.

The resulting selection screen is identical to the one for transaction "VK12" with one addition (see Figure 2.3.1).

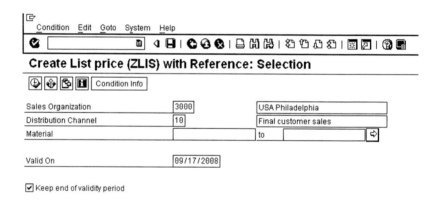

Figure 2.3.1: Create Condition Records with Reference

The field "Keep End of Validity Period" determines the Valid-To date of the new Condition Records that will be created. If this field is selected, then the "Valid-To" field of the new Condition Record is taken from the referenced Condition Record. If the field is turned off, the "Valid-To" field for the Condition Record is proposed from the customized setting of the Condition Type. In short, if the referenced Condition Record Valid-To date is 12/31/2008 and the field is turned on, the new Condition Record Valid-To date would be 12/31/2008 as well. Unchecking the field would default the 12/31/9999 date, as defined in configuration for our Condition Type as the Valid-To date. Enter your appropriate selection criteria and execute.

On the "Fast Entry" screen, the selected Condition Records are displayed. The Valid-From date defaults to the Valid-From date as set in the configuration of the Condition Type. In our case, that would be today's date. The Valid-To date is proposed as described above. Select the Condition Records that need to be changed. If you would like to create a new price that would be valid at a later date, click on the "Change Validity" 🔲 button on the bottom of the screen. Remember to use this button on the bottom instead of the identical-looking button on the top of the screen, called "Validity Periods."

On the resulting pop-up screen, change the Valid-From date to the date from which the new price should be valid. As indicated in Chapter 2.1, if you originally created your Condition Records with a Valid-To date of 12/31/9999 you will not have to change the Valid-To date during a price increase. Enter the Valid-From date from which the new price should take effect. Click the check mark and the changed Validity dates are reflected on the "Fast Entry" screen.

Now change the Condition Record amount by selecting the "Change amount" 🔲 button that looks like a calculator on the bottom of the screen. Again, only use this function if you want to increase or decrease the amount of the existing Condition Record. To change the amount of a Condition Record to a specific value, enter the desired amount manually on the "Fast Entry" screen.

In the resulting pop-up you can enter either a % in field "Percentage" or an amount in field "Absolute Amount." To increase the Condition Record value, enter a positive amount. To reduce the value, enter the amount with a negative sign, like "-1". If you are changing the Condition Record value by a percentage, rounding issues may occur. For these instances you can enter a

Rounding Rule in the field with the same name. This Rounding Rule is a piece of ABAP code that can, for example, round the changed amount to the nearest nickel.

The resulting screen shows the old and new values for each selected Condition Record (see Figure 2.2.4).

Be aware that if you change the value of a Condition Record that has Scales, you either need to use the "Change Amount" function or go to the "Scales" screen to manually adjust each Scale level. If you just manually change the value on the "Fast Entry" screen, it will only change the first Scale level of the Condition Record, leaving the other levels unchanged.

Save the Condition Records.

The example I just described explains the creation of a price from a future date on. It is also possible to reduce a price for a specified amount of time to give only a temporary price reduction. Let's use the example from our change scenario in Chapter 2.2 and execute a temporary price reduction for next month.

For all "ZLIS" material-specific Condition Records, change the Validity Period with "VK14" as described above to the beginning and end date of next month (in our case, 10/01/2008-10/31/2008). Reduce the price by 1 USD. We will review the results of this change in the next chapter when we display Condition Records.

One final note for the "Condition Record Create with Reference" option. Don't mistake it with the "Copy Condition Records" function. The difference is that when you "Create with Template," you create new Condition Records for the same Condition Table key, whereas when you copy Condition Records, you create Condition Records for a different key. How to copy Condition Records is described in Chapter 2.11.

2.4   Displaying Condition Records Using Condition Type

To display Condition Records, execute transaction "VK13" or use the SAP menu *Logistics-> Sales and Distribution-> Master Data-> Conditions-> Select Using Condition Type-> Display*. Enter the same Condition Type as in Chapter 2.3 and select the same key combination as before. Enter the appropriate selection criteria and execute.

You will see the Condition Records for the Valid-On date from the previous selection screen. This date is defaulted with the current date. You will see the Condition Records with the amounts that are valid before the executed price increase in Chapter 2.3.

To see all Condition Records for the same Condition Table key, select a Condition Record and click on the "Validity Dates" button on the top of the screen (now you are allowed to use this button). Figure 2.4.1 displays the current Condition Record highlighted and another Condition Record with the amount of the increased price.

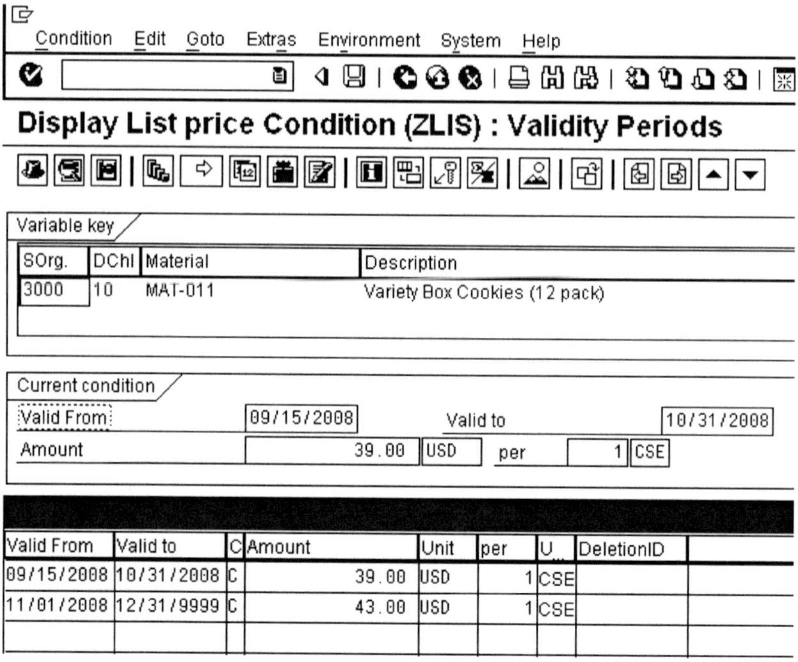

Figure 2.4.1: Display of Multiple Validity Periods in a Condition Record

You will recognize that the Validity Period for this future Condition Record starts on the date we indicated as the start of the price increase and is valid until 12/31/9999. The current Condition Record, on the other hand, has the original Valid-From date, but the Valid-To date is one day prior to the new Condition Record's Valid-From date. The SAP system automatically "expired" the current Condition Record.

For the previous example of the temporary price decrease, we have created a new Condition Record for a Validity Period within an existing Condition Record Validity Period. Just like with the price increase from a specific date on, the system would also adjust the Validity dates accordingly. Let's look at this example in Figure 2.4.2 as a comparison.

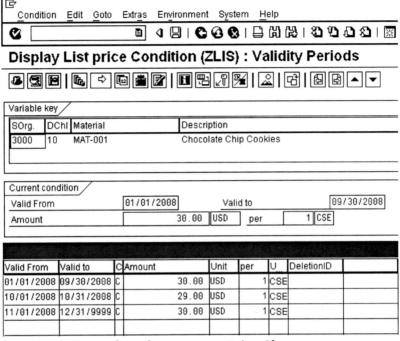

Figure 2.4.2: Display of Temporary Price Change

The original Condition Record Validity Period was from 01/01/2008 to 12/31/9999.

The Condition Record Validity Period for the temporary price decrease was from 10/01/2008 to 10/31/2008.

This resulted in the following three Condition Records:

- 01/01/2008-09/30/2008
- 10/01/2008-10/31/2008
- 11/01/2008-12/31/9999

You can see that the insertion of one new Validity Period created two new Condition Records. The first one has a Valid-To date one day prior to the start of the new Condition Record Valid-From date, and the third Condition Record has a Valid-From date one day after the Valid-To date of the Condition Record for the temporary price decrease. The system automatically adjusted these Validity dates to ensure continuous price validity.

One thing to note from a technical perspective is that although two new Condition Records were created by inserting a Validity Period, the Condition Record number ("KONP-KNUMH") is the same for both. This means both Condition Records have the same pricing information. If the rates in one of the two Condition Records are changed, it would also automatically change the second Condition Record, and vice versa.

2.4.2 The Condition Record Change Log

Changes to a Condition Record can be viewed in the change log in either the change or display transaction of a Condition Record. From any screen within the Condition Record, select menu *Environment-> Changes-> Per Condition Record*. The "Change Documents for Conditions" screen in Figure 2.4.2.1 is displayed. The tree menu displays the date and time of a change in the "Date/Time" column. In the next column, the SAP user ID and the transaction code with which the change was made are displayed. Besides this information, the Condition Type, the Condition Table for which the Condition Record was created, and the Validity Period of the Condition Record are all displayed.

If the detailed information for the change is not displayed (you would see a little folder with a plus sign on the left of the record), click on the "Expand All" button or click "F9." The sub-level for this Change Record displays the description of the change, with its respective old and new value.

Looking at Figure 2.4.2.1 for one of the "ZLIS" Condition Records, it clearly indicates that the price for material "MAT-001" was changed from USD 30 to USD 31 and, in another change, from 31 back to 30 dollars.

Change documents   Edit   Goto   System   Help

Change documents for conditions

Date Time	User TCode	Cond	Tab	Sales org. Rebate ag.	Distr. Ch1 Sales deal	Material Promotion	Validity period
09/15/2008 08:59:55	STUDENT50 VK11	ZLIS	004	3000	10	MAT-001	01/01/2008-12/31/9999

	Description	OldVal	NewVal
	Condition record has been created		
	Rate (condition amount or percentage) where no	0.00 USD	30.00 USD
	Condition unit		CSE
	Condition pricing unit	0	1
	Automatic changes in other condition records		
	Record deleted due to overlapping valid.period	01/01/2008-12/31/9999	

Date Time	User TCode	Cond	Tab	Sales org. Rebate ag.	Distr. Ch1 Sales deal	Material Promotion	Validity period
09/17/2008 10:28:06	STUDENT50 VK12	ZLIS	004	3000	10	MAT-001	

	Description	OldVal	NewVal
	Valid-From Date	01/01/2008	02/01/2008
	Rate (condition amount or percentage) where no	30.00 USD	31.00 USD

Date Time	User TCode	Cond	Tab	Sales org. Rebate ag.	Distr. Ch1 Sales deal	Material Promotion	Validity period
09/17/2008 10:31:43	STUDENT50 VK12	ZLIS	004	3000	10	MAT-001	

	Description	OldVal	NewVal
	Rate (condition amount or percentage) where no	31.00 USD	30.50 USD

Figure 2.4.2.1: Condition Record Change Log

If you would like to see changes made to more than the one Condition Record you selected, use the *Environment-> Changes-> Change Report* menu option from any of the Condition Record screens. This report can also be accessed outside of the Condition Record display or change transactions by executing report "RV16ACHD". The selection screen of this report is displayed in Figure 2.4.2.2.

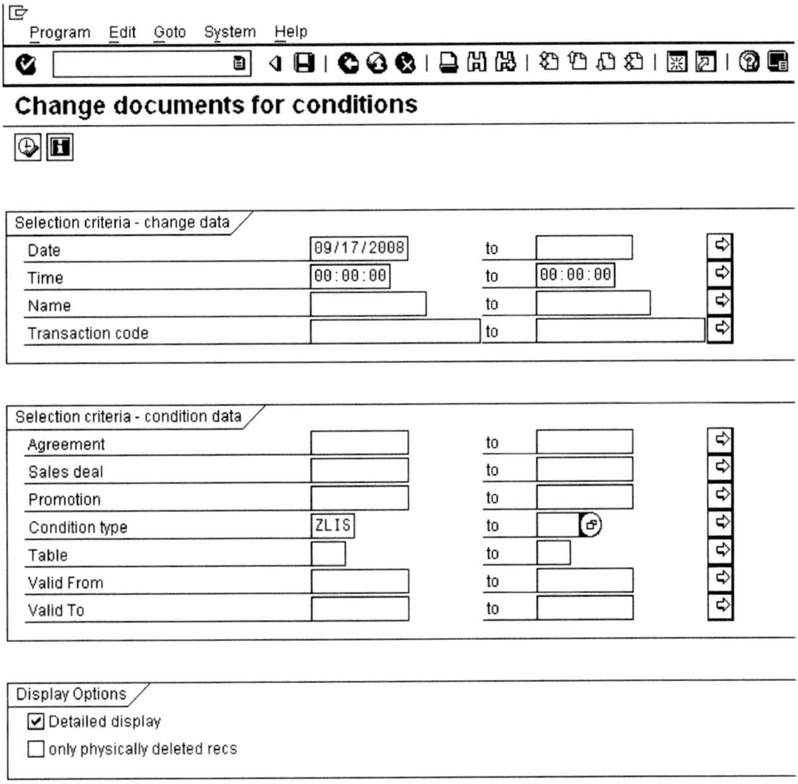

Figure 2.4.2.2: Selection Screen of Condition Record
Changes Report

I advise using as many selection criteria as possible to reduce the runtime of this report. The date of changes and Condition Type selections are a good start. Compared to the
change log in Figure 2.4.2.1, the resulting information from the
change report in Figure 2.4.2.3 truly only includes changes to
Condition Records, not the original creation of it.

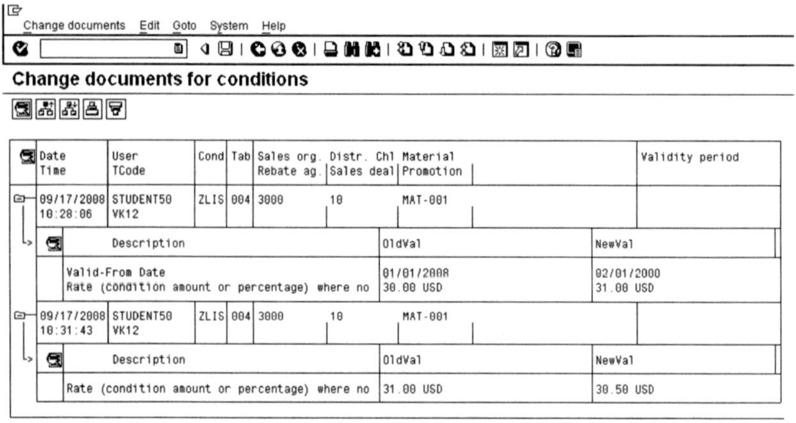

Figure 2.4.2.3: Change Log from Condition Record
Changes Report

From a technical point of view, the information for Condition Record changes is stored in the change tables "CDHDR" and "CDPOS". The change document object for pricing changes is "COND_A." This information is useful when you want to create your own change reports.

2.4.3 Condition Display

In some situations, you might want to find Condition Records for specific key fields without knowing which Condition Table in the Access Sequence the Condition Records were created for. The "Condition Info" functionality will allow the selection of Condition Records without selecting a specific Condition Table.

Using the same transaction as for displaying Condition Records ("VK13"), enter the Condition Type and click on the "Condition Information" button. All key fields of all the Condition Tables within the Access Sequence attached to the Condition Type are available as selection fields. Whatever value is entered in a particular selection field is checked against existing Condition Records. However, the resulting screen does not only display Condition Records that contain the selected field, but also all other Condition Records that don't have this field in its key.

Confused? Let's walk through an example.

Condition Type "ZLIS" has an Access Sequence with the following Condition Tables:

1) Sales Area/Customer/Material
2) Sales Area/Price List Type/Material
3) Sales Area/Customer
4) Sales Area/Material

Selecting the "Condition Information" button will provide Sales Area, customer number, material number and price list type as selection fields (see Figure 2.4.3.1).

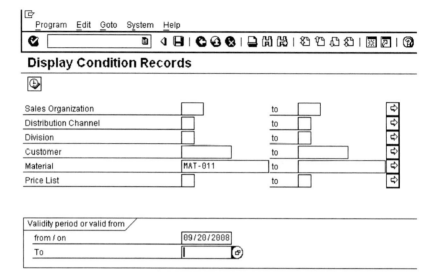

Figure 2.4.3.1: Condition Display Selection Screen

Selecting material "MAT-011" will return all pricing Condition Records of Condition Table 1, 2 and 4 that were created for this material in Figure 2.4.3.2. In addition, any Condition Records for Condition Table 3 (Sales Area/Customer) are displayed as well, since material is not a key field for this Condition Table.

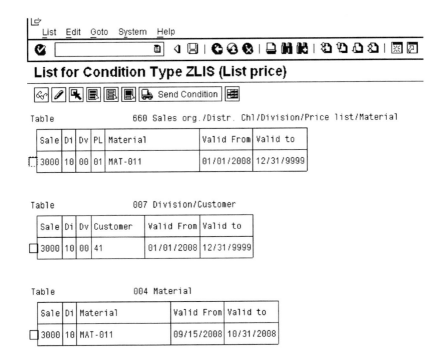

Figure 2.4.3.2: Condition Display Results

The "Condition Information" screen shows the full key of the Condition Record with its Validity Period. Unfortunately, the rate of the Condition Record is not displayed on this screen. To get this information, it is necessary to select the respective Condition Record and click on the "Display" ![btn] button or the "F5" key. This will get you to the regular "Display" screens described above. If a Condition Record should be changed from the "Condition Information" screen, select it and click on the "Change" ![btn] button or the "F6" key. This will branch into the "VK12" "Change" transaction and allow all changes to the Condition Record as described in Chapter 2.2.

Selecting the green back arrow from either transaction will return the "Condition Information" screen, from which a different Condition Record might be selected.

2.5 Pricing Reports

Another option to display pricing Condition Records is the use of Pricing Reports. These reports can be configured through IMG path *SPRO-> Sales and Distribution-> Basic Functions-> Pricing-> Maintain Pricing Report* or via transaction code "V/LA." On the resulting pop-up screen, select the "Create Pricing Report" option. Select a freely definable report ID (to follow user naming conventions, starting with a "Z") in field "Name of List" and a description for the report in field "Title." Click on the "Selected Fields" ⬛ button or click the "F5" key in Figure 2.5.1.

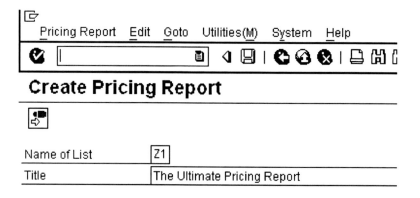

Figure 2.5.1: Naming a New Pricing Report

The Pricing Field Catalog from Chapter 1.1 is presented, just as during Condition Table maintenance. Select the fields of the Condition Table(s) that should be included in the Pricing Report. For the example report we are creating, select "Sales Organization," "Distribution Channel," "Division" and "Customer Number" as shown in Figure 2.5.2.

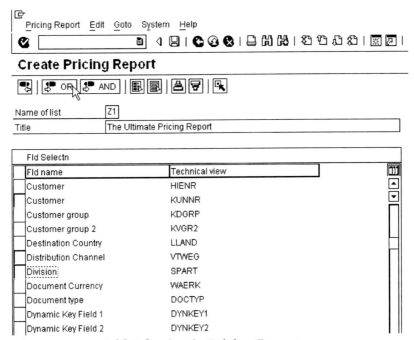

Figure 2.5.2: Field Selection in Pricing Report

After that, choose either the "OR" button ("F5") or the "AND" (Shift + F7) button. The "OR" button will result in a listing of all Condition Tables that have at least one of the selected fields in their key. For our example report, click the "AND" button, which will list only Condition Tables that include all of the selected fields in their key.

A list of all Condition Tables that include all previously selected fields is now displayed in Figure 2.5.3.

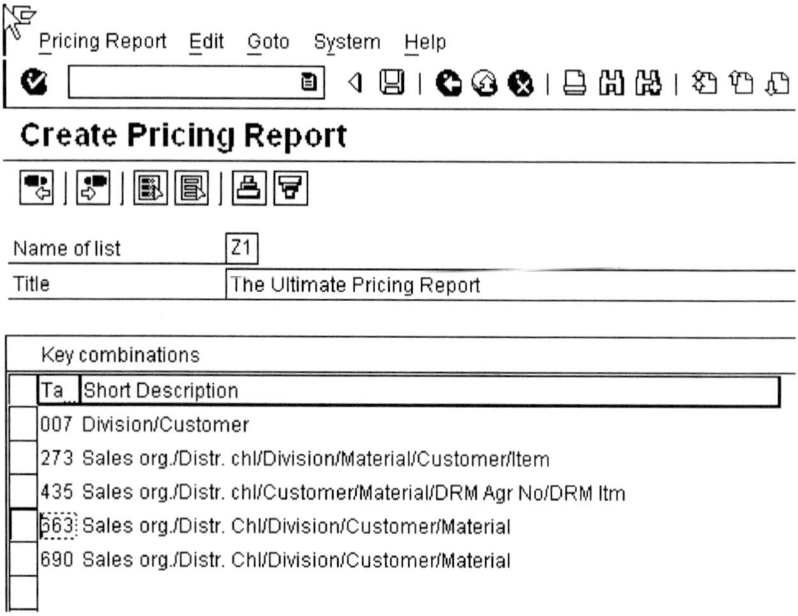

Figure 2.5.3: Selecting Condition Tables in Pricing Report

However, this list shows Condition Tables that have all of the previously selected fields and additional fields. For example, if you select "Sales Area" and "Customer Number" as the fields with the "AND" option, the results will also show Condition Tables like Sales Area, customer number and material number. For our example, we will only select our custom created Condition Table 663, and click on the "Continue to List Structure" button (or the "F5" key).

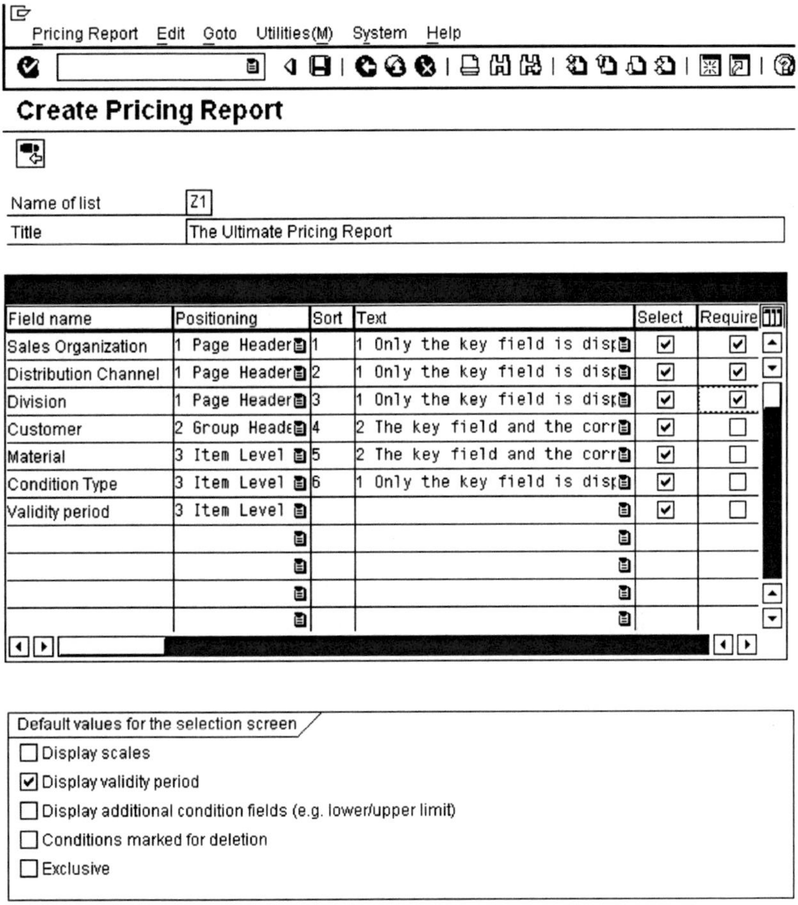

Figure 2.5.4: Field Definitions in Pricing Report

On the following screen in Figure 2.5.4 the fields of the selected Condition Tables are presented. The "Positioning" column defines where in the Pricing Report the information is supposed to appear. The available options are "Page Header," "Group Header" or "Item Level." The Page Header information will be displayed only once on the report. Fields selected on the Group Header Level, like customer number, will display all applicable information under this customer.

The "Sort" column identifies the order in which the fields should appear. The amount of information displayed per field is indicated in the "Text" column where you decide to either show the key field, only the field description, or both. Be aware that the report limits the display to 132 characters, so use descriptions only where it makes sense (for example, for a customer and material, but not for the Sales Area fields). The "Selection" column defines the fields that will be available as selection criteria. Finally, the "Required Input" column allows you to identify which of the field selections are mandatory to fill in order to run the Pricing Report.

In the "Default Values for the Selection Screen" section of this configuration screen, it is optional to define if Scales and/or Validity Periods, upper/lower limits or deleted Condition Records should be displayed on the selection screen. Select the applicable check boxes for your situation and save the report.

To execute this newly created Pricing Report, use the SAP Easy Access menu *Logistics-> Sales and Distribution-> Master Data-> Conditions-> List-> Pricing Report* or execute transaction "V/LD". Enter the Pricing Report ID and execute. The resulting selection screen in Figure 2.5.5 displays the selection fields as defined in the configuration of the Pricing Report.

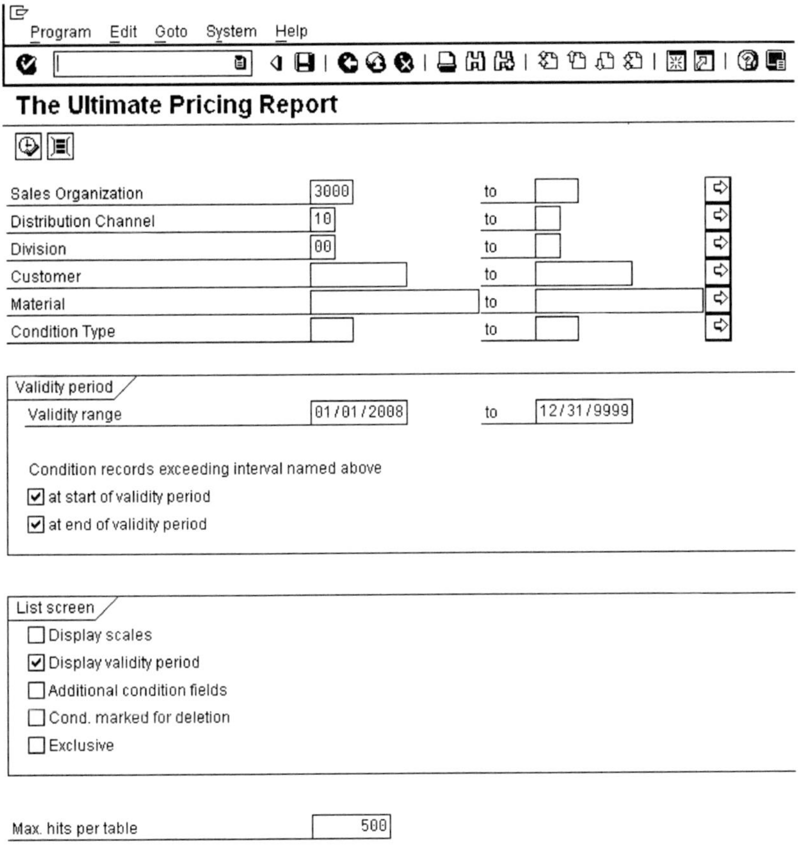

```
  ⌐
   Program   Edit   Goto   System   Help
   ◎ [                    🗎]   ◁ 🖫 │ 🄲 🄶 🄾 │ 🖴 🛗 🛗 │ 🕄 🕀 🕀 🕄 │ 🔳 🔲 │ 🄰 🖳
   The Ultimate Pricing Report
   🕀 🗊
```

Sales Organization	3000	to		⇨
Distribution Channel	10	to		⇨
Division	00	to		⇨
Customer		to		⇨
Material		to		⇨
Condition Type		to		⇨

Validity period

Validity range	01/01/2008	to	12/31/9999

Condition records exceeding interval named above

☑ at start of validity period
☑ at end of validity period

List screen

☐ Display scales
☑ Display validity period
☐ Additional condition fields
☐ Cond. marked for deletion
☐ Exclusive

Max. hits per table	500

Figure 2.5.5: Pricing Report Selection Screen

Since the Sales Area fields were defined as mandatory in the Pricing Report configuration, it is necessary to enter values in these fields. The dates for the "Validity Range" are the Validity dates that the Condition Record Valid-From and Valid-To dates have to be in. For example, if the selection dates are 03/08/2008-12/31/9999, the resulting report would not show Condition Records that started before 03/08/2008, even if the Valid-To date is in the selected date range.

To get these records, use the "At start of Validity Period" and "At e d of Validity Period" check boxes in the "Condition records exceeding interval named above" section of the selection screen. The first check box returns Condition Records that end within the Validity Period selected above, but start before that date. For example, if you would like to see all Condition Records that expire on a specific day, enter this day as the only date in the Validity range and select the "At start of Validity Period" box.

In the "List Screen Section" of the selection screen, you see the same fields as in the prior "Default Values for the Selection Screen" section of the Pricing Report configuration screen. The values from the configuration are defaults here and can be changed. Execute the report after making all necessary selections.

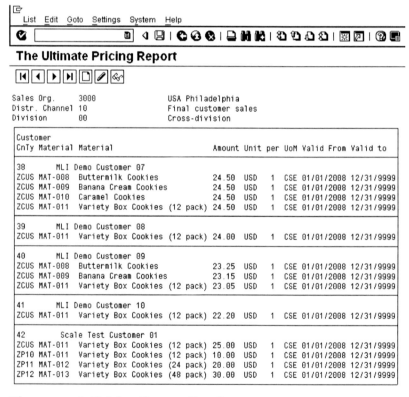

Figure 2.5.6: Pricing Report Results

Figure 2.5.6 displays the Pricing Report details. As configured in the Pricing Report, the Sales Area is displayed in the

Header section of the report. The pricing-related information is grouped by customer number, and for each customer all material-specific pricing is displayed. Looking at customer number 42, you can also see that since no specific Condition Type was defined on the selection screen, different Condition Records for different Condition Types are displayed for this customer. Of course, this is only possible if the Condition Record for these different Condition Types was created with the same Condition Table key.

2.6 Create Condition Records ("VK31")

The "Create," "Change" and "Display" transactions for Condition Records explained so far were the transactions available in the SAP releases prior to release 4.6A. The new maintenance screens starting with that release allow users to maintain Condition Records for multiple different Condition Types at the same time. The transaction codes for this maintenance correspond with the transactions from "VK11" through "VK14" and are called "VK31" through "VK34".

Let me take a step back and explain one of the reasons for creating this new maintenance screen.

Taking the example of customer/material specific prices or discounts, imagine the number of possible Condition Records that could exist if prices are set up that way. Multiply the number of customers by the number of materials and consider how many users would be needed to maintain these Condition Records.

Let's take a look again at the setup of the Condition Technique. Chapter 1.1 described the configuration of Condition Tables. Use IMG path *SPRO-> Sales and Distribution-> Basic Functions-> Pricing-> Pricing Control-> Define Condition Tables* and select "Change Condition Tables" from the following pop-up screen. For our example, we are using our pricing Condition Table "663" that consists of the following key fields: "Sales Organization," "Distribution Channel," "Division," "Customer" and "Material." Select the "Technical View" Technical view button to display the technical settings, which will allow you to change the appearance of the condition maintenance screen (accessible through transactions "VK11", "VK31", "VK12" or "VK32").

The "Technical View" of a Condition Table in Figure 2.6.1 displays the technical field names of the key fields from the Data Dictionary. The "Footer fld" column identifies which fields of the Condition Table key are maintainable on the Header and on the item level in Condition Record maintenance mode. In Figure 2.6.1, only the "Material" field is selected, which means it is maintainable on line item level. All other fields will appear on the Header level of the condition maintenance screen.

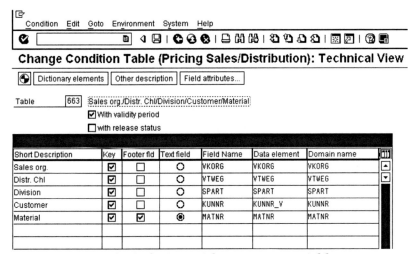

Figure 2.6.1: Technical View with One Footer Field

At minimum, the last field of the Condition Table needs to be on item level, which is why the field is grayed-out and can't be changed. However, multiple fields can be selected to be on the line item level. To better illustrate what this all means, change a Condition Record via transaction "VK12" for this Condition Table with just the "Material" field selected on the line item level.

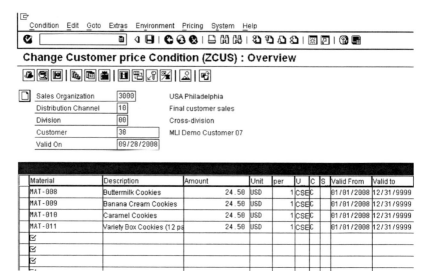

Figure 2.6.2: Condition Record with One Footer Field

As you can see in Figure 2.6.2, "Sales Organization," "Distribution Channel," "Division," and "Customer" appear on the Header level of the Condition Record maintenance screen. This means you can only maintain material prices for one customer at a time. Given the vast number of customers you might have, this would not be a desirable setup.

But before changing the appearance of the maintenance screen, let's take a look at which Condition Records are locked while prices with this Condition Table configuration are being maintained.

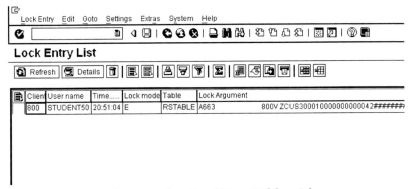

Figure 2.6.3: Lock Entry for Condition Table with
One Footer Field

Since only one customer can be changed at a time, the system locks all Condition Records for this Condition Type and Condition Table for the selected customer. This lock entry can be seen via transaction "SM12" (see Figure 2.6.3). The "Lock argument" shows the Condition Table that is being maintained (A663) as well as the Condition Type "ZCUS", Sales Area and the customer number. The "#" signs that follow indicate all Condition Records for this customer are locked. In this configuration, multiple users would be able to maintain prices for different customers.

However, it would be easier if one or only a few people do this maintenance.

Let's return to the "Technical view" configuration of Condition Table "663".

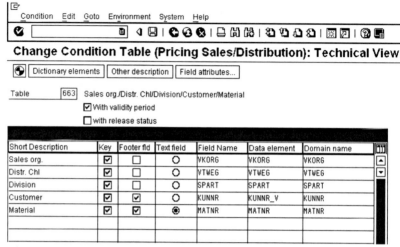

Figure 2.6.4: Technical View with Two Footer Fields

For the same Condition Table as in Figure 2.6.2 ("A663"), mark the "Footer fld" flag for "Customer" (see Figure 2.6.4) in addition to the "Material" field in "Change" mode. Once done, re-generate the Condition Table.

To see the effect of this configuration change, maintain or change prices for a Condition Type that uses this Condition Table (in our example, "ZCUS"). Figure 2.6.5 shows how these Condition Records with transaction "VK12" (Change) or "VK14" (Create with Reference) are selected. Note that in this configuration it is possible to select a range of customers. Previously, only one customer could be selected at a time, since the customer was on the Header level.

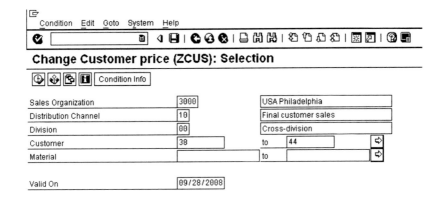

Figure 2.6.5: Selection Screen with Two Footer Fields

The resulting maintenance screen in Figure 2.6.6 now allows the maintenance of multiple customers at the same time.

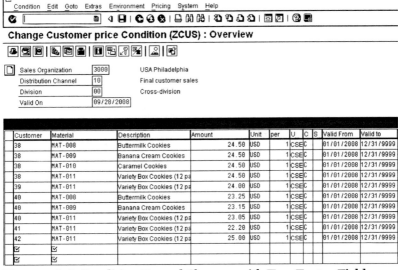

Figure 2.6.6: Condition Record Changes with Two Footer Fields

This comes in handy when prices for one material across all customers should be changed. In the previous configuration, you would have had to execute "VK12" one customer at a time (just think: 1,000 times for 1,000 customers). Instead, "VK12" only needs to be executed once for the material that needs to be changed.

The locking issue with this configuration, however, becomes apparent when we look again at the lock entry with transaction "SM12". As before, Condition Records are only locked if a user is in a "Create" or "Change" transaction. You can see in Figure 2.6.7 that every record for the selected Sales Area is now locked. Compared to the lock entry in Figure 2.6.3, customer number is not part of the lock entry anymore and therefore locks _all_ customers from being maintained by someone else. Once one user maintains this Condition Type and key combination, every other user attempting to change prices for this Condition Type and Condition Table at the same time is locked. These users would receive the message, "Conditions for the selection entered are blocked (User name)." The system will lock all Condition Records even if the first user selected a single customer or multiples in Figure 2.6.5.

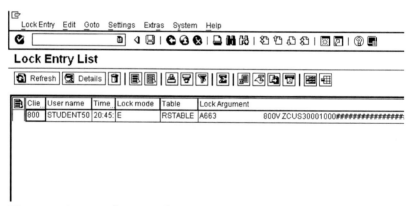

Figure 2.6.7: Lock Entry for Condition Table with Two Footer Fields

What does this have to do with the new "Pricing Maintenance" screen? The new maintenance transactions allow not only the maintenance of multiple customers by multiple users, but also the maintenance of multiple Condition Types at the same time, without locking Condition Tables.

Execute transaction "VK31" or use menu *Logistics-> Sales and Distribution-> Master Data-> Conditions-> Create* to access the screen in Figure 2.6.8.

Figure 2.6.8: Create Condition Records with "VK31"

Initially, we see that we don't have to enter any Condition Types, but rather select options from a menu tree with folders in the left column of this screen. Open all menu levels by clicking on the arrow in front of each folder. Each of the menu option represents a Pricing Report (see Chapter 2.5). These Pricing Reports are attached to an area menu displayed in the left column.

For our example, double-click on the "By Customer" option under the "Conditions" folder. This opens the information in the right window of the screen. Multiple key combinations, all of them including the customer number, are displayed. Clicking the respective folder button in front of that key combination will branch into the actual "Pricing Maintenance" screen in Figure 2.6.9.

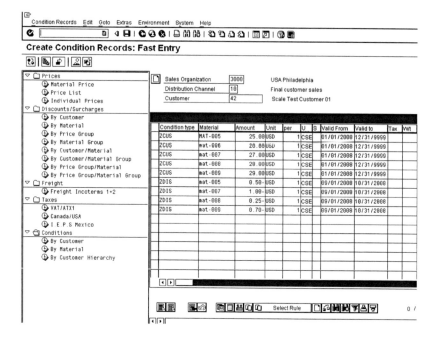

Figure 2.6.9: Creating Condition Records for Different Condition Types

The maintenance screen provides the same capabilities as the one in "VK11", like changing amounts or Validity Periods. One difference on this screen is that you are able to create your own screen variant with all pricing relevant fields. Figure 2.6.9 also shows that within the same transaction it is possible to maintain multiple different Condition Types like "ZCUS" and "ZDIS".

The folder menu on the left side is supplied by SAP and does not include any custom created key combinations. Chapter 5.11 explains how to add custom pricing Condition Tables to this tree structure.

2.7 Change Condition Records ("VK32")

Changing Condition Records with "VK32" is as versatile as the "Create" transaction. Although certain fields for the Condition Tables of these Condition Types are configured to be on Header level, Figure 2.7.1 shows that selection ranges for each of the possible Condition Table fields can be entered to select applicable Condition Records.

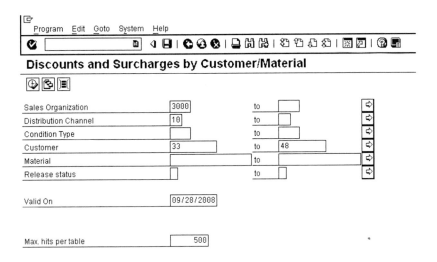

Figure 2.7.1: "VK32" Selection Screen

For our example, we are selecting a customer range and a specific Sales Organization and Distribution Channel. Execute.

The resulting Figure 2.7.2 displays all customer-related prices and discounts. All functions available in transaction "VK12" are also available for "VK32", such as copying Condition Records, mass changing of prices, etc.

Figure 2.7.2: Changing Condition Records with "VK32"

In the lower right section of the "VK32" screen, additional data can be viewed for a selected Condition Record. Initially, this view might be collapsed, but by clicking the "Display Condition Detail" 🔲 button, several tabs are displayed, just as in Figure 2.7.2. By clicking on a specific Condition Record and the mentioned button, tabs for "Validity Period," "Scales," "Condition Texts" and Condition Table "Key" information become available. Note that the information on these tabs is for informational purposes only; no data can be changed there.

To close the view of this "Additional Data" section, click on the "Compress Data Areas" 🔲 button.

2.8   Display Condition Records ("VK33")

Transaction "VK33" enables the display of Condition Records regardless of the Condition Type. The selection screen to select specific Condition Records is identical to the one in Figure 2.7.1. The "Display Condition Detail" function is also available with the same tabs as in "VK32". Although also available in "Change" mode, I want to point out the screen variant box on the top of the screen (see Figure 2.8.1).

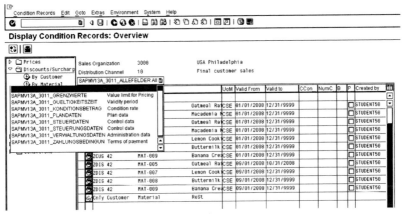

Figure 2.8.1: Display Screen Variants

The default screen variant displays all Condition Record relevant fields in one line. But clicking the pull-down for this field, several other pre-configured screen variants are available. You can either look at Validity Period relevant data only, or at rate relevant information only. Select different screen variants and see how the information in the Condition Record section of the screen changes.

2.9   Create Condition Records with Release Status

As shown during the configuration of a Condition Table, and as mentioned earlier in this book, Condition Records since SAP R/3 release 4.6A can be created with a Release Status. This status allows pricing Condition Records to be created without applying on a Sales or Billing Document. They can be used to establish an approval process for any price changes or to simulate "what if" scenarios.

To create a Condition Record with a Release Status, the Condition Table needs to be configured accordingly. Let's review again the creation of a Condition Table from Chapter 1.1.

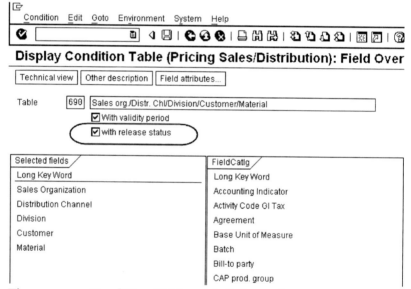

Figure 2.9.1: Condition Table with Release Status

Figure 2.9.1 displays a Condition Table for which the field "With Release Status" is checked. Several standard SAP Condition Tables were copied for release 4.6A going forward to include this Release Status. For example, the previous Condition Table we looked at, "A005" for Sales Area/Customer/ Material, is now Condition Table "A305", which has the same key fields, as well as the Release Status, in its key.

The Release Procedure, as SAP calls it, uses a Processing Status and the Release Status. The Release Statuses in the standard SAP system are pre-defined and unchangeable, since downstream processes work based on them. These Release Statuses are:

- A – Blocked
- B – Released for Price Simulation
- C – Released for Planning and Price Simulation
- Blank - Released

The Release Status regarding Price Simulation allows the applicable Condition Records to affect the values in the Net Price List report. This report is "SDNETPR0" and will be explained shortly.

The Release Status regarding Planning allows the Condition Records with that status to be included in CO-PA planning scenarios.

The Processing Status can be freely defined and is linked to a Release Status. This is done in configuration via IMG path *SPRO-> Sales and Distribution-> Basic Functions-> Pricing-> Define Processing Status*. Figure 2.9.2 displays the assignment of four freely defined Processing Statuses.

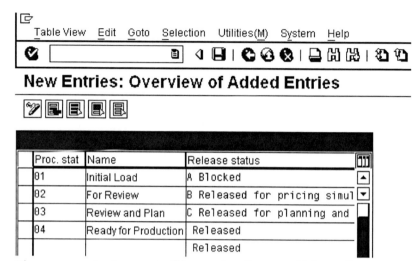

Figure 2.9.2: Assignment of Processing Status to Release Status

More than one Processing Status can be assigned to the same Release Status. This might make sense if an approval process should route a Condition Record through several Processing Statuses in a "Blocked" Release Status.

For the example in this book, Condition Table "690" (from Figure 2.9) was added to a custom Access Sequence attached to a discount Condition Type "ZDRE".

Creating Condition Records for this Condition Type with this key combination displays the Release Status fields in Figure 2.9.3.

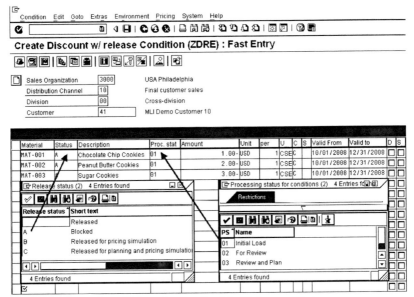

Figure 2.9.3: Condition Record with Release Status

Maintain the self-defined Processing Status from Figure 2.9.2 in column "Proc.Stat." Based on the configuration assignment of the Processing Status to the Release Status, the display-only field "Status" is populated accordingly. Initially, maintain the Condition Record with Processing Status "01" for the "Initial Load" and save the Condition Records.

To see the effects of this Release Status, let's review a Sales Order and the Net Price List report.

Create a Sales Order for the customer and materials of the Condition Records that were just created with a "Blocked" status.

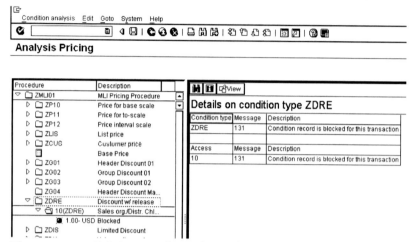

Figure 2.9.4: Pricing Analysis for Release Status

The Pricing Analysis of that line item (which is explained in detail in Chapter 3.2) and Condition Type "ZDRE" indicates in Figure 2.9.4 that the Condition Record did not apply due to the "Blocked" status in the Condition Record.

Running the Net Price List by either SAP menu *Logistics-> Sales and Distribution-> Master Data-> Conditions-> List-> Net Price List* or transaction "V_NL" offers the selection screen in Figure 2.9.5.

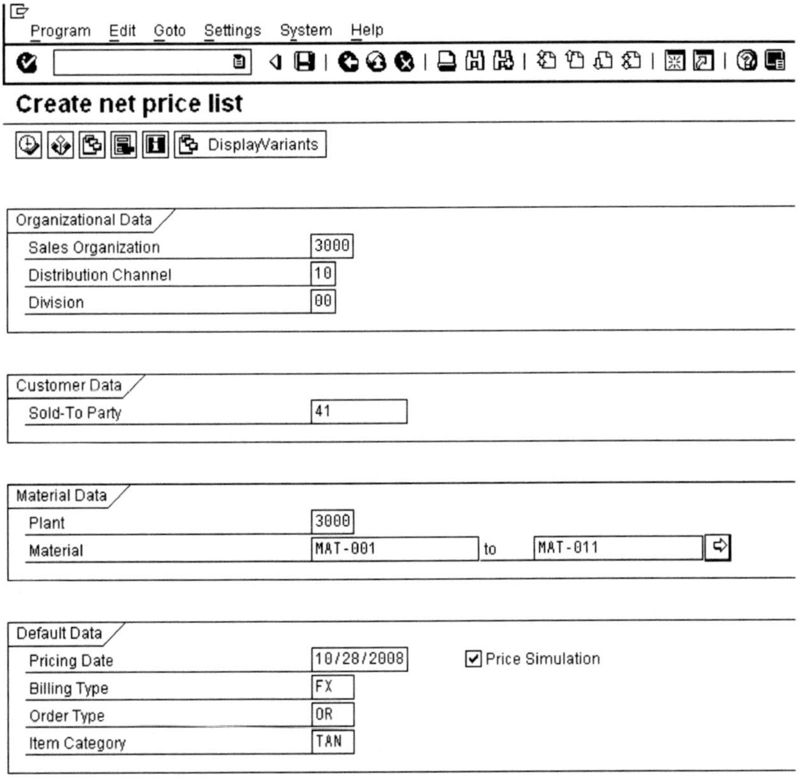

Figure 2.9.5: Selection Screen for Net Price List Report

The Net Price List simulates the Net Price for a customer and material for the quantity of one sales unit on a given Pricing Date. Enter the necessary selection criteria and the Pricing Date for which pricing should be simulated. For the Condition Records with a Release Status to have any effect on this report, make sure that selection field "Price Simulation" is checked. Execute the report.

List Edit Goto Settings Environment System Help

Create net price list

Choose | Save | Error Log

Billing Doc.	Item	Bill.qty	SU	BUn	Pricing date	Net price	Material	Description	Plant	Subtotal 1	Subtotal 2	Subtotal 3	Subtotal 4	Subtotal 5	Subtotal 6
$000000001	1	1	CSE	CSE	10/28/2008	25.00	MAT-001	Chocolate Chip Cookies	3000	25.00	25.00	25.00	0.00	0.00	0.00
$000000001	2	1	CSE	CSE	10/28/2008	25.00	MAT-002	Peanut Butter Cookies	3000	25.00	25.00	25.00	0.00	0.00	0.00
$000000001	3	1	CSE	CSE	10/28/2008	25.00	MAT-003	Sugar Cookies	3000	25.00	25.00	25.00	0.00	0.00	0.00
$000000001	4	1	CSE	CSE	10/28/2008	25.00	MAT-004	Oatmeal Cookies	3000	25.00	25.00	25.00	0.00	0.00	0.00
$000000001	5	1	CSE	CSE	10/28/2008	19.50	MAT-005	Oatmeal Raisin Cookies	3000	20.00	19.50	19.50	0.00	0.00	0.00
$000000001	6	1	CSE	CSE	10/28/2008	25.00	MAT-006	Macadamia Nut Cookies	3000	25.00	25.00	25.00	0.00	0.00	0.00
$000000001	7	1	CSE	CSE	10/28/2008	25.00	MAT-007	Lemon Cookies	3000	25.00	25.00	25.00	0.00	0.00	0.00
$000000001	8	1	CSE	CSE	10/28/2008	25.00	MAT-008	Buttermilk Cookies	3000	25.00	25.00	25.00	0.00	0.00	0.00
$000000001	9	1	CSE	CSE	10/28/2008	24.25	MAT-009	Banana Cream Cookies	3000	25.00	24.25	24.25	0.00	0.00	0.00
$000000001	10	1	CSE	CSE	10/28/2008	25.00	MAT-010	Caramel Cookies	3000	25.00	25.00	25.00	0.00	0.00	0.00
$000000001	11	1	CSE	CSE	10/28/2008	22.20	MAT-011	Variety Box Cookies (12 pack)	3000	22.20	22.20	22.20	0.00	0.00	0.00

Figure 2.9.6: Net Price List with Blocked Release Status Records

The resulting Net Price List in Figure 2.9.6 displays the simulated Net Price per material. Since the "ZDRE" Condition Records are still in "Blocked" status, they have no effect on the prices here. The Net Price List can provide even more details, but for the purpose of this book, the screen variant displayed here was created with pricing-related fields. The subtotal "1" and subtotal "2" fields show the gross and the Net Price of the material according to the configuration of the Pricing Procedure linked to the selected customer and Sales Order Type.

Go back to the previous Condition Records in "Change" mode and change the Processing Status to "02", which will change the Release Status to "A" for Price Simulation.

After that, execute the Net Price List again with the same selection criteria as before.

List Edit Goto Settings Environment System Help

Create net price list

▲ ▼ | Choose | Save | Error Log

Billing Doc.	Item	Bill.qty	SU	BUn	Pricing date	Net price	Material	Description	Plant	Subtotal 1	Subtotal 2	Subtotal 3	Subtotal 4	Subtotal 5	Subtotal 6
$000000001	1	1	CSE	CSE	10/28/2008	24.00	MAT-001	Chocolate Chip Cookies	3000	25.00	24.00	24.00	0.00	0.00	0.00
$000000001	2	1	CSE	CSE	10/28/2008	23.00	MAT-002	Peanut Butter Cookies	3000	25.00	23.00	23.00	0.00	0.00	0.00
$000000001	3	1	CSE	CSE	10/28/2008	22.00	MAT-003	Sugar Cookies	3000	25.00	22.00	22.00	0.00	0.00	0.00
$000000001	4	1	CSE	CSE	10/28/2008	25.00	MAT-004	Oatmeal Cookies	3000	25.00	25.00	25.00	0.00	0.00	0.00
$000000001	5	1	CSE	CSE	10/28/2008	19.50	MAT-005	Oatmeal Raisin Cookies	3000	20.00	19.50	19.50	0.00	0.00	0.00
$000000001	6	1	CSE	CSE	10/28/2008	25.00	MAT-006	Macademia Nut Cookies	3000	25.00	25.00	25.00	0.00	0.00	0.00
$000000001	7	1	CSE	CSE	10/28/2008	25.00	MAT-007	Lemon Cookies	3000	25.00	25.00	25.00	0.00	0.00	0.00
$000000001	8	1	CSE	CSE	10/28/2008	25.00	MAT-008	Buttermilk Cookies	3000	25.00	25.00	25.00	0.00	0.00	0.00
$000000001	9	1	CSE	CSE	10/28/2008	24.25	MAT-009	Banana Cream Cookies	3000	25.00	24.25	24.25	0.00	0.00	0.00
$000000001	10	1	CSE	CSE	10/28/2008	25.00	MAT-010	Caramel Cookies	3000	25.00	25.00	25.00	0.00	0.00	0.00
$000000001	11	1	CSE	CSE	10/28/2008	22.20	MAT-011	Variety Box Cookies (12 pack)	3000	22.20	22.20	22.20	0.00	0.00	0.00

Figure 2.9.7: Net Price List with Price Simulation Status Records

Figure 2.9.7 now clearly shows that the Net Prices for the materials for which a "ZDRE" discount Condition Record was created are now reduced by the rates in the "ZDRE" record. "Subtotal 1" for these items remained the same, but "Subtotal 2," which includes discounts, was reduced by the discount amount.

Creating another Sales Order will still show the "ZDRE" condition as blocked in the Pricing Analysis but also indicates the Condition Record was released for Planning. Once the Processing Status in the "ZDRE" Condition Records is set to "04" and therefore the Release Status set to "Released," the Condition Records will apply just like regular Condition Records on a Sales Document.

Since the Release Status is part of the key in the Condition Table, it is possible that multiple Condition Records for the same material exist with different Release Statuses. The following priorities are established in a scenario like this:

- For Pricing, only "Released" Release Statuses are active.

- For Price Simulation, first the "Release for Simulation" status ("B") applies, then the "Released for Planning and Price Simulation" status ("C"), and lastly the "Released" status ("Blank").

Sales Deals (see Chapter 4.2) also have a Release Status but no accompanying Processing Status. The Release Status from the Sales Deal will be copied into the Condition Records created within that Sales Deal. The Processing Status linked to that Release Status in configuration applies on these Condition Records. If more than one Processing Status exists for a Release Status, the first one in alphabetical order will be used.

2.10 Pricing by Pricing Reference Material

A way of reducing the number of created Condition Records is to use the Pricing Reference Material in the material master.

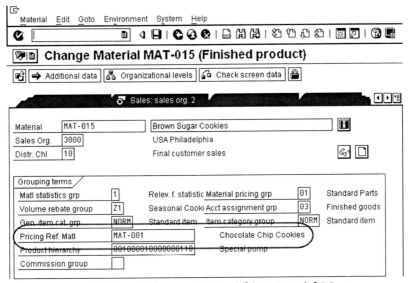

Figure 2.10.1: Pricing Reference Material in Material Master

Figure 2.10.1 displays the "Sales: sales org. 2" view of the material master for material "Mat-015". The field "Pricing Ref. Matl" shows material "MAT-001" as the Pricing Reference Material.

When creating a Sales Order, all Pricing Records that were created for material "MAT-001" apply for material "MAT-015", although no Condition Records were created for material "MAT-015". When looking at the pricing on a Sales Order line item (see Chapter 3.1) and displaying the Condition Record applied for material "MAT-015", the system would branch into the Condition Record for material "MAT-001".

For this functionality to work, it is important that the Pricing Reference Material is the source field for the "Material" field in respective Access Sequence (as shown in Figure 1.2.4).

2.11   Copying Pricing Condition Records

As already pointed out in Chapter 2.6, depending on how you have structured your Condition Tables, the maintenance of Condition Records is more or less time consuming and cumbersome. SAP provides some tools to make this maintenance easier. The copy function is one of them.

Let's assume you have customer specific Condition Records and want to duplicate these records to a number of other customers. Usually you would manually enter a separate Condition Record for each customer. The pricing copy function will show how you can easily copy one Condition Record to hundreds of records in a single transaction. Before this is possible, rules for copying Pricing Records need to be set up in configuration.

There are two rules that need to be defined: first, which Condition Tables should be copied; second, from which Condition Type to which Condition Type the copy should be allowed.

One Condition Type can be copied to one and the same, or even to a different Condition Type. The same is also true for the Condition Table copy rules.

The first configuration step is to execute IMG path *SD-> Basic Functions-> Pricing-> Pricing Control-> Copy Control for Conditions-> Copying Rules for Conditions.*

The resulting Figure 2.11.1 shows an overview of the copy rules already established in the standard SAP system. Double-click on any line to see the detailed information.

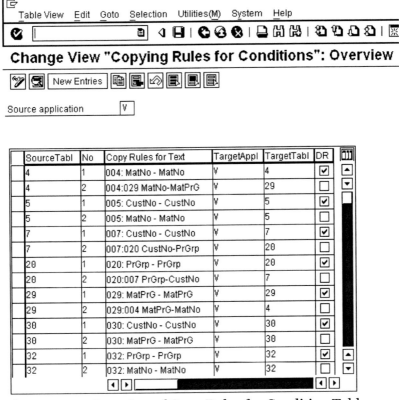

Figure 2.11.1: Overview of Copy Rules for Condition Tables

Although any available Condition Table can be selected, the system checks and only allows a combination of tables based on the following two rules: both tables have to have the same number of key fields, and the tables cannot differ by more than one field.

In the "Source Data" section of the ' "Copying Rules for Conditions": Details' screen shown in Figure 2.11.2, enter the Condition Table number that should be copied in the "Source Table" field (in our example, Condition Table "005").

Change View "Copying Rules for Conditions": Details

Change View "Copying Rules for Conditions": Details

Source applica.   V

Source data
Source table	5	Customer/Material
Sequence No.	1	005: CustNo - CustNo
Source field	KUNNR	Customer

Target data
TargetApplicat.	V	Sales/Distribution
Target table	5	Customer/Material
TargetFieldName	KUNNR	Customer

Copy control
Select.rep	RV15CC07	Copying : Customer to Customer
☑ Copy date		
☑ Default rule		

Figure 2.11.2: Detailed View of Condition Table Copy Rule

Enter a sequential number and give the copy rule a description. Select the source field that should be copied. In our example, use "KUNNR" for customer number.

According to the rules just mentioned, enter the target Condition Table in field "Target Table" (in the "Target Data" section). The "TargetFieldName" is automatically selected by the system. If you are copying the same table to itself, the Target Field will be the same as the identified source field. As in our example (copying Condition Table "005" to "005"), the customer number is the source *and* the Target Field.

In the case of different Condition Tables (remember, they can only differ by one field), SAP automatically selects the differing fields in the source and Target Field. As an example, check out the copy rule for Condition Table "007" to "020" (double-click on that line in the screen shown in Figure 2.11.1). The different field is "Customer Number" in table "007" and

"Price Group" in table "020". Even if you picked a different source field than "KUNNR", SAP would change your selection back to the customer number.

In the "Copy Control" section of Figure 2.11.2, it is important to pick a selection report in field "Select.rep". This report is needed later during the actual copy of Condition Records to select a list of new customers (or any other field) to which you want to copy your records.

SAP provides a number of standard selection reports, all starting with "RV15CC". Click on the pull-down to see which reports are available in the standard SAP system. As you can see, these are reports for just a few basic fields, like copying customer to customer, material to material, etc. To copy custom tables that include a field that is not in any of these copy selection reports, you need to create a custom report by copying and modifying one of the standard SAP reports.

To automatically default the Validity dates of the Condition Record that is being copied, select the "Copy Date" field. The Validity date is just a default and can be changed later on the "Copy Selection" screen.

It is possible to have multiple copy rules for the same Condition Table. For example, if you have a Condition Record with customer and material in the key, you might want to create a copy rule for the customer and a separate rule for material. As we will see later during Condition Record creation, you can either select a copy rule or execute the copy function without having to specify a rule. For the latter option, the default rule will be used (it is indicated by selecting the "Default Rule" field in Figure 2.11.2). Only one default rule per Condition Source Table can exist.

Following the IMG path *SD-> Basic Functions-> Pricing-> Pricing Control-> Copy Control for Conditions-> Copying Rule for Condition Types,* we can now define which copy relationships between Condition Types are allowed (see Figure 2.11.3). Enter the source Condition Type, a sequential counter, and the target Condition Type. After saving this setting, the configuration steps to copy Condition Records are now complete.

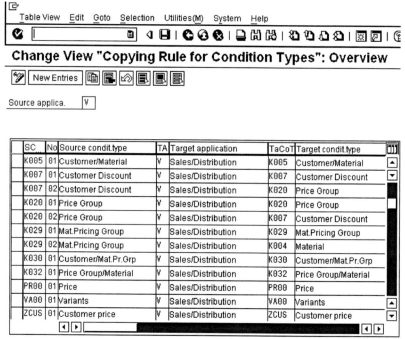

Figure 2.11.3: Copy Rule for Condition Types

You should note that if no copy rule is set up and the copy of a Condition Record is attempted, a message stating, "copying is not possible" is issued, since no rules were defined.

Condition Records can be copied in Condition Record "Change" mode (execute transaction "VK12" or "VK32" as shown in Chapters 2.2 and 2.6). You can't use the copy function in "Create" mode since there are no existing Condition Records to copy from yet.

Select an existing Condition Record of the Condition Type you would like to copy (in our example, "ZCUS"). After selecting the record in Figure 2.11.4, there are two choices.

Option one is to select the "Copy Condition" 🔲 button. This will copy the Condition Record using the default copy rule, previously identified in configuration. If no default rule was defined, the first copy rule in the configuration sequence would apply.

The other option is to click on the "Select Rule" button. This will open a pop-up from which you can select one of the configured copy rules (in the example of a customer/material record, either customer to customer or material to material, as shown in Figure 2.11.4).

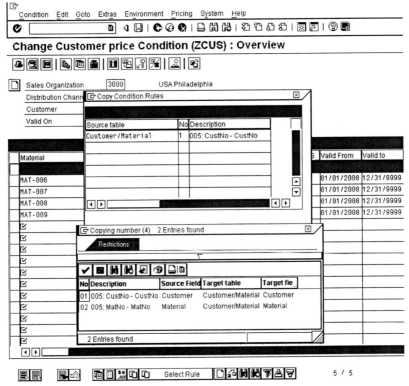

Figure 2.11.4: Selecting a Copy Rule

Regardless of which option is chosen, the "Copy Control" selection screen will be presented (see Figure 2.11.5), which is the result of the selection report that was assigned in the configuration of the copy rule (in Figure 2.11.2).

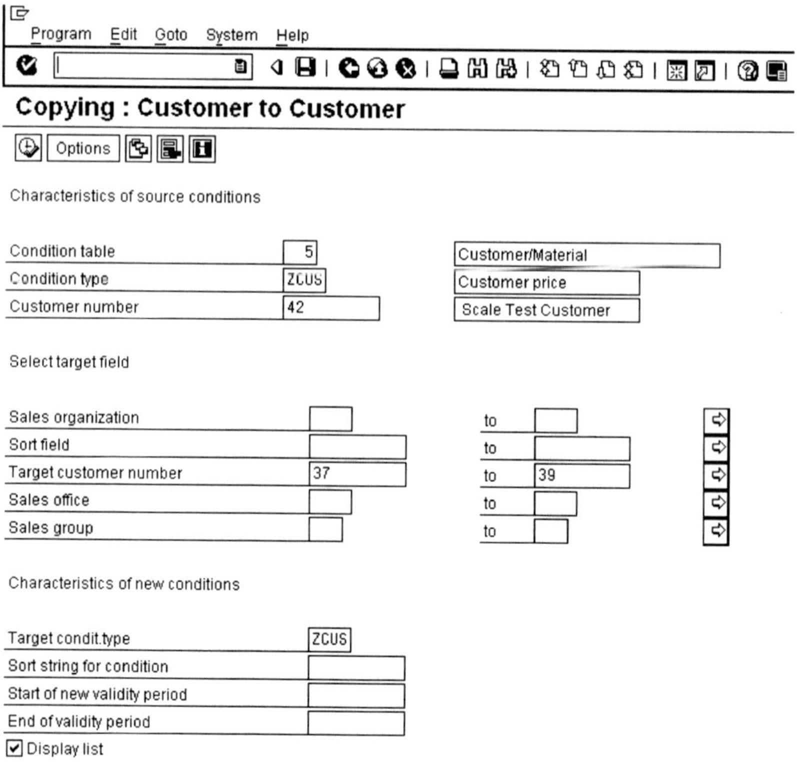

```
┌─
  Program   Edit   Goto   System   Help
  ✔  [          ]  ▣  ◁ 🗄 | 😊😊😊 | 🖥🖰🖰 | 🕮🕮🕮🕮 | 🖾🗐 | 🕜🖳
━━━━━━━━━━━━━━━━━━━━━━━━━━━━━━━━━━━━━━━━━━━━━━━━━━━━━
  Copying : Customer to Customer
  ⊕ [Options] 🖺🖺🖽
```

Characteristics of source conditions

Condition table	5
Condition type	ZCUS
Customer number	42

Customer/Material
Customer price
Scale Test Customer

Select target field

Sales organization		to	⇨
Sort field		to	⇨
Target customer number	37	to 39	⇨
Sales office		to	⇨
Sales group		to	⇨

Characteristics of new conditions

Target condit.type	ZCUS
Sort string for condition	
Start of new validity period	
End of validity period	

☑ Display list

Figure 2.11.5: "Copying: Customer to Customer" Selection Screen

Enter the customer numbers for which new Condition Records should be created in the "Target customer number" field. You have the option to select a different Validity Period for the new Condition Records as well. If you want to verify the customers for whom you will create new Condition Records, select the "Display list" field. Selecting this field presents the "Copying: Customer to Customer" screen in Figure 2.11.6, in which it is possible to select or deselect specific customers. Leaving the "Display list" field blank will present the "Pricing Record Overview" screen (see Figure 2.11.7).

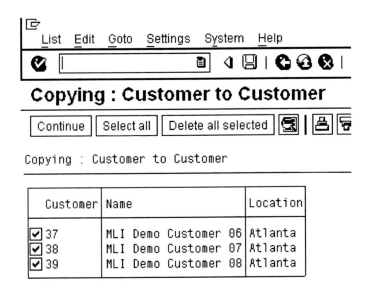

Figure 2.11.6: "Copying: Customer to Customer" Screen

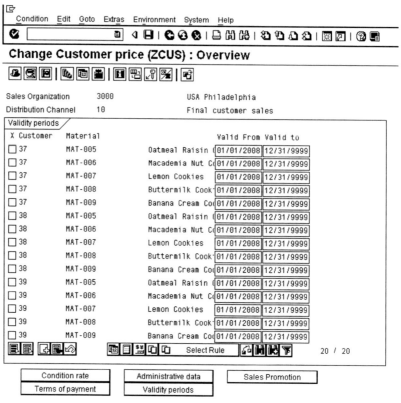

Figure 2.11.7: "Pricing Record Overview" Screen

On the "Pricing Record Overview" screen in Figure 2.11.7, you can see the original Condition Record with the original Validity Period and the newly copied records, all displaying the Validity Period entered on the previous selection screen. Saving the transaction will finally create the copied Condition Records.

This copy functionality is currently only available for pricing Condition Records. Unfortunately, it is not available to other applications that also use the Condition Technique, such as output or listings and exclusions.

2.12 Reference Conditions

Another option to reduce Condition Record maintenance is the use of Reference Conditions. No master data maintenance is necessary for this; all that is needed is a configuration setting. This is done within the Condition Type definition, accessed by IMG path *SD-> Basic Functions-> Pricing-> Pricing Control-> Define Condition Types-> Maintain Condition Types* (see Figure 2.12.1).

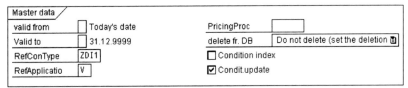

Figure 2.12.1: Reference Condition Type Configuration

Applying a Condition Type in field "RefConType" will reference the Condition Records of that Condition Type in a Sales Document. The two different Condition Types can, but don't have to, have different Access Sequences. However, in order for the reference to work, at least one Condition Table must be identical in both Access Sequences. The two Condition Types can differ in their description and their reference level in the Pricing Procedure.

In our example, we have Condition Type "ZDI2", which references Condition Type "ZDI1" (see Figure 2.12.1). The effect of this setting is that every Condition Record created for "ZDI1" would also apply for Condition Type "ZDI2". There is no need to create additional Condition Records. For example, you might want to give two discounts with the same rate for each, but for reporting purposes distinguish them by Condition Type.

Field "RefApplicatio" in Figure 2.12.1 represents the system application from which the Condition Type is referenced. In our example, we enter "V" for Sales. Another useful application of this field would be to reference a vendor price, which was created in material management, in a Sales and Distribution

Pricing Procedure. With this information, you would be able to calculate profitability. In that scenario, the reference application would be "M."

If you attempt to create a Condition Record for a Condition Type for which you have maintained a Reference Condition, the system reminds you, first when entering the Condition Type and again at save time. The message in Figure 2.12.2 states that the Condition Type you are using has a Reference Condition Type and that you should create Condition Records for that type only. You can ignore this and still create a Condition Record, but it will not have any effect on a Sales Document. The Reference Condition Record will be the one that is active.

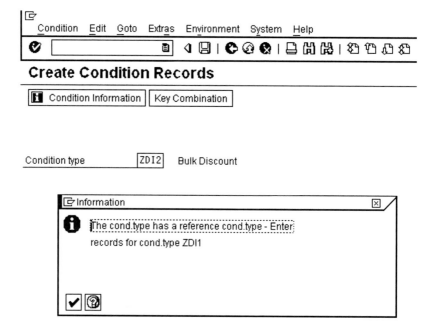

Figure 2.12.2: Message When Creating Condition Records for Reference Condition Type

In addition, it is possible to define the Condition Type that references another Condition Type with a different Condition Class or Calculation Type. Again, the values from the reference Condition Type apply on the Sales Document based on the values from the referenced Condition Type.

2.13 Pricing Limits

During Condition Record Maintenance, as well as during manual entry of Condition Types in document processing, it is possible to set limits for the value of the Condition Record. This functionality comes in handy when you want to avoid creating prices or discounts for excessive amounts (like $100,000 for a box of cookies or discounts of 1,000%). This feature is set in configuration and can be accessed with the IMG path *SPRO-> Sales and Distribution-> Basic Functions-> Pricing-> Pricing Control-> Define Condition Types.* In the following pop-up, select "Define Upper/Lower Limits for Conditions." On the next screen in Figure 2.13.1, click on "New Entries."

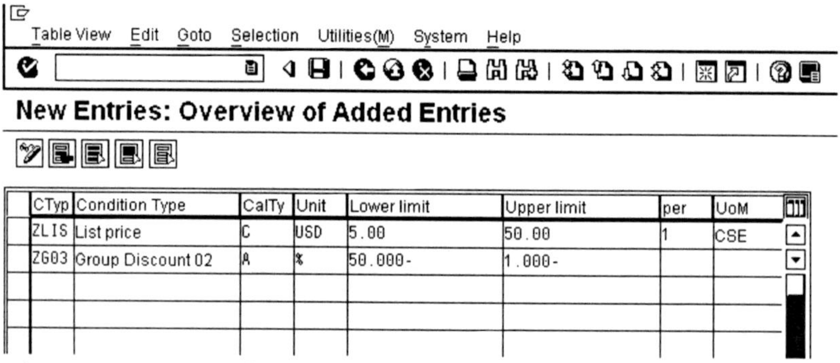

Table View   Edit   Goto   Selection   Utilities(M)   System   Help

New Entries: Overview of Added Entries

CTyp	Condition Type	CalTy	Unit	Lower limit	Upper limit	per	UoM
ZLIS	List price	C	USD	5.00	50.00	1	CSE
Z603	Group Discount 02	A	%	50.000-	1.000-		

Figure 2.13.1: Configuration of Pricing Limits

Enter the Condition Type for which pricing limits should be entered (in our example, "ZLIS" in field "Ctyp"). As the Calculation Type, enter the same value as in the Condition Type configuration ("C") in field "CalTy" since it is not defaulted from the Condition Type settings. The currency in which the pricing limits are calculated needs to be entered in field "Unit."

If a Condition Record is created in a different currency than what is maintained in the pricing limits configuration, the system converts the values to the pricing limits currency based on the valid exchange rate. Example: If the upper pricing limit for a Condition Type is set to 50 USD and the Condition

Record is maintained for 49 Euro, the system will issue an error message that the pricing limit is exceeded since the 49 Euros convert to 75.84 USD based on an exchange rate of 1:1.54778.

The values in the "Lower Limit" and "Upper Limit" fields indicate that the Condition Record Value can't have a value that is less or more than the entered values respectively. For a Condition Type that is configured to only allow negative values, such as a discount, it is important to enter the minus sign when entering the values since they are not defaulted based on the "Plus/Minus" setting of the Condition Type as they are during Condition Record maintenance. For example, if the "ZG03" discount should be allowed between 1 and 50%, "50-" will be entered as the lower limit and "1-" as the higher pricing limit.

For quantity dependent Condition Types, the Unit of Measure in which the limits are indicated has to be entered in fields "per" and "UoM." As with the currency, any value maintained in a different UoM than the limit UoM will be converted back to the pricing limit UoM.

Let's take a look how these settings apply during Condition Record maintenance. Attempt to create a new Condition Record for pricing Condition Type "ZLIS". The pricing limits are independent of the Condition Table that is chosen, so it doesn't matter which key combination is chosen. Enter the key values and a condition amount of 60 USD, which is higher than the upper limit allowed in the previous configuration step. Hit enter and the following error message is displayed, as in Figure 2.13.2: "60.00 exceeds the limit 50.00 for Condition Type ZLIS". Unless the amount is changed to a value of or under 50 USD, the Condition Record can't be saved.

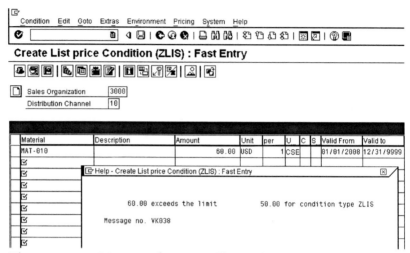

Figure 2.13.2: Message for Exceeding Pricing Limits

As mentioned before, the same check is performed for Condition Types that can be entered manually on a Sales Document, such as a Sales Order. If the manually entered value is outside the configured pricing limits, an error message is given and the Sales Order can't be saved.

As we saw in Chapter 2, lower and upper limits can also be maintained within a Condition Record. Setting the limits there is meant to maintain a limit for manual changes of the Condition Type on a Sales Document. This is different than the configuration setting for upper and lower limits in this Chapter, since these limits do not default into the Condition Record. Even if upper/lower limits are maintained in configuration, they are not displayed in these fields on the Condition Record.

2.14 Creating Condition Records with an ABAP Program

All of the previous chapters explained Condition Record maintenance carried out manually by users. During conversions or as a regular procedure to create new Condition Records, an ABAP program can be developed that creates the Condition Records. As you've seen, when creating Condition Records with either "VK11" or "VK31", Condition Tables from the Access Sequence have to be selected by the user. Due to technical restrictions, an ABAP program would not be able to place the cursor on the correct Condition Table, especially if the Access Sequence is being changed.

Therefore, transaction "VK15" provides the option to specify a Condition Type and a Condition Table in order to create Condition Records.

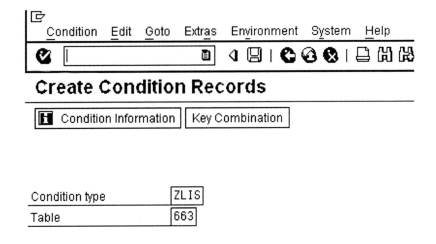

Figure 2.14.1: "VK15" Selection Screen

The ABAP program would be programmed to enter the required Condition Type in field "Condition Type" in Figure 2.14.1. Also, the Condition Table number for which Condition Records should be created needs to be specified in field "Table." The ABAP program then knows, based on the Condition

Tables, which key fields need to be entered in the Condition Record in Figure 2.14.2.

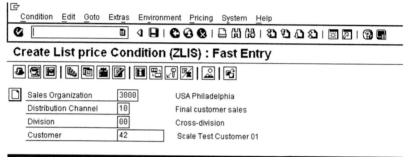

Figure 2.14.2: Creating Condition Records with "VK15"

Based on the previously specified Condition Table "663" we know the key fields are the Sales Area, the customer and the material number.

The "VK15" transaction can also be used for the manual creation of Condition Records.

Summary of Chapter 2

Using our knowledge of the Condition Technique, we were able to create the necessary master data in Condition Records several different ways.

If the Condition Type for which Condition Records should be created is known, use "VK11".

If Condition Records for multiple different Condition Types should be created, or to avoid locking issues, use "VK31".

Use "VK15" when using an ABAP program to create Condition Records.

Chapter 3: Pricing on Documents

So far, a lot of preparation work went into setting up the pricing configuration and Master Records. But as most things in SAP, the more time you spend to set up a sound pricing design and create the correct master data, the better off you are down the line. You will have more accurate pricing for your customers without a lot of manual intervention to revise incorrect information. This *Pricing Guide* will not go into all possible intricacies of Sales Order creation but will cover the pricing relevant information on the Sales Order and other Sales and Distribution documents. Please refer back to Figure 1.1 to visualize how pricing will apply on a Sales Document compared to how it was configured.

3.1   Pricing on a Sales Document

To enter a Sales Order in the SAP system, at a minimum the Sales Order Type that is created (like "OR" for a standard Sales Order), a customer and a material are required entries. As shown in the chapter on configuration, a combination of the Sales Area, the Document Pricing Procedure Indicator and the Customer Pricing Procedure Indicator determines the Pricing Procedure to be applied on the document. In addition to all the material master and customer master fields on the Sales Order that determines which pricing Condition Records apply, another important field is the Pricing Date. This date is the Valid-On date that needs to be within the Validity Period of a Condition Record in order for it to apply. Before we start with a Sales Order, let's take a look at the configuration of the Sales Order Type. In our example, it is the SAP standard delivered "OR" in Figure 3.1.1.

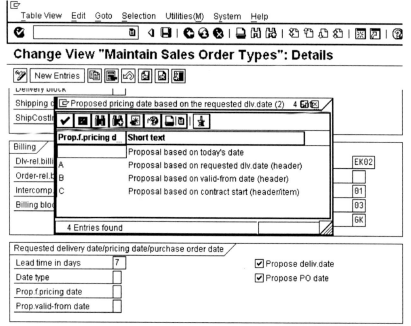

Figure 3.1.1 Pricing Date Proposal on Sales Order Type

In the "Requested Delivery Date/Pricing Date/Purchase Order Data" section of Figure 3.1, field "Prop. F. Pricing Date" defines the default Pricing Date when entering a Sales Order. The most commonly used standard default dates are the date of Sales Order entry, the requested delivery date, and the Valid-From date (when using Contracts).

For the examples in this book, I will use the Sales Order entry date as the default Pricing Date. Looking back at the configuration of a Condition Type, it is possible to use a different Pricing Date than the order Pricing Date to determine the validity of a specific pricing Condition Record. Another exception to the standard default dates: if you would like to default a date that is not part of the standard, a user exit will allow you to do so. Chapter 5.6 explains how to modify the Pricing Date based on your requirements.

Of course, the defaulted Pricing Date can be changed manually during Sales Order processing time. If a Pricing Date is manually changed, all respective Condition Records on the line items will be re-priced. Condition Types that were added manually will remain unchanged.

On the Sales Order, the Pricing Date exists on the Header of the document as well as on each line item. Figure 3.1.2 displays the Header Pricing Date on the "Sales" tab of the "Standard Order Overview" screen.

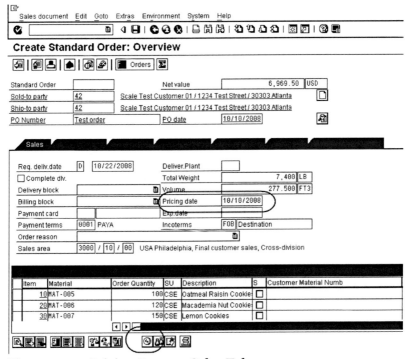

Figure 3.1.2: Pricing Date on Sales Tab

The default Pricing Date is originally the same on the Header and the line items. If the Pricing Date is changed on the Header of the document, all line items are updated with the same Pricing Date. It is also possible to change the Pricing Date on individual line items on the "Sales A" tab (as shown in Figure 3.1.3). However, if the Pricing Date on one of multiple line items is changed and the Pricing Date is subsequently changed on the Sales Order Header, the Pricing Date is only updated for the line items for which no line item Pricing Date change was previously executed.

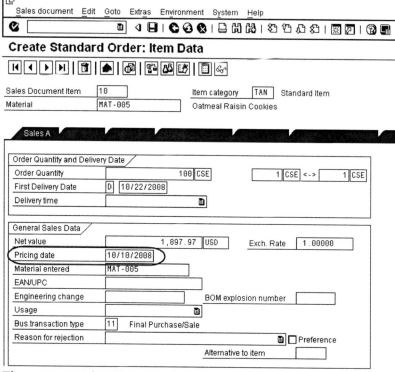

Figure 3.1.3: Line Item Pricing Date

Pricing information can be displayed on the Sales Order Header and item level. Since pricing Condition Records are always determined on line item level, we will look at pricing information on the line item level first. To get there, select a line item on the "Create Standard Order: Overview" screen and either go to *Goto-> Item-> Conditions* or click on the "Pricing" button that looks like a coin (see Figure 3.1.1). If you are in any of the other line item tabs, the pricing information is on the "Conditions" tab as shown in Figure 3.1.4.

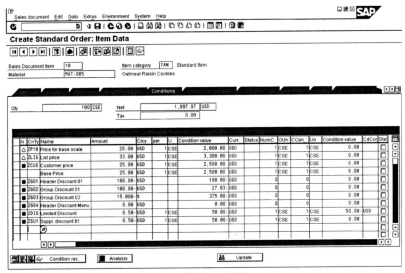

Figure 3.1.4: "Line Item Conditions" Screen

The top of the resulting conditions screen displays the material, the Sales Document line item number and the item category. The quantity in the sales UoM is also displayed. The item net value and tax amount are shown next to it.

In the main view of the conditions screen, you will see each Condition Type of the determined Pricing Procedure for which a valid Condition Record was found. In addition, you'll see all subtotals that were defined in the respective Pricing Procedure.

The first column, called "Non-Active," displays color-coded messages relating to the status of the line in the pricing display. A green light indicates that a pricing Condition Record was found and that the Condition is active. The technical field name for the active status that is checked is "KINAK", and will be blank for a green indicator. A red indicator relates to a Condition Type that has an error; the Condition Type could have been manually entered or determined by a Condition Record. The "KINAK" field has a value of "X" in that case. An amber light indicates that a Condition Type is inactive. In this case, "KINAK" has a value other than blank or "X." This column is new with SAP release ECC 6.0. Subtotal lines do not have an

133

indicator light. How a Condition Type becomes active or inactive will be discussed in a later chapter.

In the next column, labeled "CnTy", you'll see the Condition Type, and in column "Name" you'll see the Condition Type description. Subtotals don't show any information for the Condition Type; they display the name of the subtotal from the Pricing Procedure.

The "Amount" column displays the Condition Record rate. For a quantity Condition Type this would be the per unit rate. In comparison, a percentage Condition Type will show the percentage rate here. Subtotals display the rate for an item in the pricing UoM. To calculate the unit price for a subtotal, the extended value is divided by the Sales Order quantity. This might lead to rounding issues when percent Condition Types are included in the calculation and might not match the calculation when looking at just the rate values.

Example: 525 CS are ordered at $22.88 per case. A per case allowance is given in the amount of $5.04, as well as a percent discount of 1.2% of the $22.88. The system calculates the following:

$22.88 * 525 CS = $12,012
$5.04 * 525 CS = $2,646
1.2% off $12,012 = $144.14

The calculations on unit and at the extended level are:

| $22.88 | $12,012 |
| -$5.04 | - $2,646 |
-1.2%	- $144.14
$17.57	$9,221.86

The $17.57 unit price is calculated as $9,221.86 divided by 525 CS = $17.56544, rounded to $17.57. Due to the rounding, using $17.57 * 525 CS, the extended value would be $9,224.25, not $9,221.86.

The "CrCy" column shows the pricing currency. The pricing currency is the currency in which pricing Condition Records were maintained. They can be the same as or different from the document currency. In case they are different, the system performs a conversion to the document currency.

The "Per" column displays per how many units the Condition Rate applies. Usually the rate is per 1 unit, but it could also be per 100 lbs.

The "UoM" column identifies the pricing Unit of Measure. This value is copied from the pricing Condition Record. The pricing UoM can be different than the ordering sales UoM. If this is the case, the system does a conversion to the pricing UoM.

Example:	A customer orders 100 EA of a product and the pricing Condition Record is set up as 10 USD per CSE and 25 EA equal 1 CSE. The total value for this line item would be 40 USD:
	100 EA / 25 * 10 USD = 40 USD

Overwriting the pricing UoM for a price that was determined through a Condition Record will change the total value of an item.

The "NumCCO," "Oun," "CconDe" and "Un" columns display any potential UoM conversion from sales to base unit of measure. If the pricing UoM is different than the base UoM, it will display the conversion between these two UoM in these columns.

The last column on the "Line Item Conditions" screen is the "Stat" column. It identifies a pricing Condition Type as statistical. This means the value of the Condition Type does not affect the net value of an item.

The "Net Value" field in Figure 3.1.4 includes all active, non-statistical condition values for this line item. It is possible to define your business's net value differently with subtotals, but the net value displayed on this screen is the sum of all active Condition Types.

The conditions screen represents a comprehensive view of how the line item was priced. Even more information can be retrieved for the displayed pricing conditions. Select a Condition Type for which a Condition Record was found and click on the "Condition Rec." [⚭ Condition rec.] button. This will branch to the actual Condition Record to allow, for example, the display of any potential Scales. Green arrow back to return to the conditions screen. Of course, for any manually added Condition Types, it is not possible to display a Condition Record (since there isn't one).

Even more information about a displayed Condition Type can be gathered by selecting the Condition Type and clicking on the "Condition Detail" [icon] button (or double-clicking on the Condition Type).

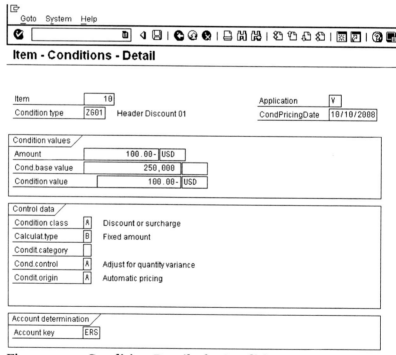

Figure 3.1.5: Condition Detail of a Condition Type

The resulting screen in Figure 3.1.5 displays the Condition Pricing Date in field "CondPricingDate" which explains for what date the system was looking for valid Condition Records.

The "Condition Values" section displays the rate of the pricing condition per pricing UoM, which could result from a Condition Record or a manually added Condition Type. The Condition Base Value explains the base for the calculation of the Condition Value. Condition Value is understood as the Condition Rate times the Condition Base Value. I will refer to Condition Value also as "Extended Value" in the course of this book. The information in the Condition Base Value depends on how the Condition Type was configured. If it is a quantity-dependent Condition Type, the Condition Base Value displays the number of units for which the Condition Value is calculated. If it is a value-dependent Condition Type, like a percentage calculation of a discount, the Condition Value will be an amount in a specified currency.

In this section, you can also see if an Alternate Calculation Type or an Alternate Condition Base Value was used to determine the Condition Value. These formulas would explain any derivation from the Condition Base Value that deviates from the standard calculation (as shown in Figure 3.1.6).

Item - Conditions - Detail

Item	10	Application	V
Condition type	Z602 Group Discount 01	CondPricingDate	10/12/2008

Condition values

Amount	100.00-	USD
Cond.base value	75,000	
Condition value	0.00	USD

AltCondBaseVal	1
Alt.calc.type	2

Figure 3.1.6: Alternate Calculation Formulas in Condition Detail

The "Control Data" section of the "Item Conditions Detail" screen in Figure 3.1.7 supplies information about the Condition Type and how it was determined. The "Condition Class" displays how the Condition Type was configured. It shows it as a price, a discount, or as taxes, for example.

The Calculation Type also refers to the configuration setting of the Condition Type. It also explains the Condition Base Value as described above.

Another field copied from the Condition Type configuration is the "Condition Category." This will help research why a Condition Type was re-priced, for example. Re-pricing and its rules will be explained in a later chapter.

"Condition Origin" identifies where the value of the Condition Type came from. If it was determined using a Condition Record, it displays an "A" for automatic pricing. A "C" indicates the Condition Type was entered manually on the Conditions screen. Use the pull-down to look at other potential origins.

In the case of an inactive Condition Type, the field "Inactive" is displayed with the respective inactive reason (see Figure 3.1.7).

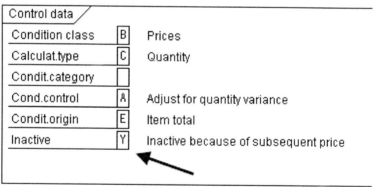

Figure 3.1.7: Inactive Condition Type

Use the pull-down for this field to display various reasons for inactive pricing conditions.

There is even more information available in the "Control Data" section, depending on certain scenarios (exclusions, multiple prices, etc.). We will explore different inactive scenarios and the additional fields in another chapter.

The "Account determination" section in Figure 3.1.5 displays the account keys for the Condition Type, which control to which G/L account the amounts for this Condition Type are posted.

If the Condition Type was determined by a Condition Record with Scales, an additional information box "Scales" is displayed on the "Conditions Detail" screen with that information (see Figure 3.1.8).

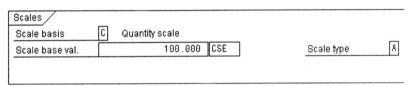

Figure 3.1.8: Scales Information on Condition Type

In Sales Order "Create" or "Change" mode, you are able to add Condition Types manually if they are configured as such. Remember which settings are needed in the Condition Type configuration for that? Correct: the Condition Type must allow manual changes and must be checked as an "Item Condition" to allow the Condition Type to be added on the "Item Conditions" screen. If it should be available to be added on the "Header Conditions" screen, it will also need to be checked as "Header Condition." Clicking on the "Insert Row" button, the cursor is positioned at the end of all Condition Types. Click on the pull-down for the Condition Type to display all Condition Types for the determined Pricing Procedure that are configured to be added manually, and available to be selected (see Figure 3.1.9).

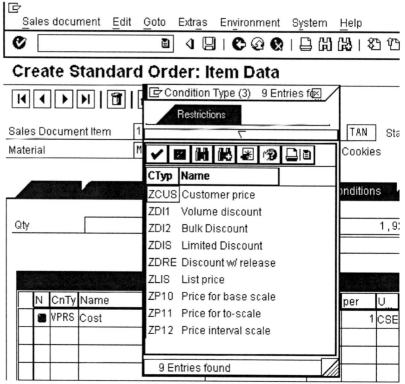

Figure 3.1.9: Adding a Condition Type Manually

You can also allow a Condition Type that can be determined via a Condition Record to be added manually at the same time.

After selecting the desired Condition Type, the rate for the Condition can be entered in the "Amount" field for the UoM of choice. The only limitation is that the pricing UoM that is chosen is maintained as an alternate UoM for the line item material if it is different than the ordering UoM. If Condition Limits are maintained for that Condition Type as described in Chapter 2.3, the entered amount needs to be within these limits, or an error message will be issued.

To delete a Condition Type, as far as it is allowed in its configuration, select the Condition Type and click on the "Delete Row" button. If a Condition Type was manually added, it can also be deleted, regardless if its deletion is allowed in the Condition Type configuration.

Additional pricing information can be retrieved by clicking on the "Analysis" button, which is covered in the next chapter.

If you are in "Create Sales Order" or "Change Sales Order" mode, an "Update" [Update] button is available. This button is grayed out in "Display Sales Order" mode. Pricing Update allows the re-pricing of that particular Sales Order line item. Chapter 3.4, "Re-pricing Sales Documents and Price Rules," will explain this function in more detail.

To display line item pricing information for another Sales Order item, simply click on the "Next Item" [▶], "Previous Item" [◀], "First Item" [◀◀] or "Last Item" [▶▶] buttons on the top of the screen. This avoids having to go back to the "Sales Order Overview" screen in Figure 3.1.2 to select another item and to click on the "Pricing" button again.

The information on the "Header Conditions" screen is similar to the one on the "Item Conditions" screen in regard to the columns displayed. One of the differences is that the "Condition Record" button is grayed out. Since Condition Records only apply on line item level, Condition Records can't be displayed on the Header. Also, there are no UoM conversion columns on the "Header Conditions" screen. On line item level, only one occurrence of a Condition Type which represents a price can be displayed. On the Header, however, the same Condition Type can be displayed multiple times if the rate of that particular Condition Type is different for certain line items. This display is applicable to SAP releases prior to ECC 6.0 only. In SAP release ECC 6.0, only one line per Condition Type is displayed on the Header with the total value of all line items summarized.

As with the "Item Conditions" screen, the "Header Conditions" screen has an "Update" button as well. After selecting it, the same list of Pricing Rules appears as on the line item. Instead of just re-pricing one line item, the Header update carries out new pricing for all line items.

By clicking the "Activate" | ▯ Activate | button, a manually entered Header Condition amount, which should be allocated to the applicable line items, is distributed to these line items according to specified rules. This functionality is described in detail in the chapter on "Group Conditions."

There are certain Condition Types that apply automatically without the determination by Condition Records. Two examples of these special Condition Types are the cost of an item and the Cash Discount.

The cost Condition Type "VPRS" is configured as Condition Category "G" for "Internal Price." The cost value is therefore read from the material valuation segment of the material master.

The Cash Discount Condition Type "SKTO" has Condition Category "E" for "Cash Discount." The Cash Discount percentage is determined from the terms of payment table. It is important that the "Cash Discount" box on the "Sales: Sales org. 1" tab of the material master is checked in order for the Cash Discount to apply on a Sales Document.

Figure 3.1.10 displays the Condition Details of the Cash Discount Condition Type "SKTO".

Control data				
Condition class	A	Discount or surcharge	☑ Group condition
Calculat.type	A	Percentage	☑ Statistical
Condit.category	E	Cash discount ⬅	
Cond.control	A	Adjust for quantity variance	
Condit.origin	A	Automatic pricing	

Figure 3.1.10 Condition Detail for "SKTO"

These special Condition Types cannot usually be changed manually. The only way a Cash Discount could potentially change is by changing the payment terms in the Sales Document.

After reviewing all applied Condition Types, save the Sales Order.

3.2   Pricing Analysis

So far I showed you how to get information about a specific Condition Type that applied on a Sales Order. Yet another tool to gather even more information on how and why pricing conditions applied (or didn't apply) is the "Analysis" tool. The Pricing Analysis can only be accessed from the "Item Conditions" screen, since the automatic pricing via the Condition Technique only occurs for line item pricing. The goal of the Pricing Analysis is a complete analysis of the Condition Access on a Sales Document.

By pressing the "Analysis" button (see Figure 3.1.4), the system simulates the re-pricing of the item with pricing rule "B" without changing any "real" pricing on the Sales Order line item. Therefore, information that is seen on the "Analysis" screen can be different than what actually applied on the Sales Order line item. The Analysis does a real-time pricing check, regardless of what applied on the line item. It is not necessary to have a Condition Type selected in order to access the "Analysis" screen.

Looking at the "Pricing Analysis" screen in Figure 3.2.1, you will see the screen is divided into three sections.

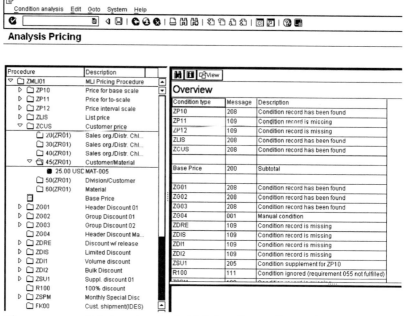

Figure 3.2.1: Pricing Analysis Pricing Procedure View

The left column (the "Procedure" window) displays all Condition Types and subtotals of the determined Pricing Procedure, the name of which is displayed on the top of the column. Contrary to the "Item Conditions" screen, every Condition Type of the Pricing Procedure is displayed here, regardless if it applied or not.

The window on the top right side of the screen displays details for a Pricing Procedure, a Condition Type or a Condition Table, depending on what information was selected in the "Procedure" window. Based on the different information it displays, its Header description changes as well. In future references, I will call it the "Details" window. It gives information about every Condition Table in the Access Sequence of a selected Condition Type (see how everything comes back together?).

The lower "Information" window on the right side of the screen displays even more information based on what was selected on the "Details" window above.

So how does all this information help us?

First, select the Pricing Procedure in the "Procedure" window (in our example, "ZMLI01"). The "Details" window then displays every Condition Type and subtotal, and indicates if a valid Condition Record was found or if one is missing. If a Condition Record was found in Analysis but did not apply on the Sales Order line item (remember, Analysis does a real-time check), it indicates that a record was found but removed. This would be the case if a Condition Record was created after the Sales Order. As you can also see in Figure 3.2.1 for Condition Type "R100", no record was found because the attached pricing requirement was not fulfilled. This is related to the pricing requirement that is attached to the Condition Type in the Pricing Procedure. An example for a requirement would be "002", which checks if the item category of the line item is relevant for pricing.

Let's take a look which pricing Condition Records applied on the Sales Order line item. If the Condition Type in the Pricing Procedure is determined by a Condition Record, a little arrow is displayed in front of it. Manual Condition Types do not have this arrow, like "ZG04" in Figure 3.2.2. Before clicking on this arrow, click on the "ZCUS" Condition Type, and the information displayed in the "Details" screen changes to the "Details" view of that Condition Type, as shown in Figure 3.2.2.

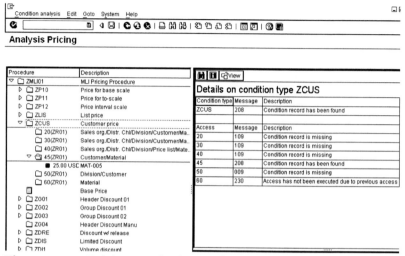

Figure 3.2.2: Pricing Analysis Condition Type View

The "Details" window shows a message if a Condition Record for the selected Condition Type has been found or not. (There are more possible messages, which we will review later.) Below that information, under the "Access" section, the Condition Tables of the Access Sequence for the selected Condition Type are displayed with their respective status, depending on whether a Condition Record was found or not. The message "Access not made (initialized field)" will occur when one or more of the Condition Table fields is not populated. This can be caused by either missing master data or, in the case of a custom Condition Table field, by incorrectly populating the custom field (see how to do this in Chapter 5.2).

A message stating, "Requirement xxx not fulfilled" indicates that the checks in the piece of code attached to the Condition Table in the Access Sequence (see Chapter 1.2) are not successfully fulfilled.

To see the detail for one particular Condition Table, now select the arrow in front of the Condition Type in the "Procedure" window. This will open another menu level and display the individual Condition Tables of the Access Sequence. Clicking on one of the Condition Tables without clicking on the arrow in front of it will again change the view in the "Details" window to the Access Sequence details. It now shows the Access Sequence Condition Table with the respective message if the Condition Record was found or not (see Figure 3.2.3).

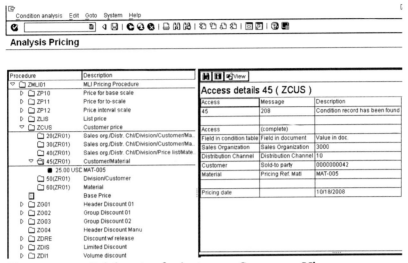

Figure 3.2.3: Pricing Analysis Access Sequence View

In the "Access" section, the individual fields of the Condition Table are displayed with the respective values populated for them in the Sales Order. This information and the displayed Pricing Date provide the data to look for a Condition Record with "VK13" or "VK33". It is possible that a Condition Record exists but not for the determined Pricing Date on the Sales Order. In the case of the "Access not made (initialized field)" message, this view will also show the field of the Condition Table that was not filled. The field value is then marked with an exclamation point.

The "Information" window on the lower right displays an extended message, stating that no Condition Record was found with the data on the Sales Document.

If a Condition Record was found, the Condition Table in the "Procedure" window will have an arrow in front of it. Click on it to open another menu level. Clicking on that new level, pre-fixed with a green button, branches into the actual pricing

Condition Record display. From there, the green back arrow will return you to the "Analysis" screen.

Special pricing conditions were mentioned in the previous chapter. As discussed, these conditions are determined without Condition Records. The "Analysis" describes how the values for these Condition Types were found in Figure 3.2.4 for Condition Types "SKTO" and "VPRS".

Net Price	200	Subtotal
SKTO	214	Percentage copied from terms of payment table
VPRS	213	Amount copied from material valuation data

Figure 3.2.4: Pricing Analysis for Special Condition Types

3.3 Optimizing Pricing on a Sales Document

As we saw in the previous chapter, the Pricing Analysis is a good way to visualize how many Condition Table accesses the system needs to make in order to determine prices and discounts for each line item. Imagine a Sales Order with 100 or more line items, and it becomes obvious that pricing is a resource intensive task.

SAP provides a way to reduce the number of accesses made, with the use of the Condition pre-step technique.

The configuration task "Optimize Access," which is often overlooked or misunderstood, will reduce the number of accesses carried out in a Pricing Procedure without altering the pricing model or the results of pricing.

Transaction "OVUo" or IMG path *SPRO-> SD-> Basic Functions-> Pricing-> Pricing Control-> Define Access Sequences-> Optimize accesses* allows the definition of the Condition Tables by Condition Type for which a Condition pre-step should be carried out.

In Figure 3.3.1, enter the Condition Type and the Access Sequence number for which a Condition pre-step should be carried out. Given our previously created list price, enter pricing condition "ZLIS" in field "Ctyp" and click on the pull-down next to field "AcNo". By entering the Condition Type in the previous field, all accesses of the attached Access Sequence of the Condition Type are displayed (see Figure 3.3.1). As you can see in this figure, the first Condition Table by Sales Area, customer and material is displayed twice since it is once configured by ship-to and once by sold-to. For "ZLIS", a preliminary step is to be executed for Access Sequence number 30 (Sales Area/Customer Sold-to/Material).

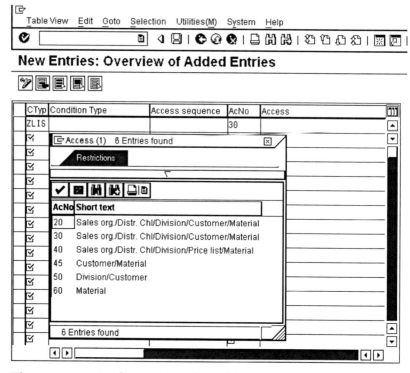

Figure 3.3.1: Configuration of Condition Pre-Step

During the pricing of a Sales Order line item, the Condition pre-step looks for valid Condition Records using the document Header data first before using line item data. Based on the example above, for the key combination of customer and material, the pre-step checks if there are any Condition Records for that Condition Type and that customer number. If there are none, the system does not continue to check for the material number of that potential Condition Record. In addition, it does not check Condition Records for that Condition Table again in the subsequent document line items, since the system already determined there are no Condition Records for that customer and Condition Type. The material numbers are therefore irrelevant. The effect of the pre-step increases the more line items there are on a Sales Document. Displaying the Pricing Analysis on the line item pricing screen shows the effect of the Condition pre-step (see Figure 3.3.2).

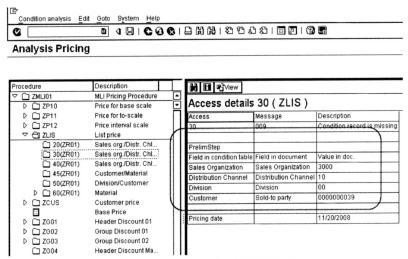

Figure 3.3.2: Condition Pre-Step for "ZLIS", Access 30

The Condition Access (40) for Sales Area, price list type and material shows a full access since this Condition Table was not defined as a Condition pre-step in Figure 3.3.1. The reason might be by design, since the price list type can differ between Header and line item(s), and Condition Records should therefore be read for each line item. However, if by design the price list type remains the same for each item of a Sales Document, it is advisable to also add this access to the pre-step configuration. As a result, this access would not be searched for subsequent line items if there are no "ZLIS" records for price list type "02", as shown in Figure 3.3.3.

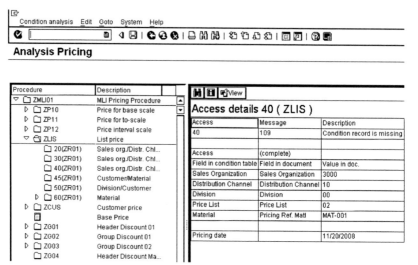

Figure 3.3.3: No Condition Pre-Step for "ZLIS", Access 40

3.4 Re-pricing Sales Documents and Price Rules

The re-pricing of a Sales Document can occur in "Create" or "Change" mode until the Sales Order is invoiced. Once invoiced, pricing changes are no longer possible.

There are several ways a Sales Document can be re-priced: by executing a manual price update, by changing certain field values or by doing a mass price change with transaction "VA05"

The reasons for needing to re-price a Sales Document could be a price increase necessitating an update of the current price in existing Sales Orders; a missing mandatory price that resulted in the incompleteness of the Sales Order; or an incorrect price does not match the Customer Expected Price.

During pricing, the system checks for all mandatory pricing conditions as indicated in the "Required" column in the Pricing Procedure (see Figure 1.4.2). If a mandatory pricing condition can't be found, the system sets the "KOMP-PRSOK" field to blank, which will result in an incomplete Sales Order. The incompletion status group attached to this incompletion field determines if delivery of the Sales Order is allowed and if the creation of a Billing Document is prevented. To view all incomplete Sales Orders due to missing mandatory pricing, execute transaction "V.01".

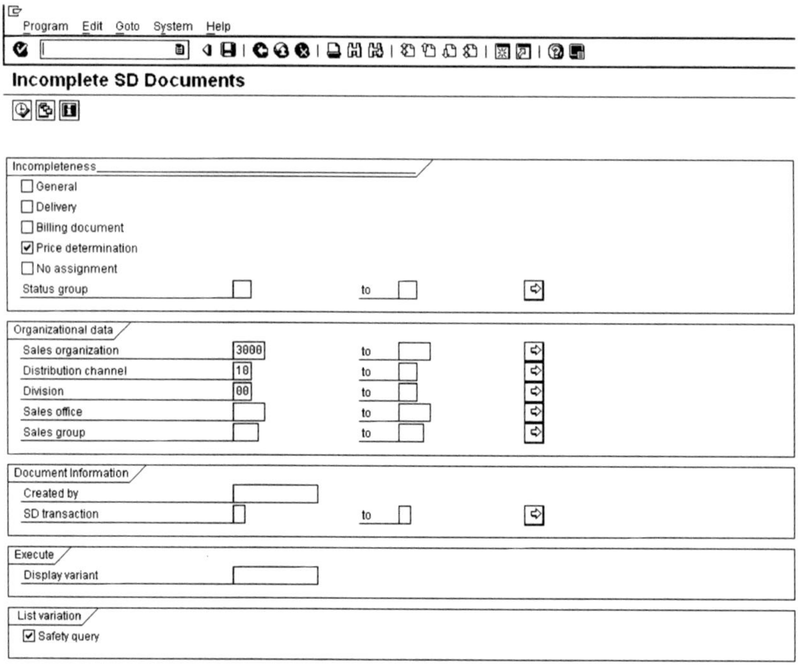

Figure 3.4.1 Incomplete SD Documents Report

The selection screen in Figure 3.4.1 provides several selection options for Sales Order incompleteness, one of them being "Price Determination." Enter the appropriate selection criteria and hit "Execute". The resulting screen in Figure 3.4.2 lists the Sales Order number, which user created the order and when, and which incompletion flags are set based on the status group configuration. Clicking on the Sales Order branches right into the incompletion log of that Sales Order from where the document can be completed.

Incomplete SD Documents

Edit incompletion | Choose | Selections

Sales Document Type	Created by	Created on	General	Delivery	BillingDoc	Pricing	Number
Order 10298	MARTINOD	07/28/2004	X	X	X	X	001
Returns 10300	MARTINOD	07/28/2004	X	X	X	X	001
Order 11955	D036882	09/29/2006	X	X	X	X	001
Order 11974	D036882	10/09/2006	X	X	X	X	001
Order 11975	D036882	10/09/2006	X	X	X	X	001
Order 11976	D036882	10/09/2006	X	X	X	X	001
Order 11986	D036882	10/11/2006	X	X	X	X	001
Order 12023	D036882	10/17/2006	X	X	X	X	001
Order 12026	D036882	10/18/2006	X	X	X	X	001
Order 12029	D036882	10/18/2006	X	X	X	X	001
Order 12136	STUDENT189	04/14/2008	X	X	X	X	001
Order 12137	STUDENT189	04/14/2008	X	X	X	X	001
Order 12213	STUDENT200	05/25/2008	X	X	X	X	001
Order 12256	STUDENT65	07/15/2008	X	X	X	X	001
Order 12458	STUDENT30	09/08/2008	X	X	X	X	002
Order 12460	STUDENT27	09/10/2008	X		X	X	001
Order 12462	STUDENT27	09/10/2008	X	X	X	X	001
Order 5000382	PDAPHARMA	01/04/2002	X	X	X	X	001
Order 5000531	ITSGLOBAL	03/08/2002	X	X	X	X	001

Figure 3.4.2: List of Incomplete SD Documents

Assuming that a Sales Order is incomplete due to a missing price at time of Sales Order creation, and a new Condition Record for that price was created in the meantime, let's explore the different options for re-pricing that Sales Document.

Re-pricing a Sales Document manually

One way of re-pricing a Sales Document is to manually trigger a re-pricing. This can be done on the Sales Document "Header Conditions" screen or the "Item Conditions" screen. Let's use the Sales Order we just saved in Chapter 3.1. Execute transaction "VA02" or go to SAP menu *Logistics-> Sales and Distribution-> Sales-> Order-> Change*. Within the Sales Order, use menu *Goto-> Item-> Conditions* to get to the line item pricing screen (seen in Figure 3.1.4). Click on the "Update" button. As a result, a pop-up offers a list of different Pricing Rules (see Figure 3.4.3).

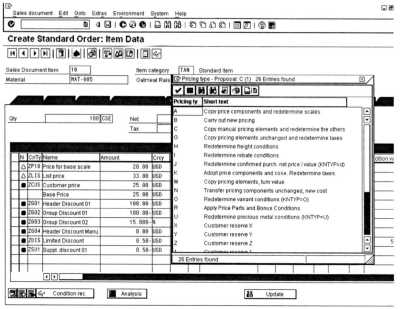

Figure 3.4.3: Pricing Types for Manual Re-Pricing

A Pricing Rule, also called a Pricing Type, defines which types of Condition Types are being re-priced. For example, Pricing Rule "H" will only re-price Condition Types with a Condition Category of "F" for freight. All other Condition Types will not be re-priced in that Pricing Rule.

Pricing Rule "C" will re-price all Condition Types that were determined by a Condition Record, but will leave any manually added Condition Types untouched.

Pricing Rule "B," however, will carry out a completely new pricing, which will remove any manually added Condition Types. There are additional Pricing Rules that are not listed during the manual re-pricing of a Sales Document, like Pricing Rule "D," which does not change any pricing. Since this does not make any sense when you re-price a Sales Document, it is not listed here. This Pricing Rule will become available when Pricing Rules are assigned in Copy Control, which will be covered in Chapter 3.10.

Select the Pricing Rule with which the Sales Document should be re-priced. On the item condition screen, the value of Condition Types for which the rate in their Condition Record was previously changed, is then altered to the new values. The re-pricing occurs for the Pricing Date that is maintained on the respective line item, which means that if a pricing Condition Record was changed for a Validity date after the line item Pricing Date, a re-pricing of that line item will have no affect on the Sales Document.

In case you are worried that users will accidentally select a Pricing Rule that should not be used, a default Pricing Rule can be established in a user exit, which is explained in Chapter 5.8.

The same re-price functionality can be executed on the Sales Order Header by using menu *Goto-> Header-> Conditions*. The same set of Pricing Rules is available as on the line item. A difference for the Header re-pricing is that a pricing condition that was entered manually on the "Header Condition" screen will not be re-priced and therefore removed when selecting Pricing Rule "B." A Condition Type entered manually on the line item would be removed with Pricing Rule "B."

Another way of manually re-pricing a Sales Document is to select menu *Edit->New Pricing Document* from the "Sales Order Overview" screen. Using this menu will not provide the pop-up screen to select a Pricing Rule but instead will re-price the Sales Document with the Pricing Rule that is maintained for the Pricing Procedure in the Pricing Procedure Configuration (refer back to Figure 1.4.1). If no Pricing Rule is maintained for the Pricing Procedure in configuration, Price Rule "B" applies as the default.

Re-pricing by changing field values

The second option is to re-price a document by changing the value of certain fields. One example is the material number. If an existing material number is changed, the SAP system executes a completely new pricing for this line item with Pricing Rule "B." A message is issued to notify the user: "New Pricing was carried out."

Automatic re-pricing of a Sales Document also occurs when one of the following fields are changed:

- Pricing Date: Re-pricing with Pricing Rule "B"
- Currency: Re-pricing with Pricing Rule "G" (only taxes and the exchange rate are re-determined)
- Ship-to: Re-pricing with Pricing Rule "G" (only taxes are re-determined), which is indicated by an informational message
- Inco terms: Re-pricing with Pricing Rule "H" (only freight Condition Types are re-determined), which is indicated by an informational message
- Payment Terms: Re-pricing with Pricing Rule "E" (only the terms of payment are re-determined)

All of these fields will re-price automatically with the mentioned Pricing Rules without offering the option to pick a Pricing Rule as in the manual re-price scenario.

It is also possible to define additional fields that would trigger an automatic re-price of the Sales Document when changed. This is done via custom code in user exits, which are explained in Chapter 5.9. For now, just be assured that changes to any fields on the Sales Order Header (DDIC Table "VBAK"), Sales Order line item (DDIC Table "VBAP") and for the Sales Order Business Data (DDIC Table "VBKD") can potentially trigger new pricing. For a complete list of fields, please refer to the Data Dictionary definitions of the mentioned tables.

Re-pricing by mass changing of Sales Orders with "VA05"

The third and last option to re-price Sales Documents is a mass change via the Sales Order list transaction "VA05".

"VA05" allows the display of a list of Sales Orders based on certain selection criteria and enables the update of multiple documents at the same time. For example, it could be that a customer received a new type of discount that applied to all products he orders. You would select all Sales Orders for a specific time frame for that one customer.

Another example could be that the price of an item changed and all Sales Orders for that particular product need to be updated. Just enter the material number in the "List of Sales Orders" selection screen as shown in Figure 3.4.4.

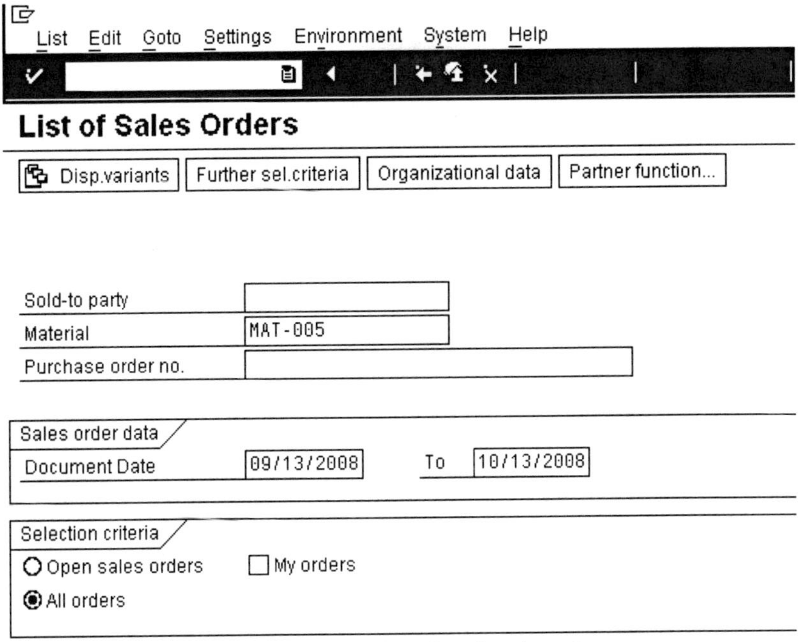

Figure 3.4.4: "List of Sales Orders" Selection Screen

Select a document date range and decide if only open orders (select the "Open Sales Orders" button) or all orders (select the "All Orders" button) should be selected. If more selection criteria are necessary, click on the "Organizational Data" and/or the "Further Selection Criteria" buttons on the top of the screen, which will allow narrower selections. After making all necessary selections, press enter.

On the next screen, either select all (by clicking the "Select All" button) or only specific Sales Orders from the "List of Sales Orders" screen in Figure 3.4.5. Then choose menu *Edit-> Mass Change-> New Pricing*.

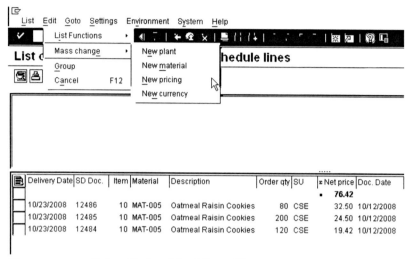

Figure 3.4.5: Sales Order List Mass Changes

A message will inform you that new pricing will be executed, and it will provide the now familiar list of Pricing Rules. Select the desired Pricing Rule, and all selected Sales Orders will be re-priced. The Net Price per line item indicated in Figure 3.4.5 will not reflect the price changed after the re-pricing is complete. There is no message issued once the pricing updates are complete; you must wait for the hourglass, which indicates the transaction is still in process, to disappear.

Instead of re-pricing individual Sales Orders, the list functionality offers a much more convenient way to get the job done.

3.5   Customer Expected Price

In certain industries, like the Consumer Product Industry, price plays an important role. It is important for the system to calculate the same price the customer expects. Discrepancies result in short payments, deductions and fees for non-matching Invoice amounts. Needless to say, countless hours and dollars are spent investigating and resolving these Invoice disputes due to differing pricing.

To catch these discrepancies up front, price Condition Types that can be added to the Pricing Procedure have been available since SAP R/3 release 2.2. Condition Type "EDI1" compares the Net Price of a line item with the Customer Expected Price that a customer sends in via an EDI transaction or one that is entered manually. Condition Type "EDI2" compares the customer expected value of a line item (price times quantity) with the value the customer claims. The configuration of the Pricing Procedure looks as follows in Figure 3.5.1.

Figure 3.5.1: Customer Expected Price Condition in Pricing Procedure

For this book, the example used will show the Customer Expected Price comparison. The "EDI1" Condition Type is usually added to the end of the Pricing Procedure. Mark the

"Manual" and the "Statistical" columns. The important configuration for this Condition Type is to add the "Alternate Calculation Type" of "09". This piece of code compares SAP's calculated Net Price (which is the sum of all active Condition Types) with the price the customer sent (see Figure 3.5.2). For the customer expected value Condition Type "EDI2", the "Alternate Calculation Type" would be "08".

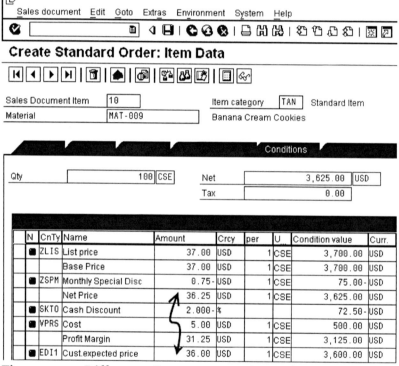

Figure 3.5.2: Difference Between Net Price and Customer Expected Price

As you can see in Figure 3.5.2, the Net Price on the Sales Order line item is $36.25, but the customer expected a price of $36.00. The customer assumed a $1.00 discount, which does not take effect until next month.

Upon saving the Sales Document, the incompletion screen shows the Customer Expected Price discrepancy (see Figure 3.5.3). Save the Sales Order as incomplete.

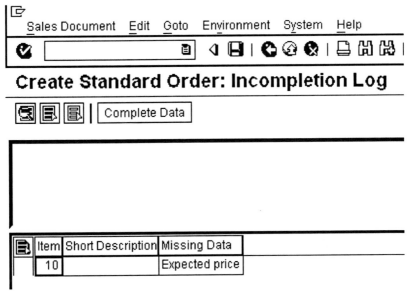

Figure 3.5.3: Incompletion Log Due To Customer Expected Price

In order to show the effect this incompletion has for the downstream processes of delivering and invoicing this order, we need to look at the incompletion configuration for the Customer Expected Price.

Use IMG path *SPRO-> Sales and Distribution-> Basic Functions-> Log of incomplete items-> Define Incompleteness Procedures*. On the following screen, select the "Sales->Item" incompletion group and double-click on the "Procedures" folder in the left column (not displayed here). Select incompletion procedure "20" and double-click on the "Fields" folder in the left column. Incompletion Procedure "20" is assigned to the standard line item category "TAN" which is used for most of the examples in this book. Figure 3.5.4 displays the document fields in this incompletion procedure. Field "CEPOK" is flagged by the "Alternate Calculation Type" if the Customer Expected Price or value does not match the system calculated value. Status group "05" in column "Status" is assigned to this incompletion field. You might also notice field "PRSOK" from the previous chapter for pricing on this screen, which is set if a mandatory pricing condition does not exist on the line item.

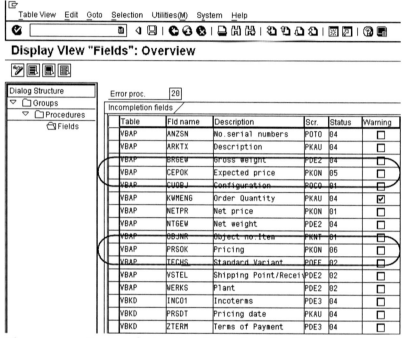

Figure 3.5.4: Incompletion Configuration for Customer Expected Price and Pricing

Using IMG path *SPRO-> Sales and Distribution-> Basic Functions-> Log of incomplete items-> Define Status Groups* defines how the system reacts during the downstream processes of a Sales Order.

Looking at Status Group "05" in Figure 3.5.5 shows that an incomplete Sales Order due to an expected price discrepancy would allow the creation of a Delivery but prevent the creation of an Invoice. Column "Delivery" is unchecked, but column "Billing doc" is checked. Some businesses might not like this configuration since although the customer is not being invoiced, they still receive their goods and might not care if they are being invoiced or not. Therefore, if the creation of a Delivery should be prevented in order to resolve the Customer Expected Price beforehand, the "Delivery" column needs to be checked as well. Instead of doing this for status group "05", which could be used for other fields in the incompletion procedure, I suggest assigning status group "06" (which is also assigned to the "PRSOK" field) to the "CEPOK" field in the incompletion procedure.

S.	General	Delivery	Billing doc.	Price	Goods movement	Picking/putaway
01	✓	☐	☐	☐	☐	☐
02	✓	✓	☐	☐	☐	☐
03	✓	☐	✓	☐	✓	☐
04	✓	✓	✓	☐	✓	☐
05	✓	☐	✓	✓	✓	☐
06	✓	✓	✓	✓	✓	☐
16	✓	☐	☐	☐	☐	✓
30	✓	☐	☐	☐	☐	☐

Figure 3.5.5: Incompletion Status Groups

Now back to the dispute we have with our customer due to the discrepancy in price. There are several ways to resolve this.

Of course it is possible that the prices, surcharges and discounts in our system are incorrect and the Customer Expected Price is correct. In that case, correct the applicable pricing Condition Records and re-price the affected line item as explained in the previous chapter. The "Alternate Calculation Type" code is executed again, and if the now calculated Net Price matches the Customer Expected Price, the incompleteness of the Sales Order is removed and the Sales Order can be delivered and invoiced.

But what if the customer was mistaken and deducted the wrong amount for a discount as in our example? Naturally, communication with the customer must occur first. If an agreement is reached that our price is correct, there are two ways of resolving the incompleteness of the Sales Order.

Option 1 is to change the value of the "EDI1" Condition Type to match the system calculated price. However, for audit reasons you might want to keep the value that the customer sent in. In that case, you need to release the incomplete Sales Order.

To do that, execute transaction "V.25" or use SAP menu *Sales and Distribution-> Sales-> Information System-> Worklists-> Release Customer Expected Price*. Figure 3.5.6 displays the selection screen, which, unfortunately, doesn't offer many selections. Select the Sales Area and execute the transaction.

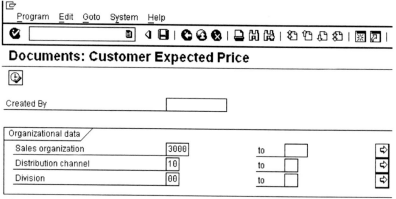

Figure 3.5.6: Customer Expected Price Release Report

The resulting Figure 3.5.7 displays all Sales Orders with incomplete line items. It shows the Customer Expected Price and the system calculated Net Price.

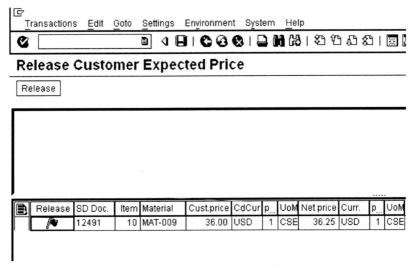

Figure 3.5.7: Released Customer Expected Price

By double-clicking the Sales Order number in column "SD Doc.", you will be able to access the Sales Order in "Change" mode. If the system price needs to be corrected, you could execute a manual re-pricing of the Sales Order. Click on the green back arrow to return to this work list. Select the Sales Order line items that you want to release, then select the "Release" button. The "Release" column will show a release flag as seen in Figure 3.5.7. After that, you need to save your releases to keep the original "EDI1" value but allow the creation of a Delivery and an Invoice.

If you want SAP to compare a different value than the system calculated Net Price to the Customer Expected Price, you can create a custom "Alternate Calculation Type." Just replace the Net Price with your desired subtotal.

3.6 Condition Exclusions

So far we have examined how each pricing condition in the Pricing Procedure is checked in a Sales Order for valid Condition Records. In this chapter, I will discuss how some applied Condition Records can exclude other Condition Records. For example, you might not want to give a discount to a customer if a low customer price was already applied on a Sales Order.

Prior to SAP R/3 release 4.0A, it was only possible to exclude Condition Records based on the setting of the Exclusion Flag in other Condition Records. As we saw in Chapters 1.3 and 2.1, an exclusion indicator can be set either in the configuration of the Condition Type (see Figure 1.3.7) or on an individual Condition Record (see Figure 2.1.3). The setting on the Condition Type would result in the setting of the exclusion indicator as a default for each created Condition Record of this Condition Type. Let me explain the functionality of this exclusion indicator with the following example.

A price Condition Record is maintained by customer and material number. Customer 1 pays 150 USD, customer 2 only 100 USD for a product. Set the exclusion indicator manually in the Condition Record for 100 USD. A separate discount Condition Record would give both customers a 10% discount from their list price. Since customer 2 only pays 100 USD for the product, we don't want to give him the 10% discount on top of the already reduced price. Attach requirement "002" to the discount Condition Type in the Pricing Procedure in column "Reqt." This pricing requirement checks that no exclusion indicator exists for that line item and only then allows the application of the discount. The Condition Record for 150 USD does not have an exclusion indicator and therefore allows the discount condition to be applied.

On the other hand, since we maintained the exclusion indicator for the 100 USD Condition Record, the requirement "002" prevents the application of the discount condition. Be aware that all other Condition Types in the Pricing Procedure that either have requirement "002" attached or are checking for the existence of the exclusion indicator will also not apply due to the failed requirement check.

As you can tell, this procedure is not as flexible as business requirements might require, so SAP introduced a new Condition Exclusion procedure with SAP R/3 release 4.0.

The configuration for this procedure can be found in the IMG path *SPRO-> Sales and Distribution-> Basic Functions-> Pricing-> Pricing Control-> Condition Exclusion-> Condition Exclusion for Groups of Conditions*. In the next pop-up, select "Define Condition Exclusion Groups." In this configuration step, Exclusion Groups can be freely defined. The Exclusion Group in field "ExGr" is a four-character field. To protect custom Exclusion Groups from being overwritten during an upgrade, enter Exclusion Groups starting with "Z." Enter a description in field "Name" for the Exclusion Group as shown in Figure 3.6.1.

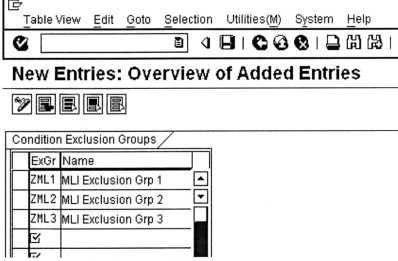

Figure 3.6.1: Condition Exclusion Groups

Next, Condition Types that need to be part of any exclusion calculation need to be assigned to the respective Exclusion Group. Go to IMG path *SPRO-> Sales and Distribution-> Basic Functions-> Pricing-> Pricing Control-> Condition Exclusion-> Condition Exclusion for Groups of Conditions*. In the following pop-up window, select "Assign Condition Types to the exclusion groups." Click on the "New Entries" button.

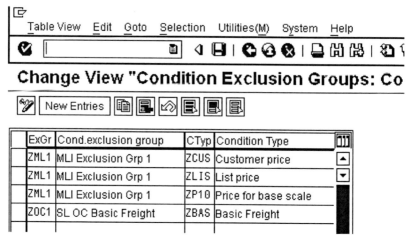

Figure 3.6.2: Assignment of Condition Types to Exclusion Groups

In field "ExGr"in Figure 3.6.2, enter the Exclusion Group to which Condition Types should be assigned. In field "CTyp" enter the Condition Type that should belong to the listed Exclusion Group. The descriptions of both the Condition Type and the Exclusion Group are displayed automatically. Multiple Condition Types can be assigned to the same Exclusion Group. A Condition Type can also be assigned to more than one Exclusion Group. In the next configuration step, we will go deeper into the logic of different scenarios for which Condition Types to assign to which group and for which exclusion.

Exclusion Rules are assigned to a specific Pricing Procedure. Multiple Procedures can use the same rule(s), but they can also have their own exclusion logic.

To assign exclusion rules to a Pricing Procedure, go to IMG path *SPRO-> Sales and Distribution-> Basic Functions-> Pricing-> Pricing Control-> Condition Exclusion-> Condition Exclusion for Groups of Conditions*. From the following pop-up, select "Maintain Condition Exclusion for Pricing Procedures."

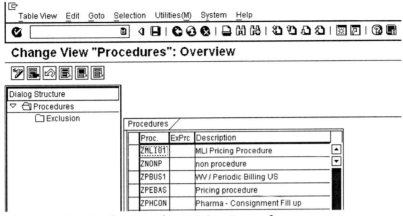

Figure 3.6.3: Exclusions for Pricing Procedures

Select the appropriate Pricing Procedure in the "Proce-dures" window in Figure 3.6.3 and double-click on the "Exclu-sion" folder in the left window pane.

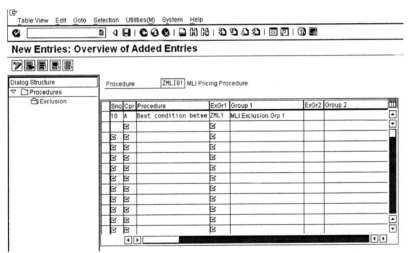

Figure 3.6.4: Assign Exclusion Procedure to Pricing Procedure

Select the "New Entries" button to display Figure 3.6.4.

The "Sno" column identifies a sequential number for the different possible Exclusion Rules. The Exclusion Rules assigned to a Pricing Procedure are processed in that sequential order.

The "Exclusion Procedure" is entered in the "Cpr" (Condition Exclusion Procedure) column. This Procedure defines the rules of the exclusion. The Exclusion Group that was defined in the first configuration step is entered in field "ExGr1".

The following Procedures are available in SAP ECC release 6.0.

Procedure "A" ("Selection of the most favorable Condition Type within a Condition Exclusion Group"): If three price Condition Types are assigned to an Exclusion Group and this rule is selected, the system will pick the lowest price condition as the active Condition Type. In the case of discount Condition Types, the most favorable one for the customer (the highest discount) is chosen.

Procedure "B" ("Selection of the most favorable Condition Record for a Condition Type, if several valid Condition Records exist"): The system looks for all valid Condition Records of *one* Condition Type and selects the one with the lowest value. For this option to work, the exclusion indicator in the Access Sequence for this Condition Type has to be de-selected.

Procedure "C" ("Selection of the most favorable of two Condition Exclusion Groups"): In this option, all Condition Types of each Exclusion Group are accumulated and the totals are compared. The group with the least value is the one for which Condition Types will remain active. In this scenario, you might have a price in Exclusion Group 1 that is higher than in Exclusion Group 2, but the discount condition from Group 1 might reduce the total of the Exclusion Group 1 more than the discount condition from Group 2. The result would be that the Condition Types of Exclusion Group 1 will apply. In this scenario, the Exclusion Group 2 would be entered in field "ExGr2".

Procedure "D": If any Condition Type from the first Exclusion Group applies in the Sales Document, all Conditions Types found in the second Exclusion Group are set to inactive.

Procedure "E": Same as Procedure "B," only the least favorable Condition Record within a Condition Type is active.

Procedure "F": Same as Procedure "C," only the least favorable of two Condition Exclusion Groups is selected. This means the Condition Types of the Exclusion Group with the highest value will remain active.

Procedure "L": Same as Procedure "A," only the least favorable Condition Type within an Exclusion Group remains active. This Procedure is not available in SAP releases prior to ECC 6.0.

The columns for Exclusion Group 1 ("ExGr1") and Exclusion Group 2 ("ExGr2") identify the Exclusion Groups for the respective Exclusion Procedure. The second Exclusion Group column is only applicable for Procedures "C," "D" and "F."

Now that the Exclusion Rules are defined, Sales Orders can be entered. To understand the impact of the Exclusion Rules, it is important to first understand how standard SAP handles multiple price Condition Types on the same Sales Order line item. Assuming valid Condition Records exist for three prices that all exist in a Pricing Procedure (namely "ZP10", "ZLIS" and "ZCUS"), the system allows only one price to be active on a line item. In the absence of Exclusion Rules, the last price Condition Type in the Pricing Procedure sequence will remain active. As seen in Figure 3.6.5, this would be the "ZCUS" Condition Type, although it is not the lowest price.

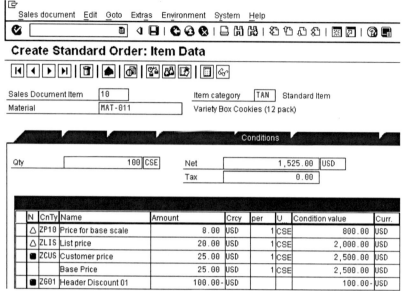

Figure 3.6.5: Multiple Prices on a Sales Order Line Item

Looking at the Condition Type detail of the "ZLIS" Condition Type, the inactive flag in field "Inactive" ("KOMV-KINAK") is set to "Y," meaning this pricing condition is inactive due to a subsequent price (see Figure 3.6.6). The last price that applied for that line item will not have an inactive indicator and is therefore active.

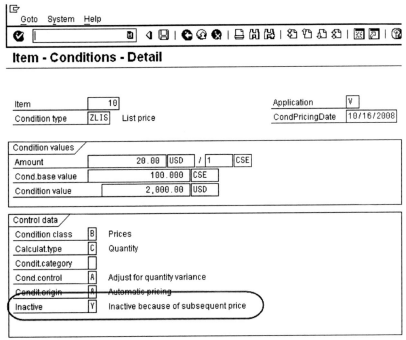

Figure 3.6.6: Inactive Reason for Multiple Prices

In comparison, enter a line item for which Condition Types apply as part of our Exclusion Group "ZML1" (which includes Condition Types "ZP10", "ZLIS" and "ZCUS"). Remember, we defined the Exclusion Procedure to select the most favorable Condition Type out of the specified group with Exclusion Rule "A." In our example, "ZP10" has the lowest price of 8 USD. Although the "ZLIS" and "ZCUS" Condition Types apply after this pricing condition, they are both set to inactive due to the Exclusion Procedure. This is also indicated by the yellow triangle in front of the Condition Type (see Figure 3.6.7).

Figure 3.6.7: Price Exclusion for Best Price

Looking again at the details of the excluded Condition Type "ZLIS", the inactive flag is now set to "A," indicating that the condition was inactivated due to Exclusion Rules (see Figure 3.6.8). This indicator is set if any of the above mentioned Exclusion Procedures apply.

Control data		
Condition class	B	Prices
Calculat.type	C	Quantity
Condit.category		
Cond.control	A	Adjust for quantity variance
Condit.origin	A	Automatic pricing
Inactive	A	Condition exclusion item

Figure 3.6.8: Inactive Reason for Exclusion Rule

176

3.7 Condition Update

As I mentioned earlier in the configuration chapter of the Condition Type, it is possible to turn on the "Condition Update" field for a Condition Type.

There are two purposes for selecting this option. The first is to track the use of a Condition Record. The Condition Update allows you to see what amounts and quantities applied for that particular Condition Record within the Validity Period of the Condition Record.

The second reason to turn on Condition Update is to limit the application of a Condition Record by certain criteria. One option is to define the maximum number of Sales Orders on which a Condition Record can apply. It is also possible to limit the total dollar amount or a specified number of quantities for which the Condition Record applies.

To enable these limitations, turn on the "Condition Update" field in the Condition Type; for our example, "ZDIS" (see Figure 3.7.1).

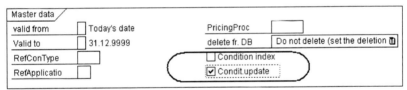

Figure 3.7.1: Condition Update Flag in Condition Type

Then create a Condition Record for that Condition Type. Enter all applicable key fields, rates and Validity Periods as shown in Chapter 2. Go to the "Additional Data" screen. As you can see in Figure 3.7.2, the selection of "Condition Update" in the Condition Type now displays additional fields on that screen. They can be found in the "Limits for Pricing" box.

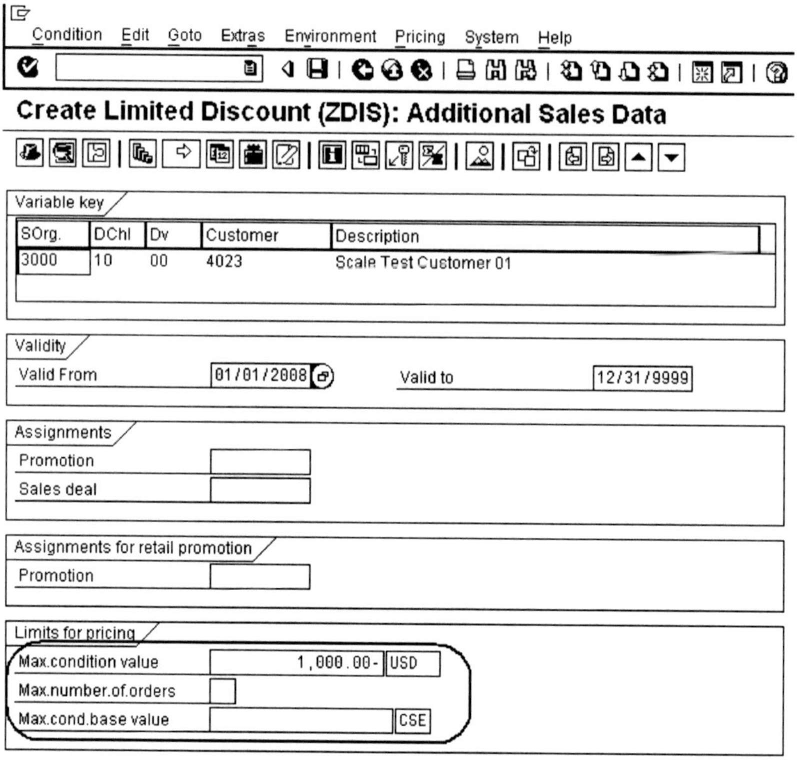

Figure 3.7.2: Condition Update Limit Fields

The "Max.Condition Value" field allows the setting of a maximum dollar amount up to which the Condition Record can apply. This feature is mostly used for discount Condition Types.

Example: The maximum amount is set to $1,000. Three Sales Orders are created. On each Sales Order, the amount applied for that Condition Record is $400. The system accumulates these values and compares them to the maximum value. The first two Sales Orders would allow the $400 discount to be applied. On the third Sales Order, though, only $200 would apply. Any Sales Order thereafter would not have any amounts applied.

The second limitation is for a maximum number of Sales Orders. This can be used for discount, surcharge or price Condition Types. You can set a number between 1 and 3 in field "Max.number.of.orders."

Example: You want to give an introductory price to a new customer for the first two Sales Orders they are placing. The first two Sales Orders after the Condition Record is saved will apply this price. Any Sales Orders thereafter will inactivate the price.

The last option to limit the application of a Condition Record value is by the number of units. This option will only display for quantity-, volume- or weight-dependent Condition Types. Enter the maximum number of units for which the Condition Record should apply in field "Max.Cond.Base Value." The UoM for that maximum amount is the same as the pricing UoM of the Condition Record.

Example: You would like to offer a discount to a customer for the first 1,000 units they buy. Three orders are entered, each for 400 units. The first two will have the discount applied for 400 units each. The third Sales Order only applied the Condition Record value for the first 200 units, since the cumulative quantity has now reached 1,000 units.

All three limit fields could possibly be maintained on a Condition Record simultaneously. The system will use the value for which the limit is reached first to determine further applications of the discount or price and disregard the others. So, even if a maximum of three orders were set up in addition to a maximum value of $1,000, but the first order reached this maximum amount limit, the discount would not be applied to any subsequent order.

To show this functionality in an example, create a new Condition Record for Condition Type "ZDIS". Go to the "Additional Data" screen and enter a Maximum Condition Value of "$1,000-". The "-" sign is important since a discount is given. If a special price should be given to the customer instead, the value in this field would be positive. Generally speaking, assign the same sign for the limit as the pricing condition has when it applies on a Sales Document. Save the Condition Record.

Every Sales Order on which this pricing condition applies will track against the limit of $1,000. The discount amount that applies for our pricing condition will be accumulated during the Condition Record Validity Period. In our example, the customer places Sales Order 1 and 2 for 80 units each. The applied discount of 5 USD per unit for Condition Type "ZDIS" is $400 per Sales Order. Since this amount is below the set maximum value of $1,000, the full amount is deducted from the gross value of the Sales Order. On order 3, the number of units is also 80, and the related "ZDIS" discount should be $400. However, since the remaining available dollar amount is only $200 ($1,000 - $800 already deducted), only $200 can be deducted from the Sales Order line item.

Figure 3.7.3 shows the "Condition Detail" screen of pricing condition "ZDIS" on the third Sales Order. The "Maximum Amount" indicator displays value "X," which indicates that the set maximum value limit of the Condition Record has been exceeded. The Condition Value for this Condition Type is shown correctly as $200.

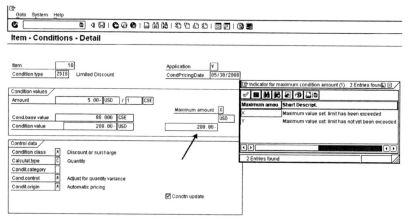

Figure 3.7.3: Maximum Condition Value Reached

In order to see the current state of how much value has been accumulated for a pricing Condition Record, go to the Master Record itself. Display the pricing Condition Record with transaction "VK13" or "VK33" and go to menu *Extras-> Cumulative values*. Note that if the Condition Record did not apply on any Sales Orders yet, the following message is given: "No Condition Update From the Sales Order Exists."

If, however, the Condition Record did apply on a Sales Order, you see at first the applied values for Sales Orders (see Figure 3.7.4). The accumulated Condition Value (here $1,000 in the pricing currency) and the accumulated Condition Base Value (here the total for the 3 orders of 80 units each = 240 CSE) are displayed by posting period.

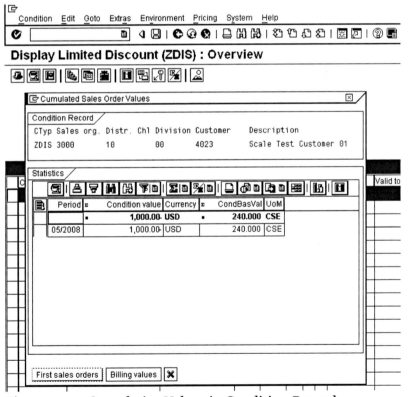

Figure 3.7.4: Cumulative Values in Condition Record

In order to see the last three Sales Orders on which the Condition Record applied, click on the "First Sales Orders" button, which will display the Sales Order numbers in Figure 3.7.5.

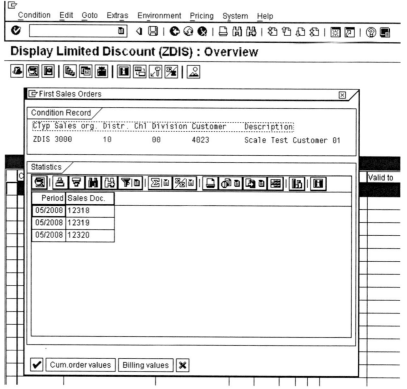

Figure 3.7.5: Last Three Orders in Condition Record

Click the "Billing values" button to display applied amounts on Billing Documents.

Although Billing Documents are tracked as well, there is one issue worth noting. The update functionality works nicely on the Sales Order; however, if your pricing model is designed to re-determine pricing at billing time, the limits are not taken into account there. So in our example, the full $400 would have applied at invoice time and not the limited amount as shown in Figure 3.7.3 on the Sales Order. OSS note 74794 describes this functionality as "not yet implemented" (as of SAP release ECC 6.0), and offers a custom work-around for this issue. A standard work-around for this problem would be to configure the Pricing Rule to not re-price at invoice time. Of course, your business rules might render this option moot.

As mentioned before, it is not necessary to maintain any limits in the Condition Record. Just by turning on the Condition Update option in the Condition Type, the system will start keeping track of the use of this Condition Record. This is useful for reporting and analysis.

The data for the Condition Update for Sales Orders is stored in one SIS structure, "S071". Invoice-related data for the same Condition Record is updated in SIS structure "S060". As soon as a Condition Record applies on a saved Sales Order, a record is written to SIS table "S071".

The key to link the Condition Record to the corresponding "S071" entry is the Condition Record number in field "KNUMH" of the respective Condition Table. Figure 3.7.6 displays the fields in this SIS table, like the "Condition Value" (the current applied amount) and "Condition Base Value," as well as the last three Sales Orders on which this Condition Record applied.

Data Browser: Table S071 Select Entries   24

Cl.	Srce	Ver	CondRecNo	No	Month	D	W	P	F	P	Curr	Condition value	CondBasVal	Sales Doc.	NoOf	Sales Doc.	NoO	Sales Doc.	No
800	000				12/2003						USD	758,780.00	3,439,406.66	0000009704	8	0070000067	24	0070000070	7
800	000	0000006764	1	08/1996							USD	0.00	0.00		0		0		0
800	000	0000019101	1	01/2002							USD	644.66-	5,372.20	0035000023	1	0035000028	1		0
800	000	0000024190	1	03/2003								34.67	3,466.67	0000008745	2	0070000066	1		0
800	000	0000025245	1	03/2003							EUR	10.00-	1,000.00-	0000008745	1	0070000066	1		0
800	000	0000025666	1	03/2003							USD	0.00	0.00		0		0		0
800	000	0000025667	1	03/2003							USD	0.00	0.00		0		0		0
800	000	0000029133	1	12/2003							UOD	500.00	100.00	0070000072	1		0		0
800	000	0000029134	1	12/2003							USD	4,000.00	400.00	0070000072	1		0		0
800	000	0000031127	1	05/2005							USD	800.00	40.00	0070000073	1		0		0
800	000	0000032065	1	02/2006							USD	1,241.40	10.00	0000011750	1		0		0
800	000	0000032074	1	02/2006							USD	2,358.66	10.00	0000011751	1		0		0
800	000	0000032074	1	04/2006							USD	2,356.00	10.00	0000011786	1		0		0
800	000	0000032101	1	04/2006							USD	0.00	0.00		0		0		0
800	000	0000032550	1	04/2006							USD	0.00	0.00		0		0		0
800	000	0000032566	1	04/2006							USD	3,400.00	20.00	0000011787	1	0000011803	1		0
800	000	0000032643	1	04/2006							USD	1,700.00	10.00	0000011785	1		0		
800	000	0000033480	1	10/2008								1,000.00-	0.00	0000012495	1	0000012497	1	0000012498	1
800	000	0000033587	1	10/2008							USD	397.50	0.00	0000012484	1	0000012495	1	0000012497	
800	000	0000033588	1	10/2008							USD	580.00	0.00	0000012495	1	0000012497	1	0000012498	1
800	000	0000033666	1	11/2008							EUR	399,480.00	133,160.00	0000012509	2	0000012510	1	0000012511	1
800	000	0000033672	1	10/2008							EUR	4,000.00	2,000.00	0000012507	1	0000012508	1		0
800	000	0000033673	1	11/2008							EUR	5,100.00	1,020.00	0000012536	1	0000012538	1	0000012539	1
800	000	0000033686	1	11/2008							EUR	231,100.00	23,110.00	0000012524	1	0000012525	1	0000012526	1

Figure 3.7.6: Cumulative Records in SIS

As with any other SIS structure that is updated in the system, its performance impact needs to be considered. Only turn on Condition Update for the Condition Types that need to have limits or that need to be tracked. OSS note 931467 discusses the performance aspects for updating SIS structure "S071". If limits are maintained within the Condition Record, the update rule for the SIS structure needs to be "V1" for "Synchronous" update. The reason is that you want to update the structure at the same time the document is posted in the system in order to have up-to-date information for the next Sales Order. To set the update rule in your SIS, configure the update (transaction "OMO1") to "V1" for "Synchronous" update.

If you would like to read more about Condition Updates, OSS Note 615370 describes the Condition Update functionality in great detail.

3.8 Scale Pricing in Sales Documents

The configuration of pricing Scales – or brackets, as they are sometimes called – in Condition Types was discussed briefly in Chapter 1.3. In the Condition Type configuration, go to the "Scales" box to look at the Scale-related configuration options. Please refer to Chapter 1.3 for detailed explanations of these options.

Scales are maintained in pricing Condition Records. The type of Scale and how it is to be used in a Pricing Record is defined in the respective Condition Type. For the example scenarios in this book, I created three new pricing Condition Types: "ZP10", "ZP11", and "ZP12".

Before we get into the application of these Scale Condition Records on a Sales Document, I would like to expand the explanation of the Scale Type in the Condition Type configuration.

As mentioned, there are three types of standard SAP Scale Types: "Base Scale," "To-Scale" and "Graduated-to Interval Scale."

Base-Scale (called *From-Scale* in previous SAP R/3 releases): This is the most commonly used Scale Type for a descending Scale. For example, it defines that for a quantity Scale, the Scale level starts *from* a specified quantity. The last Scale level of a Base Scale Condition Record would specify that all quantities above that specified quantity will be assigned the price set for that Scale level.

To-Scale: This Scale Type works in reverse of the Base-Scale. You define up to which quantity a certain price applies. If your Sales Order quantity is above that quantity, the system will look for the next Scale level quantity. A potential issue to avoid for this Scale Type is that the last Scale level might have an insufficiently low quantity. If, for example, the last Scale level is 100 units, that means up to 100 units will receive the respective Scale level price. If the order quantity were 120 units, the system could not determine a price, since no Scale level for this quantity exists. Only a Scale for *up to* 100 units was defined. Therefore, I recommend entering an artificially high quantity like 99,999 for these "To-Scale" Condition Records.

Graduated-to Interval Scale: This Scale Type is a variation of the "To-Scale." For both the "Base-Scale" and the "To-Scale," the order quantity of an item determines one price that applies to each unit of this line item. Graduated Scales, however, allow you to apply different prices for the same item depending on the quantity of the scale bracket. Let's look at an example.

To	5 EA	10 USD
	10 EA	9 USD
	20 EA	8 USD

In a regular To-Scale, an order quantity of 12 EA would apply a price of 8 USD for each of the 12 EA for a total line item value of 96 USD. In a Graduated Scale, the following prices apply:

For the first 5 EA, the price is 10 USD per EA.
For EA 6-10, the price is 9 USD.
For EA 11-12, the price is 8 USD.

The total line item value would therefore be 111 USD:

50 (5 * 10) + 45 (5 * 9) + 16 (2 * 8)

Multiple prices of the same Condition Type will apply for the same line item. The same issue as for the To-Scale applies to the Graduated Scale, in regard to the last Scale quantity. The difference for the Graduated Scale is that prices will apply up to the last Scale quantity, and after that, no prices will apply.

Taking the previous example Scale, an order quantity of 25 units would price the first 20 items at the appropriate levels, but not the final 5 units. This is actually more dangerous than the To-Scale. Assume your Sales Order line item incompletion procedure is configured to make your line item incomplete if no net value exists. Since the 20 units in the Graduated Scale would therefore have a net value, the Sales Order line item would not be incomplete. In comparison, a missing price in the To-Scale scenario would make the Sales Order incomplete and prevent it from being shipped. You would essentially give away free product of 5 units with a Graduated Scale that is maintained like in our example, which I'm sure you would agree is not desirable.

Leaving the Scale Type blank in the configuration of the Condition Type will allow you to specify the type of Scale in the maintenance of the respective Condition Record. However, if you specify either a From-, To- or Graduated Scale in the Condition Type, this will be the only type available during Condition Record creation. The "Scale Type" field in the Condition Record is then unavailable for input if a Scale Type is specified in configuration.

After configuring the Condition Type(s), the Scales in the respective Condition Records can be created. This is done with the same transactions as for regular Condition Record maintenance. Enter the Condition Type (in our example for the Base-Scale condition "ZP10") and select the desired key combination. Enter the key fields of the Condition Record. In order to create Scales, select the Condition Record and click on the "Scales" button on the top of the screen. This will display the "Scales" screen as shown in Figure 3.8.

In the "Variable Key" section of the screen, the key combination of the Condition Record is displayed.

Depending on what Scale Type was configured for the Condition Type you are maintaining Condition Records for, the "Scale Basis" and the "Check" fields are displayed in the "Control Data" box. You also see the Condition Record Validity Period next to this data in the "Validity" box.

In the "Scales" section, enter three Scale levels with the respective prices. As can be seen in Figure 3.8, the Scale Type indicates "From," which means prices apply beginning with the respective Scale quantity. Since the Scale is defined as descending, the price is reduced as more units are ordered. The Scale Type for a To-Scale or a Graduated Scale will display "To" in the Scale Type column. Although the "ZP10" Condition Type was maintained with a UoM of "PC," the Scale quantity

UoM of CSE is defaulted from the base UoM of the material in the Condition Record key, here "CSE."

If you have maintained several levels and wish to delete a Scale level, position the cursor on the level you would like to delete and click on the "Delete Row" 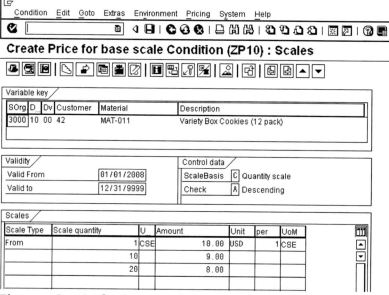 button. On the other hand, if you would like to insert a Scale level, position the cursor on the line above which you would like to insert the new level and click on the "Insert Row" button. If you inserted multiple Scale levels without entering any data for them, you can remove them all at once by pressing the "Remove Empty Scales" button.

Once all Scale brackets are entered, save the Condition Record.

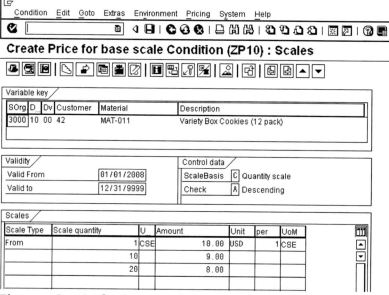

Figure 3.8.1: Scales in a Condition Record

When changing Condition Records that have Scales maintained and when executing a price increase, remember to always use the "Change Amount" function (see Figure 2.1.2

in the chapter on Condition Record maintenance) after selecting all applicable Condition Records. Just changing the price on the "Fast Entry" screen in Figure 2.1.2 will change only the first level of the Scale.

To show the application of Scales on a Sales Document, the following Condition Records were created for each of the Scale Types discussed so far:

Base-Scale

From	1	CSE	10	USD
	10	CSE	9	USD
	20	CSE	8	USD

To-Scale

To	10	CSE	20	USD
	20	CSE	18	USD
	30	CSE	16	USD

Graduated Scale

To	10	CSE	30	USD
	20	CSE	27	USD
	30	CSE	22	USD

Enter a Sales Order for three line items, each one corresponding with one of these Scales: Item 1 for a Base-Scale quantity of 15 CSE, item 2 for a To-Scale quantity of 5 CSE, and item 3 for a Graduated Scale quantity of 25 CSE.

Item 1 for 15 CSE falls into the second Scale bracket of the Base-Scale and has a price of 9 USD per unit applied (see Figure 3.8.2).

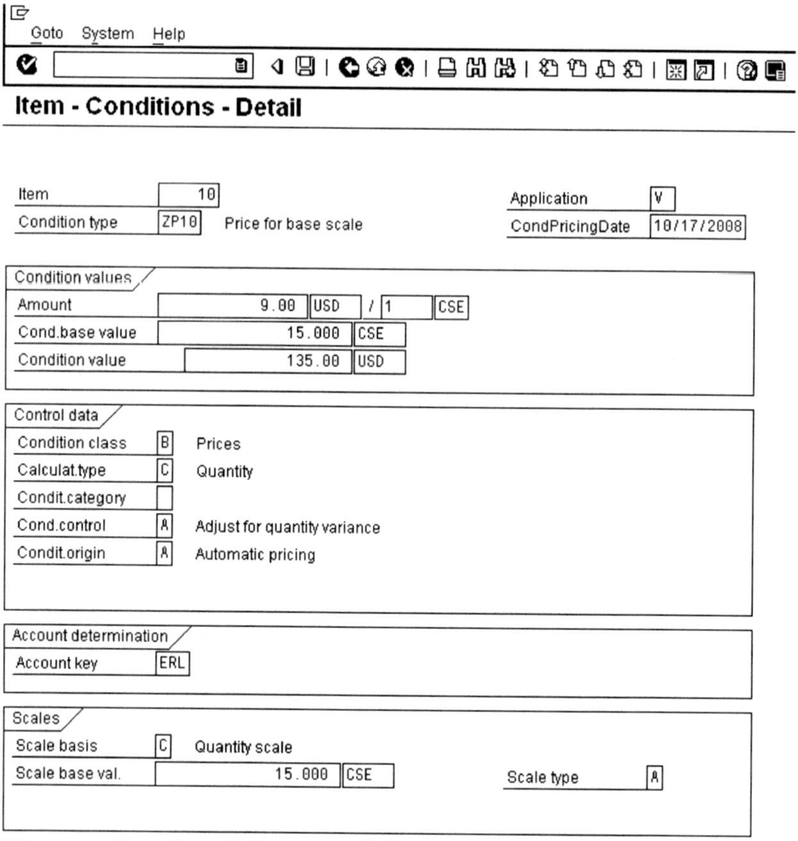

Figure 3.8.2: Condition Detail for Scale Condition Type

Item 2 for 5 CSE doesn't even reach the second Scale level and has the highest Scale price of 20 USD applied to it.

Compared to the previous items, line item 3 has three prices applied to it. Since it is a Graduated Scale and 25 CSE were ordered, the first 10 CSE apply with a price of 30 USD per unit, the second 10 CSE have a price of 27 USD, and the remaining 5 CSE are priced at 22 USD per unit. Figure 3.8.3 displays how the line item pricing appears on a Sales Order for this Graduated Scale.

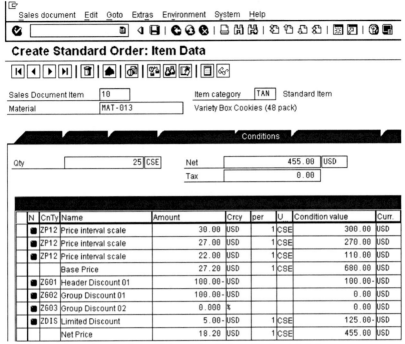

Figure 3.8.3: Scale Conditions in Sales Order Pricing

Displaying the Condition Details for the last "ZP12" Condition Type shows the Graduated Scale information in Figure 3.8.4. It shows this price applied for the Graduate Scale bracket between 20 and 30 units.

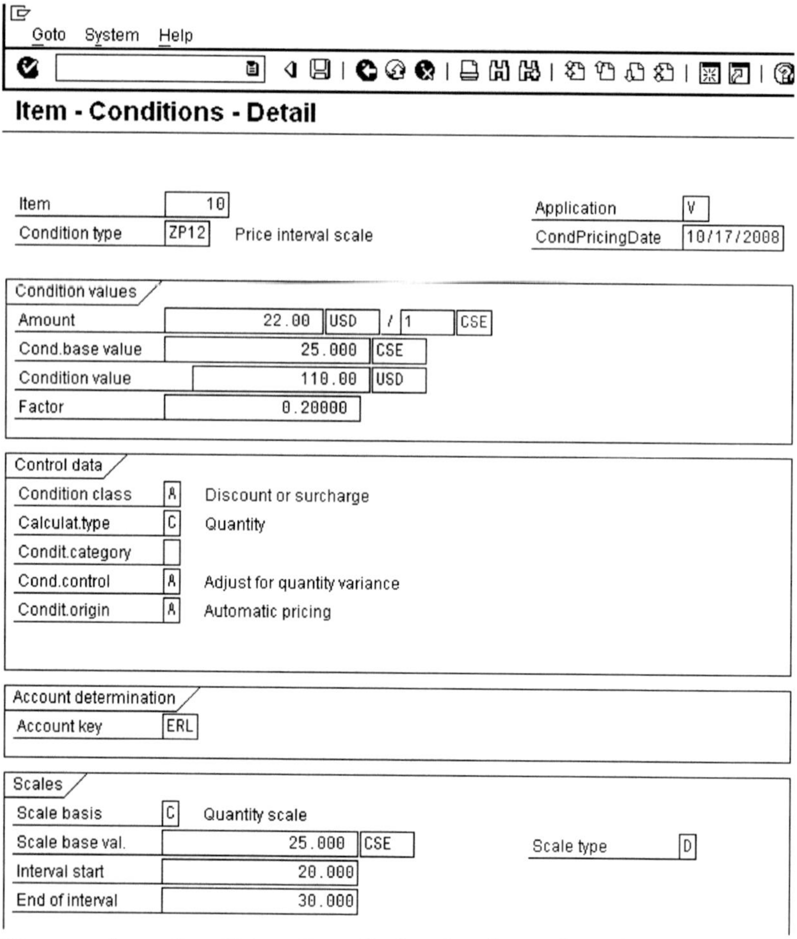

Goto   System   Help

Item - Conditions - Detail

| Item | 10 |
| Condition type | ZP12   Price interval scale |

| Application | V |
| CondPricingDate | 10/17/2008 |

Condition values

Amount	22.00	USD	/ 1	CSE
Cond.base value	25.000	CSE
Condition value	110.00	USD
Factor	0.20000

Control data

Condition class	A	Discount or surcharge
Calculat.type	C	Quantity
Condit.category		
Cond.control	A	Adjust for quantity variance
Condit.origin	A	Automatic pricing

Account determination

| Account key | ERL |

Scales

Scale basis	C	Quantity scale
Scale base val.	25.000	CSE		Scale type	D
Interval start	20.000
End of interval	30.000

Figure 3.8.4: Condition Details for Graduated Scale
Condition Record

3.9 Group Conditions

The example in Figure 3.8.2 shows a simplistic Scale scenario for which each Scale Condition Record applied is based on the quantity of the individual line item. Given the Scales setup above, an item quantity of 10 units per line item would have resulted in the lowest Scale bracket for most of the line items.

But what if the Scale should be based on the total quantity of the Sales Order? To accomplish this, Group Conditions need to be utilized: the line item quantities need to be grouped together to make up the Scale base for the Scale Condition Record. Instead of 10 units for a line item, the total quantity of all line items (10+10+10=30) would be the Scale Basis and result in the price for a higher Scale bracket.

In the example of the Base-Scale in Chapter 3.8, 8 USD instead of 10 USD per unit would be applied to the line item. The trick here is that the Condition Type needs to be set up as a Group Condition. This is done in the configuration settings of the Condition Type. As a side note, Graduated Scales cannot be used for Group Conditions. Also, Rebate Condition Types can't be defined as Group Conditions.

The combination of line item values is just one function of the Group Condition. Another one is the distribution of an amount to multiple line items.

The configuration of Group Conditions occurs in the configuration of the Condition Type (see Figure 3.9).

In scenario 1, let's observe a percentage Condition Type "ZG01" that is not configured as a Group Condition and is entered on the "Header Conditions" screen of a Sales Document. The example Sales Order has three line items, all for a quantity of 10 units. If a 10% discount is entered as the rate on the Header, each Sales Order line item will have the 10% discount applied. The same would be true if the Condition Type were configured as a fixed-amount condition. But this is just one way an absolute amount on the Header can be applied to the line items.

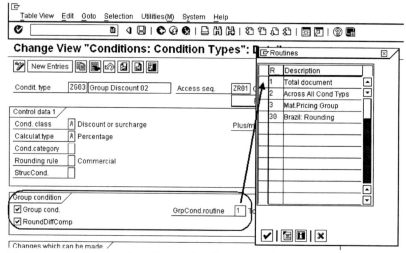

Figure 3.9.1: Group Condition Configuration in Condition Type

In example 2, a different Condition Type "ZG02" is configured as a line item condition and applies by customer for a flat amount of $100. This Condition Type is configured as a Group Condition. Looking initially at the "Item Conditions" screen, you can see that the Condition Rate has applied, but no extended amount is shown as allocated to that line item. Since the Group Condition logic is executed at the Header level, you need to go to the "Header Conditions" screen first and then go back to the line item in order to see the allocated amount. Even if you don't do that, the correct pricing will apply at Sales Order save time, since the Header pricing logic is executed at that time.

How are the $100 allocated? In the absence of allocation rules that were configured in the Pricing Procedure, the total amount is distributed by the net value of the line items. For a Sales Order with three line items (with $200, $300, and $500 net value), the $100 would get allocated with $20 for line 1, $30 for line 2, and $50 for line 3. With different net values, rounding differences can occur during the distribution of absolute amounts. The system automatically evens these out by allocating rounding differences to the item with the greatest net value. So for a Sales Order with two line items, item 1 for

2,000 USD and item 2 for 1,000 USD, a 100 USD Header discount would allocate 66.67 USD to item 1 and 33.33 to item 2.

To allocate by a different measure than net value, use the "Alternate Condition Base Value" field in the Pricing Procedure configuration (see Figure 3.9.2).

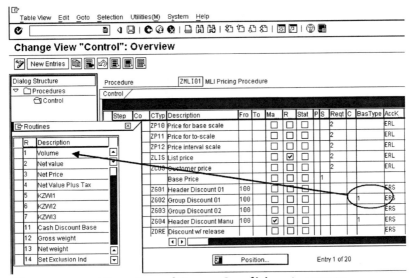

Figure 3.9.2: Allocation of Group Condition Amounts

In our example, we are allocating $100 by the volume of each line item. Figure 3.9.2 also displays other values that could allocate the fixed amount. Of course, if your required value is not listed, you can create a new custom formula with transaction "VOFM". Use the *Formulas->Condition Base Value* path and create a new formula in the customer reserved namespace (starting at number 500).

The third example brings us back to our Scale problem from earlier, where we wanted to base the Scale on the sum of all line items. Figure 3.9.3 displays the Condition Record for the Group Condition Type "ZG03". It is set up by customer and kicks in if at least 30 units are purchased.

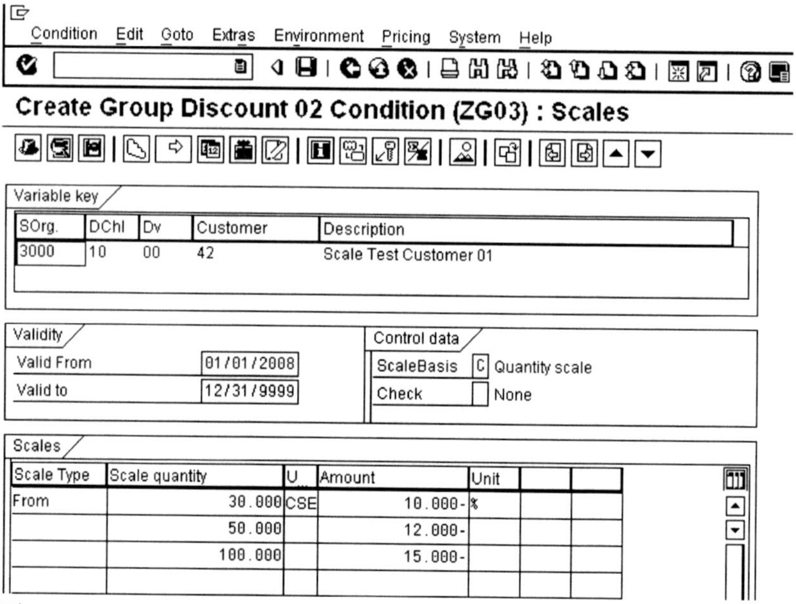

Figure 3.9.3: Group Condition Record

Creating a Sales Order for three items with a quantity of 10 units each wouldn't bring in the discount in our previous Scale scenario. However, looking at Figure 3.9.4, it is obvious that although only 10 Units were ordered for line item 10, the 10% discount for Condition Type "ZG03" applied. This is due to the fact that two more line items for 10 EA were created and that all quantities were grouped together.

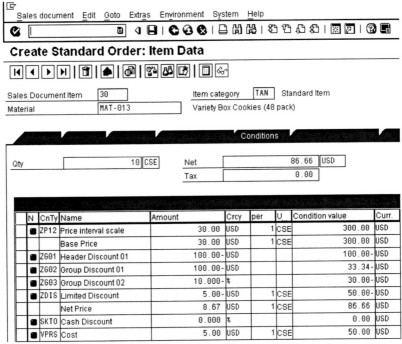

Figure 3.9.4: Group Conditions on a Sales Order

Figure 3.9.4 also shows the first Scale scenario, where $100 from the "Header Conditions" screen was applied to each line item. The "ZG02" Condition Type in Figure 3.9.4 shows the second example that allocated $100 by volume.

I mentioned earlier that it is necessary to go to the "Header Conditions" screen in order to see the allocation of a Group Condition to the line items. If at least one Condition Type is configured as a Group Condition AND as a Scale Condition, this manual step is not necessary. The reason is that the system needs to go to the Header pricing logic to gather the total quantity of the Sales Order to determine the appropriate Scale. In the case of a Condition Type that is relevant for Scales and that is a Group Condition, the system basically executed step *Header->Conditions*, and therefore the allocated amounts for Condition Types that don't have Scales can be seen as well.

If the Sales Order has line items with different sales UoMs, all will be converted to the Scale UoM.

Go to *Header->Conditions* and double-click on the "ZG03" Condition Type to see the Scale Basis on the "Condition Details" screen. In Figure 3.9.5, the "Scales" box shows that the Scale Base Value is 30 units. Therefore the Scale bracket "From" 30 units applied.

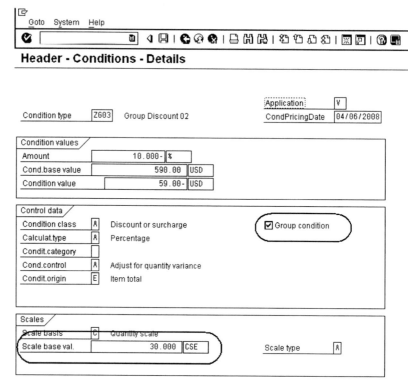

Figure 3.9.5: Group Condition Indicator on Condition Details

Although I did not get into pricing on a Billing Document yet, I would like to address an issue here with Scales that can occur during invoicing. Let's look again at example three with the three line items of 10 units each and the "ZG03" Condition Type applied with 10% on each line item. If the Sales Order is delivered as ordered, the Invoice will have the same "ZG03" discounts as on the Sales Order. However, if the order is delivered partially or in three separate deliveries, the Invoice results might differ, depending on the Pricing Rule used in copy control. We discussed Pricing Rules earlier, but let's re-visit two of them here.

If the Pricing Rule is "C," which re-prices all automatically determined Condition Types and retains the manually added ones, and the Sales Order was delivered with three separate deliveries and each Delivery invoiced individually, Pricing Rule "C" causes the Scales of Condition Type "ZG03" to be re-determined. The total quantity for this Invoice is only 10 units, so the "ZG03" discount would not apply because it did not reach the first Scale level quantity.

In another scenario, the Pricing Rule is "D," which means to copy all pricing unchanged. The Scale Basis is retained and the "ZG03" Conditions Type still applies, although the total Invoice quantity is only 10 units.

So what can you do if your business wants to re-price AND still keep the Scales? There are two options. One would be to create a custom Pricing Rule which would re-determine pricing without re-determining Scales. The other option would be to create a custom Scale Base formula that would base the Scale at invoice time on the Scale Base of the respective Sales Order. Chapter 5.5 explains the creation of this kind of rule in more detail.

Group Conditions and its application on Sales Documents can sometimes be a bit tricky. OSS notes 24944, 39034, 63070, and 109708 explain in more detail common issues and resolutions for Group Condition Scenarios and have references to other related OSS notes for this subject.

3.10   Pricing in a Billing Document

The pricing screens on a Billing Document are identical to those on the Sales Order. Manual re-pricing, adding and deleting Condition Types works exactly the same way as on the Sales Order, so there is no need to explain this functionality again. Please refer to Chapter 3.1 for the details.

What does merit further explanation, however, is how the Invoice is priced compared to the Sales Order.

Chapter 3.4 explained in detail the Pricing Rules during a manual or mass re-price of the Sales Document. For some rules, all pricing conditions are re-determined; sometimes only freight conditions are re-calculated. Since most Invoices are created via a batch job and there is no manual intervention, the Pricing Rules for the Billing Document are maintained in the copy rules for the Billing Document. There, we distinguish between order-related billing (copy rules from Sales Document to Billing Document) and delivery-related billing (copy rules from Delivery Document to Billing Document).

The order-related copy rules are maintained with transaction "VTFA" or IMG path *SPRO-> Sales and Distribution-> Billing-> Billing Documents-> Maintain Copying Control for Billing Documents-> Copying Control: Sales Document to Billing Document*. The Delivery-related copy rules are configured with transaction "VTFL" or IMG path *SPRO-> Sales and Distribution-> Billing-> Billing Documents-> Maintain Copying Control for Billing Documents-> Copying Control: Delivery Document to Billing Document*.

The available Pricing Rules or Pricing Types are identical for order- and delivery-related billing; therefore, I will only explain the delivery-related billing Pricing Rules.

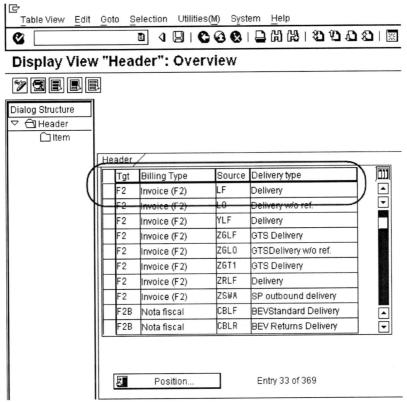

Figure 3.10.1: Copy Rules for Invoices

Since automatic pricing occurs on the line item level, the Pricing Rules are maintained on the item category level of the copy control. From the main billing copy rules in Figure 3.10.1, select the Billing Type "F2" and Delivery Type "LF" combination. Then double-click on the "Item" folder in the left window pane. Switch to "Change" mode by clicking the "Display->Change" button. Select the standard item category "TAN" and double-click on that item category. Figure 3.10.2 displays the configuration options of the line item copy rule. For our purpose, we are focusing on the fields in the lower right.

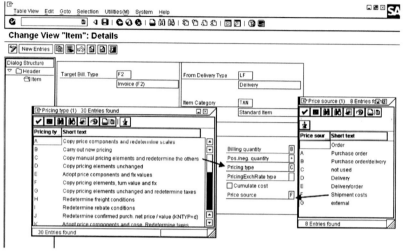

Figure 3.10.2: Item Category Pricing-Related Copy Rules

The field "Pricing Type" defines the Pricing Rule with which the line item is priced on the Billing Document. Select the pull-down next to that field to see the list of available Pricing Rules (see Figure 3.10.2).

As you can see, there are more Pricing Rules available than during the manual re-price function in Chapter 3.4. For example, Pricing Rule "D" in the copy control copies the pricing from the Sales Order unchanged, even if prices or discounts in the applied Condition Records would have changed during the time before billing occurs. Of course, this Pricing Rule is not available during manual re-pricing since it makes no sense to re-price without changing any prices.

Most commonly used is Pricing Rule "C," which keeps all manually applied pricing conditions but re-determines all automatic ones.

Pricing on the Billing Document is based on the Pricing Date of the Billing Document. The Pricing Date in the standard SAP system is the Pricing Date of the Sales Order. In case you would like to use a different date as the Pricing Date, a user exit, explained in Chapter 5.7, can be used to accomplish that.

The "Pricing Exchange Rate Type" field controls which currency exchange rate is used at billing time when the pricing currency is different than the document currency. It is possible to copy the exchange rate from the Sales Order with value "A" or re-determine the exchange rate at billing time by either the billing, pricing, service rendered or the current date. Click on the pull-down next to the field to see all available options.

The "Price Source" field controls from which reference documents (Sales Order, Delivery, etc.) the pricing conditions are copied, and in which sequence. A blank entry in this field will copy the pricing information from the Sales Order. If pricing was configured and maintained on the Delivery Document, which is not covered in this book, Price Source "E" would copy these Condition Types to the Invoice in addition to the ones from the Sales Order. Price Source "F" copies the freight-related Condition Types from the Shipment Cost Document to the Invoice in addition to the ones from the Sales Order. The important thing for both the Delivery and Shipment Cost Price Source rules is that the Condition Types from those applications have to be named the same as the ones on the Sales side in order to be copied.

Although the configuration of pricing in a Shipment Cost Document is not covered in the scope of this book, I would like to explain the scenario with a Shipment Cost Document mentioned above.

The Shipment Cost Document serves as a tool to calculate actual shipment costs, which takes into account distances between transportation legs, tariff zones, transportation types and equipment such as containers or pallets. Pricing is configured separately for Shipment Cost Documents and has priceable elements unique to a shipment, such as departure or destination point, which are not available on a Sales Document.

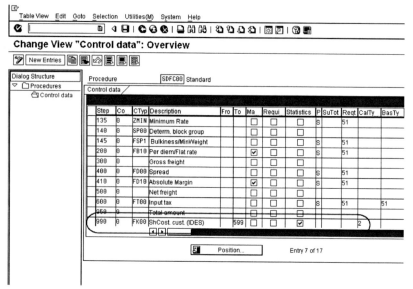

Figure 3.10.3: Shipment Cost Pricing Procedure

Figure 3.10.3 displays a Shipment Cost Pricing Procedure. Several Condition Types related to freight are included in that Pricing Procedure. Condition Type "FK00" is configured as statistical at the end of the procedure and includes the total net freight value.

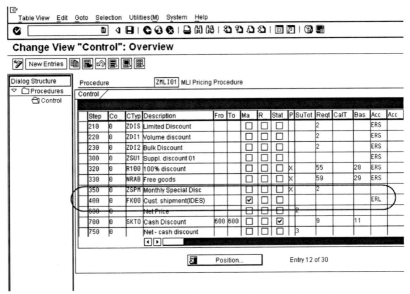

Figure 3.10.4: Freight from Shipment Cost on Regular Pricing Procedure

Figure 3.10.4 again displays our regular Pricing Procedure "ZMLI01", this time with the "FK00" Condition Type included for the Shipment Cost. It is important to set the "FK00" condition in this Pricing Procedure is as a manual Condition Type. This, together with the Price Source "F" setting in the copy rule, copies the calculated freight cost over to the Billing Document. A pre-condition for that copy to occur, however, is that the Shipment Cost Document is calculated completely.

Looking now at an actual Invoice in Figure 3.10.5, it shows that the freight is copied into the Invoice as a statistical value. The "FK00" Condition Type can then be referenced by a non-statistical Condition Type that would effectively charge the customer for the freight.

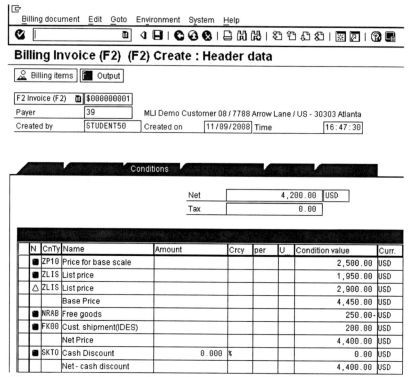

Figure 3.10.5: Freight from Shipment Cost Document on Invoice Header Condition Screen

As seen in Chapter 1.5, a Document Pricing Procedure Indicator can be assigned to a Billing Type, which could differ from the Document Pricing Procedure Indicator of the corresponding Sales Order Type. Any Pricing Procedure Indicator assigned to a Billing Type will trigger new pricing at billing time.

Summary of Chapter 3

Chapter 3 finally showed how all the pricing master data from Chapter 2 that was created based on the configuration in Chapter 1 applied on Sales Documents. You learned how to manipulate the pricing on a Sales Document and how to reprice documents, as well as how to display information regarding how pricing applied on these documents.

Chapter 4: Special Processes Using the Pricing Condition Technique

Chapters 1 - 3 covered the setup and application of day-to-day pricing-related processes. This chapter dives into the more specialized pricing applications that also use the Condition Technique.

4.1 Free Goods

One of the most requested pricing functionalities in the SAP releases prior to 4.0 was the "buy one get one free" scenario. Development or manual work-arounds were necessary to accomplish this functionality.

As we have seen in the chapter about Scales, it is possible to give a better price to a customer if quantities are purchased in bulk. In addition, the Graduated Scales allow the assignment of different prices to different order quantities.

The Free Goods functionality offers the opportunity to give a customer product free of charge, based on specific purchase requirements. For Free Goods, two different scenarios have to be distinguished: Inclusive Bonus Quantity and Exclusive Bonus Quantity.

Inclusive Bonus Quantity

This is also called Inclusive Free Goods, since a proportion of the Sales Order quantity is given away as Free Goods, meaning the customer does not have to pay for it. He only pays for some of the goods requested; the rest of the goods are free of charge.

The Unit of Measure of the materials delivered as Free Goods will also match the UoM of the ordered material.

Example:	A customer orders 100 boxes of cookies. Since the customer ordered a full pallet, 10 of these 100 boxes will be free of charge, meaning the customer only has to pay for 90 boxes.

Exclusive Bonus Quantity

This scenario is also known as Exclusive Free Goods and means that, in addition to the goods ordered, a specified quantity of materials is given away as Free Goods. The additional quantities in excess of the ordered quantities are delivered as Free Goods. The customer pays for the goods ordered and is given extra goods free of charge.

Contrary to the Inclusive Free Goods scenario, the materials given away as Free Goods can be either the same material as the material ordered or a different material. In the Inclusive scenario, the ordered and Free Goods are always the same material.

Example:	A customer orders 100 boxes of Vanilla Cookies. In additional, he will receive 10 boxes of Chocolate Chip Cookies free of charge. He will receive a total of 110 boxes but will only pay for 100.

4.1.1   Free Goods Configuration

The configuration steps for the Free Goods functionality are similar to those for pricing. The Condition Technique is used as well, so I will not go into great detail for every step of the configuration but will only point out the differences for the Free Goods functionality.

In order to build Condition Tables, a separate Field Catalog is available, accessed via IMG path *SPRO-> Sales and Distribution-> Basic Functions-> Free Goods-> Condition Technique for Free Goods-> Maintain Field Catalog.* All fields available for the pricing Field Catalog are also available for the Free Goods Field Catalog.

The Free Goods Condition Tables are created the same way as a pricing Condition Table via IMG path *SPRO-> Sales and Distribution-> Basic Functions-> Free Goods-> Condition Technique for Free Goods-> Maintain Condition Tables.* The only difference is that there is no Release Status available for the Free Goods Condition Table. After the Condition Table is generated, the Condition Table number starts with "KOTN" instead of "A" as with the pricing Condition Table.

The Access Sequence is created just like a pricing Access Sequence via IMG path *SPRO-> Sales and Distribution-> Basic Functions-> Free Goods-> Condition Technique for Free Goods-> Maintain Access Sequences.* The difference here is that there is no exclusion indicator for the Condition Tables in the Access Sequence.

A big difference exists between the Condition Type configuration of the Free Goods Condition Type and the one for pricing. Go to IMG path *SPRO-> Sales and Distribution-> Basic Functions-> Free Goods-> Condition Technique for Free Goods-> Maintain Condition Types.* The only options that are available here (as shown in Figure 4.1.1.1) are to assign an Access Sequence to the Condition Type, as well as assign a default date for the Valid-From and the Valid-To date for the later creation of a Free Goods Condition Record. The same date options as for the "Valid-From" and "Valid-To" fields in the pricing Condition Type configuration are available.

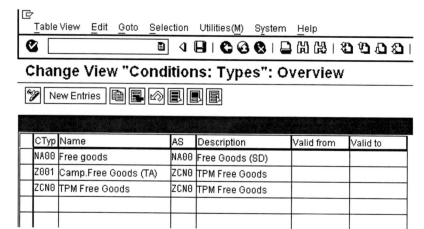

Figure 4.1.1.1: Free Goods Condition Types

Another difference compared to pricing is the configuration of the Free Goods Procedure. This is maintained with IMG path *SPRO-> Sales and Distribution-> Basic Functions-> Free Goods-> Condition Technique for Free Goods-> Maintain Pricing Procedures*. As can be seen in field "Usage" in Figure 4.1.1.2, the Procedures for Free Goods have a different usage indicator, namely "N" compared to usage "A" for pricing. On this screen, there is also no transaction-specific Pricing Procedure Indicator and no "Pricing Type" field, as is the case with a pricing-related Pricing Procedure.

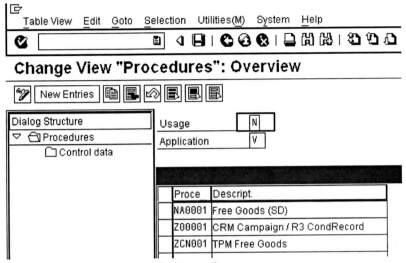

Figure 4.1.1.2: Free Goods Procedures

By selecting a Free Goods Procedure and double-clicking the "Control Data" folder in the left window pane, the detail of the Pricing Procedure shows that only a step and counter number, the Free Goods Condition Type, as well as a potential requirement can be maintained (see Figure 4.1.1.3). These requirement options are unique to Free Goods and don't include any of the pricing-related requirements. The Free Goods requirements can be maintained via transaction "VOFM" with menu *Requirements->Free Goods*.

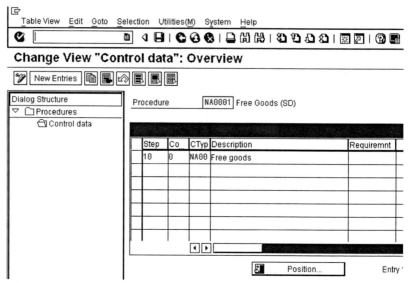

Figure 4.1.1.3: Free Goods Pricing Procedure

In addition to the Free Goods Procedure, additional configuration is necessary in the regular Pricing Procedure in which Free Goods are calculated.

The standard Condition Type "R100" discounts 100% of the sales price of the item that is given away as Free Goods. Figure 4.1.1.4 displays the configuration of the "R100" Condition Type in Pricing Procedure "ZMLI01". Requirement "55" ensures the 100% discount only applies on Free Goods items by checking for Pricing Type "B" of the item category. Condition Base Value "28" automatically applies a 100% discount without having to create a Condition Record for it.

Pricing Condition Type "NRAB" is required if a Free Goods scenario is used where no item is generated for the Free Goods quantity (Free Goods category "3" in the Free Goods Condition Record). In this scenario, the discount is given on the main item. To accomplish this, it is necessary to maintain pricing requirement "59" and Condition Base Value "29" for the "NRAB" Condition Type in the respective Pricing Procedure (see Figure 4.1.1.4). This formula calculates the discount based on the Free Goods factor of the Free Goods Condition Record (see later in Figure 4.1.2.1). The "NRAB" Condition Type also has the Condition Category "f," which ensures that this Condition Type is re-determined every time the main item quantity changes, since this could have an affect on the Free Goods quantity. (For example, the quantity could go below the minimum order quantity, which would not allow for any Free Goods.)

Procedure		ZMLI01	MLI Pricing Procedure												
Control															
Step	Co	CTyp	Description	Fro	To	Ma	R	Stat	P	SuTot	Reqt	CalTy	BasTy	AccK	Accru
150	0	ZG04	Header Discount Manu	100		☑	☐	☐				2	1	ERS	
200	0	ZDRE	Discount w/ release			☐	☐	☐						ERS	
210	0	ZDIS	Limited Discount			☐	☐	☐			2			ERS	
220	0	ZDI1	Volume discount			☐	☐	☐			2			ERS	
230	0	ZDI2	Bulk Discount			☐	☐	☐			2			ERS	
300	0	ZSU1	Suppl. discount 01			☐	☐	☐						ERS	
320	0	R100	100% discount			☐	☐	☐	X	55		28		ERS	
330	0	NRAB	Free goods			☐	☐	☐	X	59		29		ERS	
000	0		Net Price			☐	☐	☐	2						

Figure 4.1.1.4: Free Goods Condition Types in Pricing Procedure

As with the Pricing Procedure in pricing, the Free Goods Pricing Procedure needs to be assigned to a combination of Sales Area, a customer Pricing Procedure Indicator and a Document Pricing Procedure Indicator. IMG path *SPRO-> Sales and Distribution-> Basic Functions-> Free Goods-> Condition Technique for Free Goods-> Activate Free Goods Determination* enables this function. Figure 4.1.1.5 displays the Free Goods Procedure assignment. The combinations of fields for assignment are the same as for pricing. The difference for Free Goods is that no pricing Condition Type can be defaulted as in Figure 1.5.6 for pricing. For our example, the standard Free Goods Procedure "NA0001" is assigned to Sales Area "3000/10/00", document Pricing Procedure Indicator "A" and customer Pricing Procedure Indicator "M."

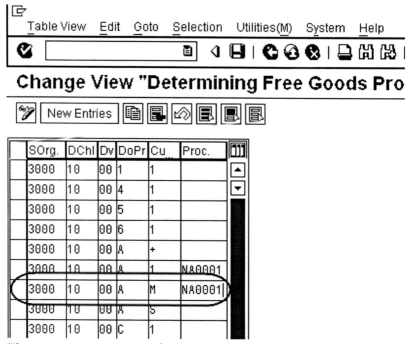

Figure 4.1.1.5: Free Goods Procedure Assignment

Items that are delivered as Free Goods have to be identified as such. A Free Goods item is displayed as a separate line item on a Sales Order. It is a sub-item of the main Sales Order line item. The Free Goods items are also Delivery-relevant and are copied to the Billing Document. The item category for the Free Goods item is defined with IMG path *SPRO-> Sales and Distribution-> Basic Functions-> Free Goods-> Determine Item Category For Free Goods Item.* In the standard SAP system, this item category is "TANN." Figure 4.1.1.6 shows the assignment of the "TANN" item category for Sales Order Type "OR," item category group "NORM," usage "FREE" (for Free Goods) and the higher level item category "TAN."

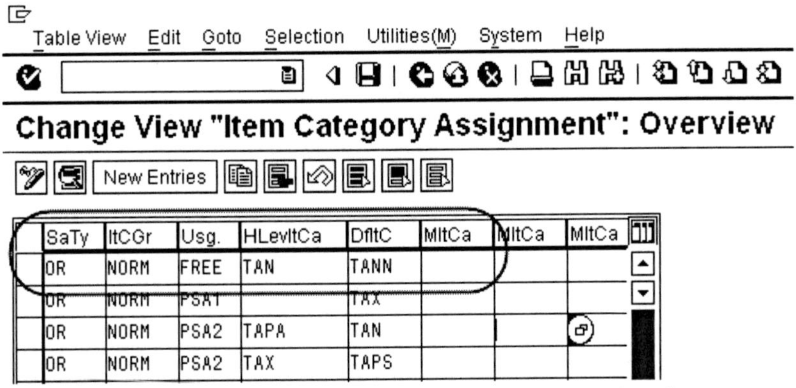

Figure 4.1.1.6: Free Goods Item Category Determination

This means the Free Goods item, if set up, will be a sub-item of a regular item with item category "TANN."

The "TANN" item category must also be configured correctly from a pricing perspective. This is done with IMG path *SPRO-> Sales and Distribution-> Basic Functions-> Free Goods-> Control Free Goods Pricing-> Control Pricing For Free Goods Item Category.* This configuration step defines if pricing is carried out for a line item of that item category. The standard item category "TAN" and all other regular item categories have an "X" for standard pricing in field "Pricing." The Free Goods item category "TANN," however, has to have value "B" in this field (see Figure 4.1.1.7). The "Statistical Value" field in the same figure defines if the value of the line item should be taken into account or not when the net value of the item is determined. Since we want to affect the net value, this field is left blank.

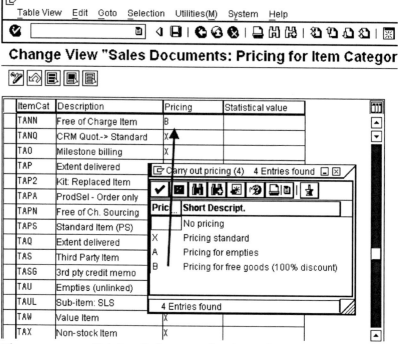

Figure 4.1.1.7: Pricing Relevance for Item Category

Another configuration step to set up Free Goods is the determination of how the cost of the Free Goods item should be copied to the main item. This is done in copy control from the Delivery to the Billing Document. Use either transaction "VTFL" or the IMG path *SPRO-> Sales and Distribution-> Basic Functions-> Free Goods-> Control Free Goods Pricing-> Set Transfer of Costs To Main Item*. Select the copy control for your respective Delivery and Billing Document Types and select the appropriate item category for the Free Goods item (in our example, "TANN"). Select field "Cumulate Cost" (see Figure 4.1.1.8) so the cost of these items is copied to the main item.

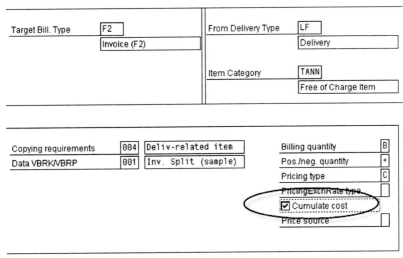

Figure 4.1.1.8: Cumulate Cost for Free Goods

4.1.2   Setting up Inclusive Free Goods Condition Records

To create a Free Goods Condition Record, either execute transaction "VBN1" or use the SAP menu path *Logistics-> Sales and Distribution-> Master Data-> Conditions-> Free Goods-> Create*. On the resulting screen, enter "NA00" as the Free Goods Condition Type in field "Discount Type." Since only one Condition Table exists for the Access Sequence assigned to Free Goods Condition Type "NA00", Figure 4.1.2.1 is displayed after pressing enter.

The only valid key combination for "NA00" is Sales Organization, Distribution Channel, Customer and Material. In the top part of the screen, enter a Sales Organization, a Distribution Channel and the customer number of who should receive the Free Goods. In addition, maintain the Valid-From and Valid-To dates in the respective fields.

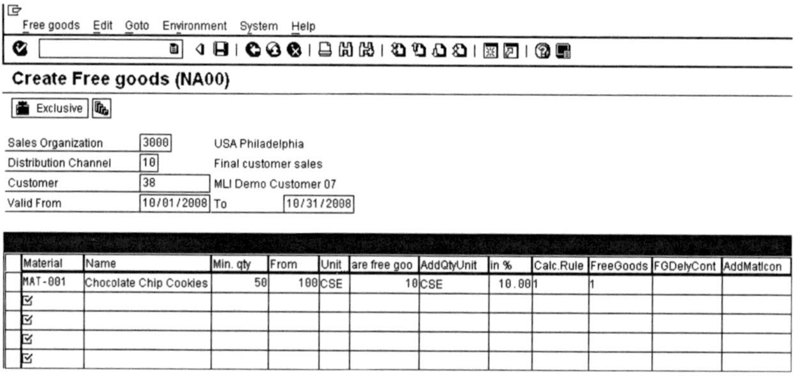

Figure 4.1.2.1: Free Goods Inclusive Record

The default type for the Free Goods Condition Record is the "Inclusive Free Goods" type. To switch to the "Exclusive Free Goods" type, click on the "Exclusive" button on the top of the screen. But first let us take a look at an Inclusive record.

Enter the material number on which Free Goods should be based in field "Material." The "Min. Qty" field defines the minimum quantity of this material that needs to be purchased in order for Free Goods to kick in. In other words, if the minimum quantity is defined as 100 and only 50 units are ordered, no Free Goods will be given.

The "From" field defines the Free Goods quantity. The description of this field is a bit misleading since it is not the quantity of the goods that are given away free of charge, but the base quantity the Free Goods are determined from.

Example:	For every 100 units, 10 units are given away as Free Goods. The 100 units will be maintained in the "From" field.

The Unit of Measure of the Free Goods quantity is entered in field "UnitFG". Although a material number is part of the Condition Table key, its base UoM is not defaulted as it is during the creation of a pricing Condition Record and has to be entered manually.

The quantity of Free Goods given away is maintained in field "are free goo." (No, we are not giving away goo - come on, SAP, couldn't you have a better label description for this field?) Looking again at our example above, the 10 units that should be given away as Free Goods need to be entered in this field.

The "AddQtyUnit" field maintains the UoM for the Free Goods given away. For an Inclusive Free Goods Condition Record, this UoM has to be the same as in field "UnitFG". If you attempt to enter a different UoM, the system will issue a respective error message.

The "in %" column shows the Free Goods percentage rate and is also called "Free Goods Factor." For an Inclusive Free Goods Condition Record, it is calculated as: Free Goods quantity * Additional Free Goods Quantity / 100. In our example, that would be: 100 * 10 / 100 = 10%. This factor is important for Free Goods category "3" in field "Free Goods" for which no additional Free Goods line item is being generated, but the Free Goods discount is calculated on the main line item.

The "Calc.Rule" field defines the Calculation Type for determining the Free Goods quantity. The standard SAP system delivers three of these rules. Rule "1" is automatically defaulted. Even if you removed the rule and hit enter again, rule "1" defaults. The rule is best explained again with an example:

Example:	For every 100 units, 4 units are Free Goods. A Sales Order is entered for 230 units.
	Free Goods quantity = 100 units Additional quantity = 4 units Document quantity = 230 units

Calculation Rule "1," called "Proportional" or "Pro Rata," determines the number of Free Goods as 9:

$$230 / 100 * 4 = 9.2, \text{ rounded down} = 9 \text{ units}$$

Calculation Rule "2," named "Unit reference," only takes full increments of the Free Goods quantity into account. The calculation here is: 200 /100 * 4 = 8 units

The last standard Calculation Rule "3" ("Whole Units") is the most stringent. It only allows Free Goods to be calculated if the document quantity is a multiple of the Free Goods quantity. Since the Sales Order quantity of 230 units is not a multiple of 100, no Free Goods are allowed. Only document quantities of 300, 400, etc. would calculate Free Goods. These rules and any custom rules that need to be added can be maintained via transaction "VOFM" with menu *Formulas-> Calc.rule RebateInKd.*

The "FreeGoods" field defines if the Condition Record is for an Inclusive (value "1" or "3") or an Exclusive (value "2") Free Goods scenario.

The "FGDelyCont" field (Free Goods Delivery Control) controls if and how the Free Goods line item is copied to a Delivery Note. A blank entry, which is the default, allows the Free Goods item to be delivered regardless of the main Sales Order line item. Other options: the main item has to be partially or fully delivered in order to deliver the Free Goods line item, or the Free Goods item is delivered proportionally to the Delivery quantity of the main item.

Example:	If 10 Free Goods items are delivered for every 100 regular items, only 1 Free Good item would be delivered if only 10 regular items are available at delivery time.

After all necessary data is entered in the Free Goods Condition Record, save the record.

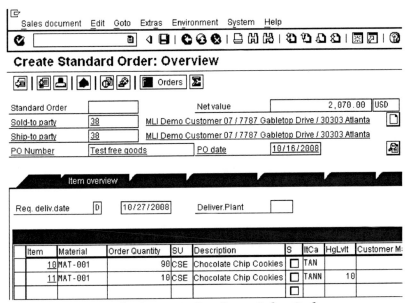

Figure 4.1.2.2: Inclusive Free Goods on Sales Order

Entering a Sales Order for the customer and material for which the Free Goods Condition Record was created nicely displays the regular and the Free Goods item in Figure 4.1.2.2. Although item 10 was originally entered with an order quantity of 100 CSE, the system finds the Free Goods Condition Record, identifies it as an Inclusive Condition Record and therefore changes the order quantity for line item 10 to 90 CSE and adds the Free Goods sub-item with the Free Goods quantity of 10 CSE. As you can see in column "HL Itm" (Higher Level Item), line item 11 refers to the main line item 10.

4.1.3 Setting Up Inclusive Free Goods Condition Records Without Item Generation

A different flavor of the Inclusive Free Goods Condition Record is one for which no additional Free Goods line item should be generated. In this scenario, the same Condition Record is created as in Figure 4.1.2.1 with the exception of value "3" in field "FreeGoods." The resulting Sales Order then only displays one line item with the originally ordered quantity of 100 CSE. Looking at the pricing of this line item in Figure 4.1.2.3 shows that the "NRAB" discount of 10% (which is the Free Goods factor as displayed in the respective Free Goods Condition Record) applied on the main item.

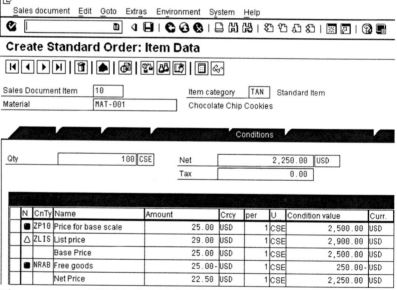

Figure 4.1.3.1: NRAB Condition for Free Goods Factor

Looking at the pricing detail of the "NRAB" Condition Type in Figure 4.1.3.2, we see the variant factor is 10, as indicated in the respective Free Goods Condition Record.

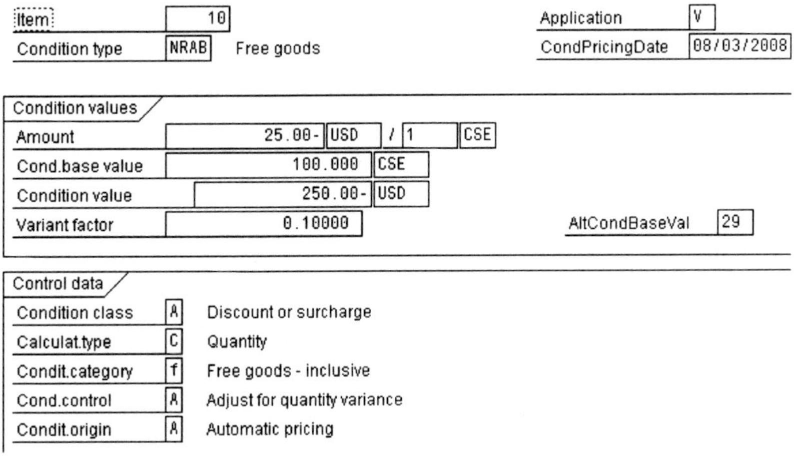

Item	10		Application	V
Condition type	NRAB	Free goods	CondPricingDate	08/03/2008

Condition values

Amount	25.00-	USD	/	1	CSE
Cond.base value	100.000	CSE			
Condition value	250.00-	USD			
Variant factor	0.10000		AltCondBaseVal	29	

Control data

Condition class	A	Discount or surcharge
Calculat.type	C	Quantity
Condit.category	f	Free goods - inclusive
Cond.control	A	Adjust for quantity variance
Condit.origin	A	Automatic pricing

Figure 4.1.3.2: "NRAB" Variant Factor

223

4.1.4 Setting Up Exclusive Free Goods Condition Records

The Exclusive Free Goods Condition Record also comes in two variations. First, we will set up a Condition Record that will give additional quantities of the same material as Free Goods. The transaction to maintain this record is the same as the Inclusive Free Goods Record. As mentioned above, click on the "Exclusive" button to switch to Exclusive Free Goods Condition Record maintenance. This option adds an additional field "AddMat FrGd" for the option to add an additional material for Free Goods, and a field for the respective material description (see Figure 4.1.4.3). The "AddMat FrGd" field is grayed-out after the Condition Record view is switched from Inclusive to Exclusive, due to the default Inclusive rule in field "Free Goods." Switch this rule to rule "2" for Exclusive, as in Figure 4.1.4.1. This opens up field "AddMat FrGd". For the first Exclusive scenario, leave this field blank.

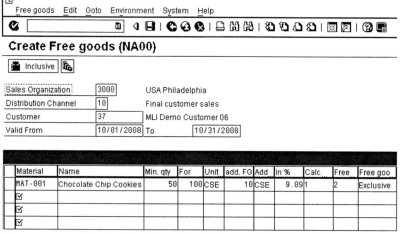

Figure 4.1.4.1: Exclusive Free Goods Record for Same Material

In comparison to the Inclusive Free Goods Record, the "in %" amount for the Exclusive Free Goods Condition Record is calculated as: Additional Free Goods Quantity * 100 / (Free Goods quantity + the Additional Free Goods Quantity). In our example, that would be: 10 * 100 / (100 + 10) = 9.09%

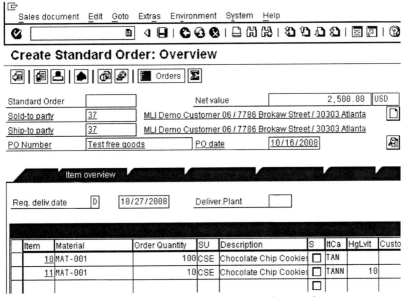

Figure 4.1.4.2: Exclusive Free Goods on Sales Order

Figure 4.1.4.2 of a Sales Order displays the same material twice, but compared to the Inclusive scenarios, line item 10 shows the originally ordered quantity of 100 CSE and a second line item with the 10 CSE of Free Goods.

The second Exclusive Free Goods scenario involves a different Free Goods material than the one originally ordered. Looking at Figure 4.1.4.3, we can see that for each ordered Chocolate Chip Cookies of 100 CSE, 10 CSE of Peanut Butter Cookies are given away as Free Goods.

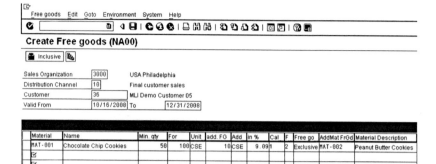

Figure 4.1.4.3: Exclusive Free Goods Record for Different Material

Looking in Figure 4.1.4.4 at the application of this Condition Record in a Sales Order, the only difference to the first Exclusive scenario is that the second line item is for a different material. Line item 10 still has the originally ordered 100 CSE and the second line item is for the 10 CSE free of charge.

In all scenarios that generated a separate Free Goods item, the second line item is a sub-item of the originally ordered line item. This is evident when looking at column "HL Itm" for the higher level item. For line item 20, the higher level item number is 10, linking this item to the main item.

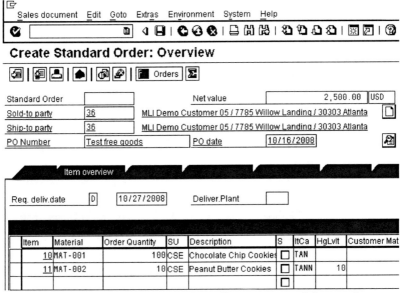

Figure 4.1.4.4: Free Goods with Different Material on Sales Order

Also identical for all the Free Goods scenarios is the pricing of the Free Goods line item. The item that is originally ordered prices as any other regular item of your Pricing Procedure. However, as can be seen in Figure 4.1.4.5 of the Free Goods line item, the pricing of the Free Goods item is different. On this line item, the "R100" 100% discount Condition Type applies. This is due to the pricing requirement that checks for the "carry out pricing" flag "B" of Free Goods item categories, which is item category "TANN." In Figure 4.1.4.5, only a base price "ZP10" applied, but the "R100" discount can refer to any subtotal in a Pricing Procedure that is made up of multiple Condition Types.

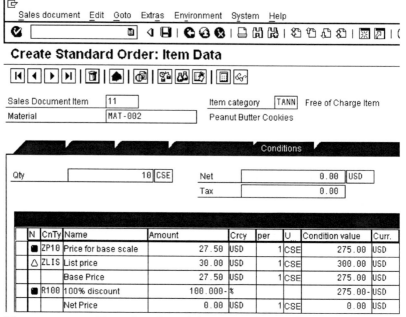

Figure 4.1.4.5: Free Goods Pricing on Sales Order

As helpful as the Free Goods functionality is, there are certain limitations I would like to point out:

- Free Goods can only support a 1:1 ratio between an ordered item and a Free Goods item. For example, it is not possible to define that the purchase of material 1 results in Free Goods materials 2 and 3. Also, the scenario that bases Free Goods material 3 on the purchase of material 1 and material 2 is not supported.

- Free Goods are not supported in combinations with material structures such as product selection, Bill of Material (BOM), variants with BOM explosion, etc.

- Free Goods are only supported for Sales Orders with document category "C." Quotations or Inquiries are therefore not supported.

- Free Goods are not supported for deliveries without reference to a Sales Order, such as the "NL" Delivery Type.

- Free Goods cannot be used in make-to-order production, third-party order processing or scheduling agreements.

4.2   Promotions and Sales Deals

In previous chapters I mentioned the use of discounts several times. There are countless reasons why discounts are given to customers. Pricing Reports or the regular Condition Record display transactions provide tools to review these Conditions. However, if you want to track the use of specific discounts in more detail, the Promotions and Sales Deal functions that SAP delivers can assist with these requirements.

Promotions and Sales Deals group price allowance Condition Records together. This functionality will let customers track the volume of transactions for these Sales Deals to determine the level of success of a Promotion.

Before setting up Promotions and Sales Deals, decisions need to be made regarding their organizational structure. Should they be organized by product groups (for example, all non-fat cookies or all variety cookies) or by time frames (weekly, monthly, quarterly)? Should they apply to all customers or only to a select group of customers?

A Promotion can have one or more Sales Deals attached to it. It serves as an umbrella over the Sales Deals. The Promotion drives no functionality other than serving as an organizational element. All linked Sales Deals must have a Validity Period within the Validity Period of the Promotion. However, Sales Deals can also be used without being linked to Promotions. Sales Deals will affect pricing on documents, since Pricing Records are created within a Sales Deal.

For the example in this book, we will set up a Promotion with monthly specials in which we temporarily reduce the price for a certain type of cookies.

Configuration of Promotions and Sales Deals

First, we configure a Promotion. Since a Promotion does not drive any functionality in the system, the configuration options for it are limited. You define a Promotion Type with IMG menu path *SPRO-> Sales and Distribution-> Basic Functions-> Pricing-> Pricing Agreements-> Define Promotions-> Maintain Promotion Types* (see Figure 4.2.1).

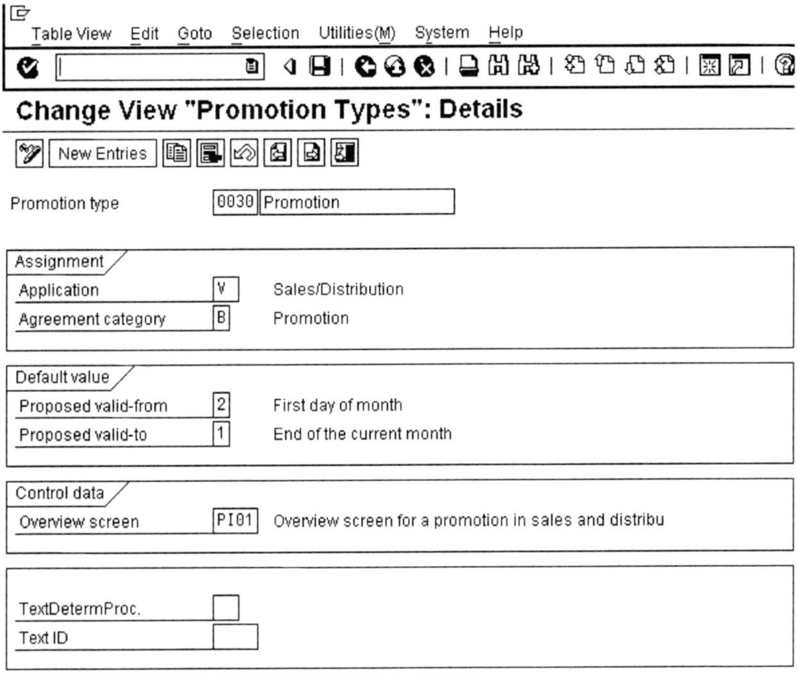

Figure 4.2.1: Promotion Configuration

You can define "Proposed Valid-From" and "Proposed Valid-To" dates, as well as link the Promotion Type to a text procedure in field "TextDeterm.Proc". This is useful if you would like to send promotion letters with specific text to your customers. We will use the standard SAP Promotion Type "0030" for our example.

Like the Condition Type texts, the Promotion Text Determination can be maintained with the IMG standard text configuration transaction "VOTXN". Entering a specific "Text ID" will default a text window for this text type at Promotion creation time. Any other text types of the identified text procedure can still be accessed, though.

The Sales Deal configuration looks similar to that of the Promotion, but it has a few more options (see Figure 4.2.2). To define a new Sales Deal Type or change an existing one, select IMG path *SPRO-> Sales and Distribution-> Basic Functions-> Pricing-> Pricing Agreements-> Set up Sales Deals-> Define*

Sales Deals-> Define Sales Deal Types. There is no configuration option available (and therefore no limitation) to define which Sales Deal Type is allowed for which Promotion Type.

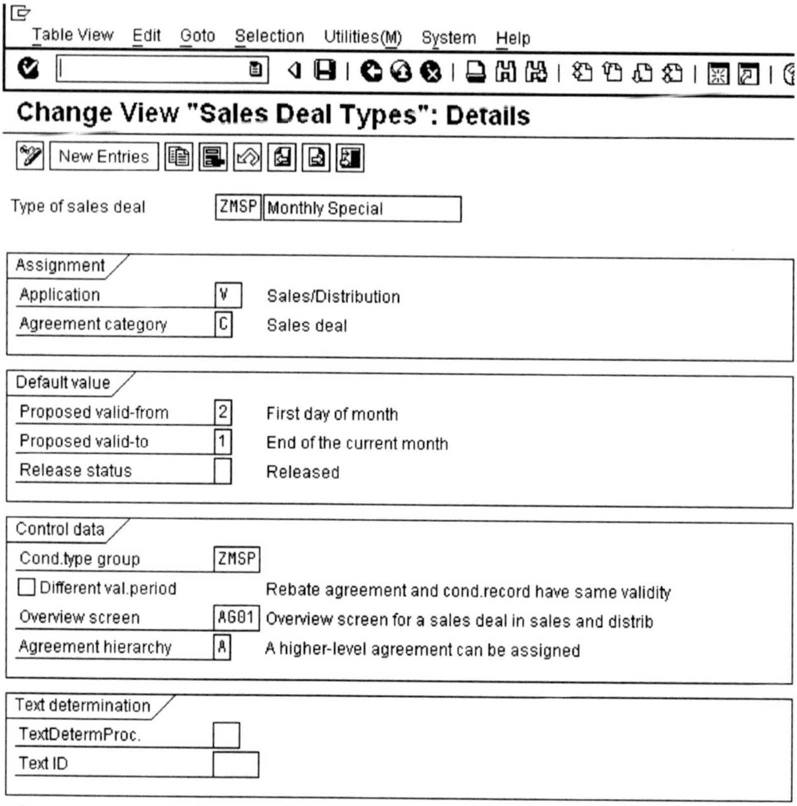

Figure 4.2.2: Sales Deal Type Configuration

As in the Promotion configuration, you can define defaults for the Validity Period of the Sales Deal. Since we would like to create monthly Sales Deals for our example, we'll use the "First day of the month" setting in the "Proposed Valid-From" field.

Since we will create pricing Condition Records from within the Sales Deal, we have the option to set a default "Release status" on the Sales Deal level that will be copied into each linked Condition Record. As mentioned earlier in the chapter about Condition Records, this is the default Release Status that would be copied into a Sales Deal and the Condition Records that are created from within that Sales Deal. For our example, we will leave this field blank.

The Condition Type Group cannot be linked to the Sales Deal Type in the configuration of the Sales Deal Type, but it will be assigned in a subsequent configuration step (see "Assigning Condition Types to Condition Type Groups" in Figure 4.2.5). The setting for field "Different val. Period" relates to the Condition Records within the Sales Deal. A blank field means the Validity Periods of the Sales Deal and the Condition Records have to be the same; a checked field allows them to be different.

The "Agreement hierarchy" field determines if you can or should assign a Promotion to a specific Sales Deal. The following values are available:

- Blank = No higher level agreement can be assigned. The "Promotion" field (see Figure 4.2.9) is not available during the creation of a Sales Deal. However, if you create a Sales Deal with reference to a Promotion (as in Figure 4.2.8), the system allows it despite this setting.

- "A" = A higher level agreement can be assigned. The "Promotion" field is available when a Sales Deal is created (copying from a Promotion is still possible). Entering the Promotion number there and pressing enter will copy the values from the Promotion (like payment terms, value data) into the Sales Deal.

- "B" = A higher level agreement must be assigned. The "Promotion" field is mandatory during the Sales Deal creation.

As with the Promotion, you can assign a text procedure and a default text ID to a Sales Deal.

In the next configuration step, a Condition Type Group needs to be defined in order to group together the Condition Types that should apply within the Sales Deal. The Condition Type Group is defined in the IMG menu path *SPRO-> Sales and Distribution-> Basic Functions-> Pricing-> Pricing Agreements-> Set up Sales Deals-> Condition Type Groups-> De-*

fine Condition Type Groups (see Figure 4.2.3), or transaction "VB(3".

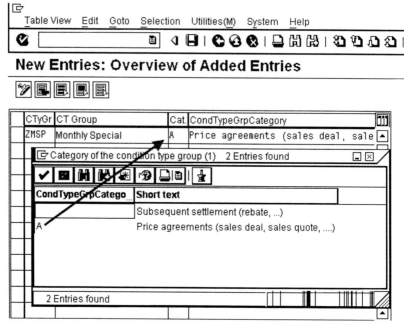

Figure 4.2.3: Create Condition Type Group for Sales Deals

It is important to enter an "A" in the "Cat." field (Category). This defines the Condition Type Group as relevant for Sales Deals as opposed to a blank entry for Rebates, which will be discussed in the next chapter. For our example, we are creating a "Monthly Special" Sales Deal Condition Type Group "ZMSP".

To assign Condition Types and their applicable Condition Tables to a Condition Type Group, go to IMG path *SPRO-> Sales and Distribution-> Basic Functions-> Pricing-> Pricing Agreements-> Set up Sales Deals-> Condition Type Groups-> Assign Condition Types/Tables To Condition Type Groups* or execute transaction "VB(4" (see Figure 4.2.4).

New Entries: Overview of Added Entries

CTyGr	Cond.type group	Cntr	CnTy	Condition type	No.	Table
ZMSP	Monthly Special	1	ZSPM	Monthly Special Disc	663	Sales org./Distr. Chl/Divi
ZMSP	Monthly Special	2	ZSPM	Monthly Special Disc	660	Sales org./Distr. Chl/Divi
ZMSP	Monthly Special	3	ZSPM	Monthly Special Disc	4	Material
		☑			☑	
		☑			☑	
		☑			☑	
		☑			☑	

Figure 4.2.4: Assign Condition Types and Tables to
Condition Type Groups

The "Cntr" field (Condition counter) controls the order in which the Condition Tables appear in the "Condition" section of the Sales Deal (see Figure 4.2.10). Enter the applicable Condition Types in field "CnTy" and its Condition Table number(s) in field "No.". You can assign multiple Condition Types that can have different Access Sequences. It is also not necessary to list all Condition Tables of an Access Sequence. Only the ones for which Sales Deal pricing Condition Records should be created need to be listed here.

Every existing pricing Condition Type, except Rebate conditions, is available to be assigned to a Condition Type Group. For our example, we're using a custom-created discount Condition Type "ZSPM" with some of the Condition Tables of our previously created Access Sequence "ZR01".

I strongly recommend creating Condition Types that should only be used for Sales Deals to distinguish them from regular Condition Types.

The final configuration step assigns the Condition Type Group to the Sales Deal. Use IMG path *SPRO-> Sales and Distribution-> Basic Functions-> Pricing-> Pricing Agreements-> Set up Sales Deals-> Condition Type Groups-> Assign Condition Type Groups/Sales Deals* or execute transaction "VB(5" (see Figure 4.2.5). This link is also displayed in the configuration of the Sales Deal in Figure 4.2.2. If no Condition Type

Group is assigned to a Sales Deal Type, the message "Condition Type Group is incomplete" will be displayed when the creation of a Sales Deal is attempted later.

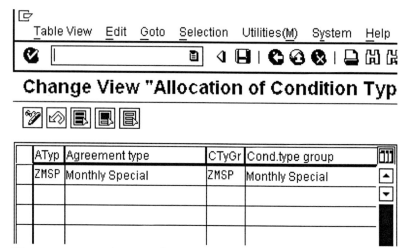

Figure 4.2.5: Assign Condition Type Group to Sales Deal Type

Enter the Sales Deal Type in field "Atyp" (Agreement Type) and the previously created Condition Type Group in field "CtyGr".

Setting up Promotions and Sales Deals

After completing the Sales Deal configuration, we are ready to create our first Promotion. Either execute transaction code "VB31" or use SAP menu *Logistics-> Sales and Distribution-> Master Data-> Agreements-> Promotion-> Create*. On the initial screen in Figure 4.2.6, enter the Promotion Type. The Sales Area for which the Promotion should be valid can be entered by clicking on the "Organizational Data" 🗖 button. Alternatively, a Promotion can be created with reference to an existing Promotion by clicking on the "Create with Reference" Create with Reference button.

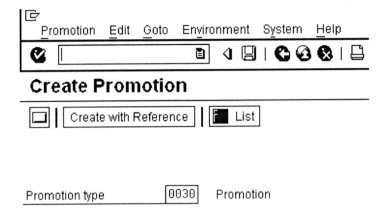

Figure 4.2.6: Creating a Promotion

Clicking on the "List" button branches into transaction "VB35", which allows you to display a list of Promotions.

Press enter to display the detail information for the Promotion (see Figure 4.2.7).

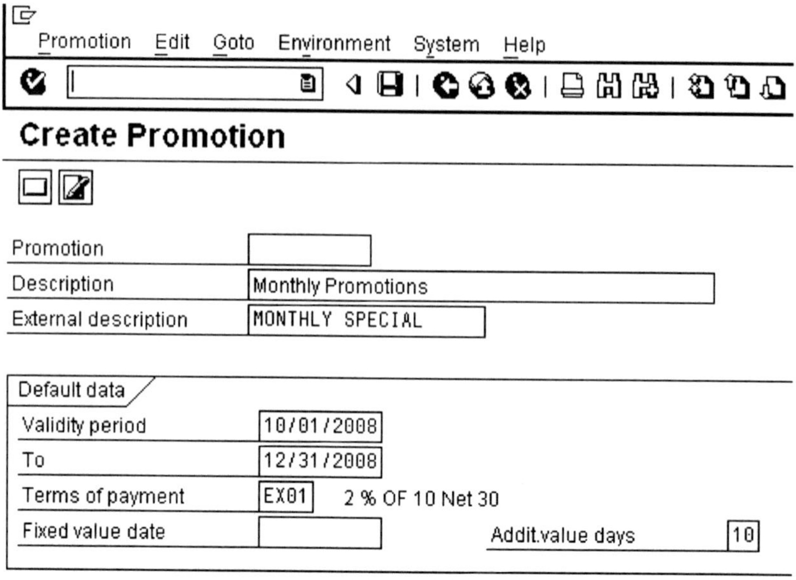

Create Promotion

Promotion	
Description	Monthly Promotions
External description	MONTHLY SPECIAL

Default data

Validity period	10/01/2008	
To	12/31/2008	
Terms of payment	EX01	2 % OF 10 Net 30
Fixed value date		Addit.value days 10

Figure 4.2.7: Promotion Details

Give the Promotion a meaningful name in the "Description" field to distinguish it better later. For example, it is possible to have weekly, monthly, quarterly or yearly Promotions. For our example, we will create a Promotion for our monthly Sales Deals. In addition, an "External description" could be entered and used on outgoing Promotion letters, for example. The "Valid-From" and "Valid-To" dates are defaulted based on the Promotion configuration settings but can be manually changed here.

It is optional to define special payment terms and value dates for this Promotion. These values will be copied into a Sales Deal (if the Sales Deal references a Promotion), and from there into the Sales Order line item where they will overwrite the default settings from the customer master. For example, if customers should receive a higher cash discount for promotional purposes, or additional days to pay their Invoices, you could define this in fields "Terms of payment," "Fixed value date" or "Addit. Value days." Note that you can only enter a fixed value date *or* additional value days, but not both. If you do, the system will inform you with an error message. Save the Promotion and note the document number.

Individual Sales Deals are set up with transaction "VB21" or via SAP menu *Logistics-> Sales and Distribution-> Master Data-> Agreements-> Sales Deal-> Create*, as we will.

Enter the Sales Deal Type and your organizational data by clicking on the "Organizational Data" button in the screen shown in Figure 4.2.8. You can create the Sales Deal with or without reference to either another Sales Deal or a Promotion. Referencing a Promotion will copy the Validity dates, as well as the defined payment terms and value dates (as far as they were maintained in the Promotion). Copying a Sales Deal will also copy any Condition Records that were created within the referenced Sales Deal.

Figure 4.2.8: Creating a Sales Deal

In the screen shown in Figure 4.2.9 you can assign a more specific name to the Sales Deal than what was defined in the Promotion. Add the name of the month in the "External Description" field and create one Sales Deal per month using the "Create with reference" functionality. If a Promotion was referenced, the defined Sales Deal Validity Period must be within the Validity Period of the Promotion. If the Sales Deal was not created with reference to a Promotion on the previous screen, it is possible to link these two documents manually by entering the Promotion document number in field "Promotion" in Figure 4.2.9. This would overwrite any values in these fields that had been maintained so far; however, it would not overwrite the Sales Deal Validity Period. You will get a warning message if you referenced a Promotion that would change the payment terms or the value dates to values other than those in the Sales Deal.

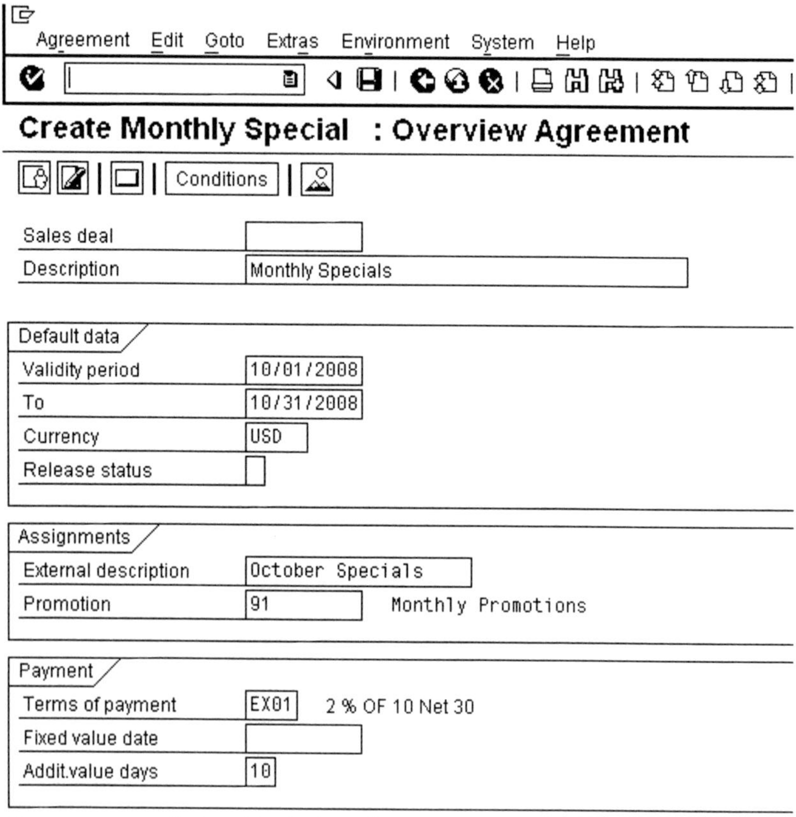

Figure 4.2.9: Sales Deal Details

After completing all necessary fields, select the "Conditions" | Conditions | button.

Similar to Rebate functionality, all Condition Types and Condition Tables that were assigned to the Condition Type Group (in Figure 4.2.4) are displayed in the sequence in which they were defined.

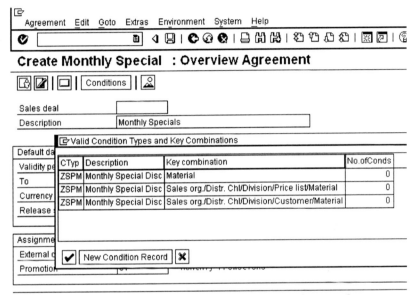

Figure 4.2.10: Available Condition Types in Sales Deal

Select the Condition Type and Condition Table you wish to maintain. For our example, we will select the "ZSPM" Condition Type (in Figure 4.2.10) and the "Material" key combination. Select that line and then click on the "New Condition Record" button.

The resulting Figure 4.2.11 should look very familiar; it is the regular Condition Record maintenance screen. This means all Pricing Record maintenance functionality is available to you, as if you were creating a pricing Condition Record with transaction "VK11" or "VK31". You can maintain Scales, set limits for cumulative conditions, maintain Free Goods or copy Condition Records.

An alternate way to create a Sales Deal pricing Condition Record is with transaction "VK11" or "VK31". To manually link the Sales Deal to the pricing Condition Record, enter the Sales

Deal number in field "Sales Deal" on the "Additional Data" section of the pricing Condition Record (see Figure 2.1.4). This would also reference and pull in the Promotion linked to that Sales Deal. In addition, the Validity Period that was maintained for the pricing Condition Record would be overwritten with the Validity Period of the Sales Deal.

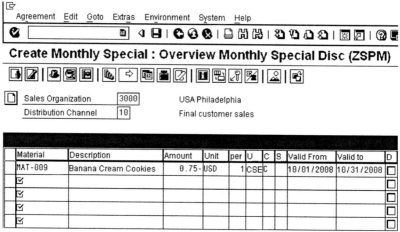

Figure 4.2.11: Sales Deal Condition Record

Either save the Condition Record (and therefore the Sales Deal), or use the green back arrow to go back to the "Valid Condition Types and Key Combinations" screen (shown in Figure 4.2.10) to maintain additional pricing Condition Records for this Sales Deal.

One more thing worth mentioning is that if you create different Sales Deals for the same Condition Type, the system doesn't allow overlapping Validity Periods (unlike in Rebates). For example: Sales Deal 1, Condition Type "ZMSP" has a Validity Period of 08/01/2008-08/31/2008. In Sales Deal 2, you attempt to create a Condition Record for "ZMSP" for 08/10/2008-08/20/2008. This will result in an error message and will not automatically create new Condition Records, as it would for non-Sales Deal related pricing Condition Records.

Promotions and Sales Deals on Sales Documents

Once all Sales Deals are set up in the system, the created Condition Records will apply on every applicable Sales Order and Invoice. In case payment terms and/or value data were maintained on the Sales Deal Master Records, they will show on the "Billing" tab of the "Sales Order Item Data" screen (see Figure 4.2.12).

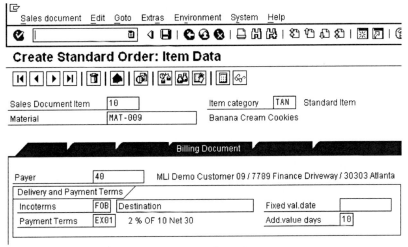

Figure 4.2.12: Billing Data on Order Line Item

The default payment terms of the customer Master Record (our example customer has payment terms "CT20") have been overwritten with "EX01", and "Add. Value Days" of "10" have been entered.

If two different Condition Types from two different Sales Deals apply on the same line item and the payment terms of these two (or more) Sales Deals are different, the Sales Deal data of the last Sales Deal Condition Type that was used in the Pricing Procedure will apply.

To identify if a Sales Deal applied on a Sales Order line item, go to the "Conditions" tab of that line item (see Figure 4.2.13). Unless the Condition Type description identifies it by its description as a "Promo" or "Deal," or unless unique Sales Deal Condition Types are used (see my previous comments under "Assigning Condition Types to Condition Type Groups"), you don't know if a Condition Type is part of a Sales Deal. However, since we know that we created a "ZMSP" Condition Record as part of a Sales Deal, we select that Condition Type and click on the "Condition Record" button as described in the "Pricing on a Sales Document" chapter.

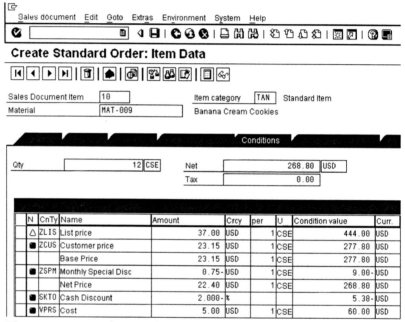

Figure 4.2.13: Sales Deal Pricing on a Sales Order

This will display the applied Condition Record. From here, select the "Additional data" button (see Figure 4.2.14).

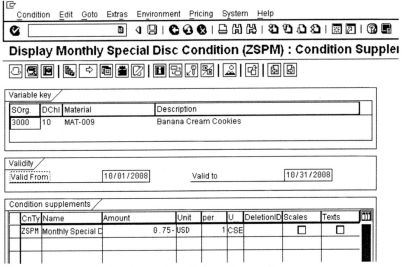

Figure 4.2.14: Sales Deal Condition Record

Figure 4.2.15 shows you the "Additional Data" section of the previously created pricing Condition Record. In the "Assignments" section, the Promotion and Sales Deal number are displayed.

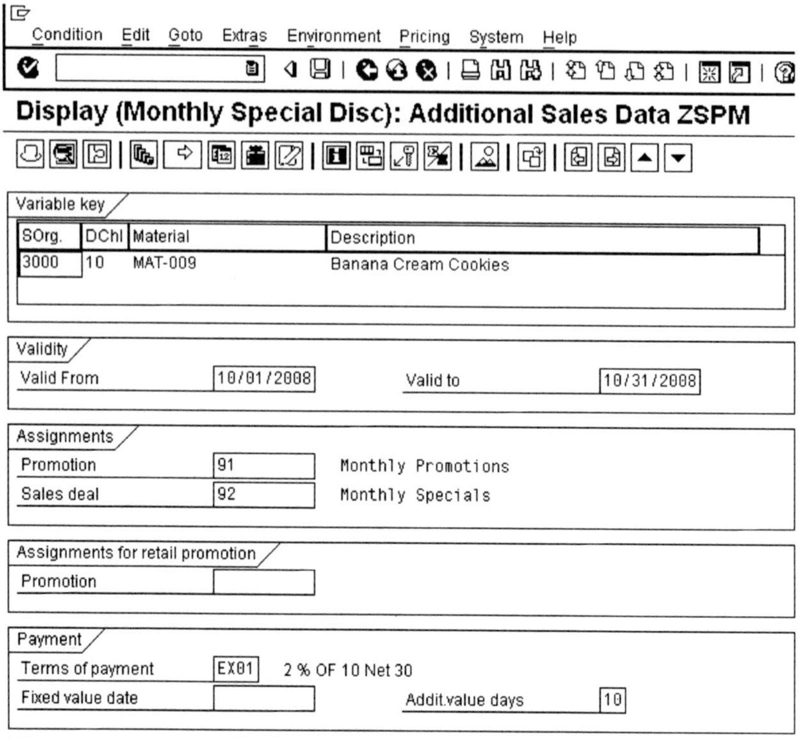

Figure 4.2.15: Applied Promotion and Sales Deal

Compared to Rebates, which will be discussed in the next chapter, the analysis capabilities for Promotions and Sales Deals are minimal at best. There are no standard transactions or standard reports to show on which document line items a specific Sales Deal or Promotion had applied. To retrieve this information, you would need to program custom reports. But before I show you how to get to this information, let's review what is available in the standard system first.

As mentioned earlier, transaction "VB35" will list Promotions, and transaction "VB25" will list Sales Deals. The resulting lists allow the option to branch into the individual agreement(s) by double-clicking on them. However, you will not be able to see Sales Order or Invoice line items that have been applied for a given Sales Deal.

Figure 4.2.16 displays a Promotion Agreement for which several Sales Deals have been created. You can see them in the "Assigned Sales Deals" section from which you can branch into the individual Sales Deals by clicking on a Sales Deal number.

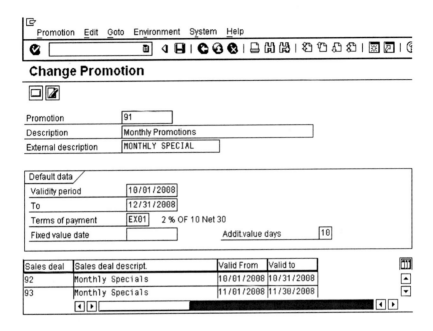

Figure 4.2.16: Multiple Sales Deals of a Promotion

In order to analyze which document line items had a Sales Deal applied, you will need to develop a custom report as explained in Chapter 5.10.

4.3 Rebates

Besides Sales Deals, Rebates are another common way for companies to pay their customers in return for fulfilling certain requirements. The classic example is the car manufacturers. They give their car dealerships a rebate at the end of the year, depending on how many vehicles they sold. These monies are not paid at the time of invoice (off-Invoice), like with the Sales Deal, but at the end of a specified period.

SAP provides a basic set of Rebate functionality to manage the most common Rebate scenarios. This book will discuss and guide you through the standard configuration of Rebates, how to plan and set them up, and most importantly, how to track and pay out Rebate payments.

Rebate functionality was first available in rudimentary form in SAP R/3 version 2.1. With SAP R/3 release 3.0, that functionality received a significant overhaul. Throughout future releases, some enhancements have been made to the Rebate functionality. I will point out the different features added throughout the releases.

Rebates use the same Condition Technique as pricing but with Rebate-specific features.

For our purposes, we will assume we want to give a customer a 5% discount on everything they buy (Rebate Condition Type "BO03"). In addition, we will give away another discount if the customer reaches a certain amount of net sales for the year for a specific group of products ("BO01"). After these Rebates are set up, the Rebate conditions will apply on applicable Invoices as accruals instead of off-Invoice discounts. The Rebate Agreement tracks the applied amounts, which can then be reviewed anytime in the Rebate Agreement. Once a payout of any Rebate amount to the customer occurs, a Rebate Settlement will be created, which is represented by a credit memo request. This reverses accrued amounts and pays the actual monies to the customer in the form of either a check or a credit memo.

4.3.1 Rebate Configuration

The configuration section for Rebates in the IMG can be accessed via IMG path *SPRO-> Sales and Distribution-> Billing-> Rebate Processing.* Some of the configuration transactions are shared with the related pricing ones, but it is easier to remember this central configuration path to access the entire Rebate-related configuration.

Before starting to configure Rebates, three settings have to be made in order to enable the Rebate functionality:

- The Payer partner of the customer participating in a Rebate program needs to have the "Rebate" field checked in the customer master on the *Sales Area-> Billing Document* tab (see Figure 4.3.1.1).

- The Billing Type must be marked as relevant for Rebates in IMG path *SPRO-> Sales and Distribution-> Billing-> Rebate Processing-> Activate Rebate Processing-> Select Billing Documents for rebate processing* (see Figure 4.3.1.2).

- The Sales Organization must be marked as relevant for Rebates in IMG path *SPRO-> Sales and Distribution-> Billing-> Rebate Processing-> Activate Rebate Processing-> Activate Rebate Processing for sales organizations* (see Figure 4.3.1.3).

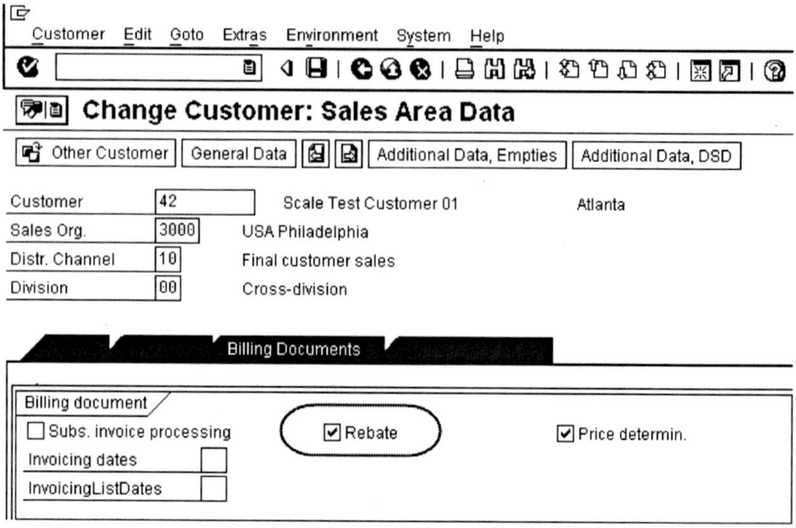

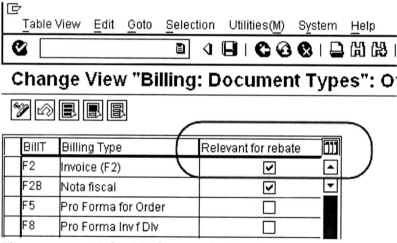

Figure 4.3.1.1: Rebate Flag on Customer Master

Figure 4.3.1.2: Rebate Relevance for Invoices

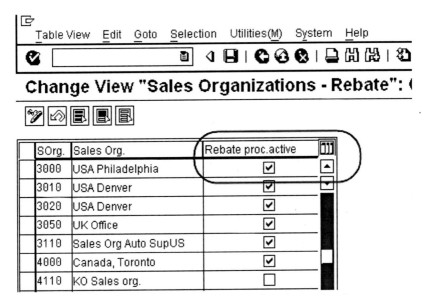

Figure 4.3.1.3: Rebate Relevance for Sales Organization

The system will issue respective messages if you try to process any Rebate-related transactions without any of these settings.

Rebates use the Condition Technique but distinguish themselves from pricing by applying to transactions over time, versus on a transaction-by-transaction basis.

Rebates have their own Field Catalog and their own Condition Table naming conventions. There could potentially be two Condition Tables with the number "001" (one for pricing and one for Rebates) which could have different key fields. If you want to query these tables with transaction "SE16", you need to use the technical names: "A001" for pricing and "KOTE001" for Rebates.

It isn't necessary to go into detail about the Rebate Field Catalogue since it works the same way as for pricing. To access it, use IMG path *SPRO-> Sales and Distribution-> Billing-> Rebate Processing-> Condition Technique for Rebate Processing-> Field Catalog for Rebates.*

To create, change or display Rebate Condition Tables, access IMG path *SPRO-> Sales and Distribution-> Billing-> Rebate Processing-> Condition Technique for Rebate Processing-> Maintain Condition Tables for Rebates.* In Condition Table creation there is no option for Validity Periods or Release status like in pricing, as can be seen in Figure 4.3.1.4.

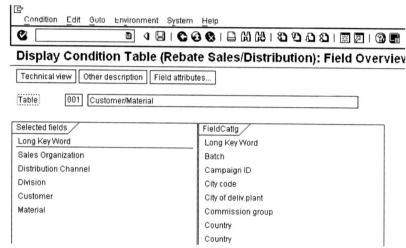

Figure 4.3.1.4: Rebate Condition Table

To create Rebate-related Access Sequences, use IMG path *SPRO-> Sales and Distribution-> Billing-> Rebate Processing-> Condition Technique for Rebate Processing-> Maintain Access Sequences.* You will recognize the screen (see Figure 4.3.1.5) from previous chapters, since it is the same as for pricing. In order to distinguish pricing- and Rebate-specific Access Sequences, enter "1" in field "Ty." (Category) for Rebate-specific Access Sequences.

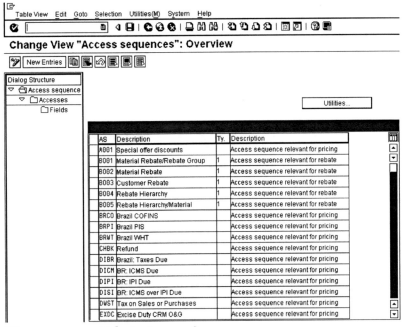

Figure 4.3.1.5: Rebate Access Sequences

For the exercises in this book, we will use some of the standard delivered Access Sequences. Select Access Sequence "BO01" and double-click on the "Accesses" tab.

The big difference between the Rebate and the pricing Access Sequence is that there is no "Exclusion" flag available for Rebate-related Access Sequences (as you can see in Figure 4.3.1.6). This means multiple Condition Tables of an Access Sequence could apply at the same time for the same Condition Type.

SAP offers a "New Rebate Procedure" which would allow the "Exclusion" flag to be turned on. This is available since SAP R/3 release 4.5A. OSS note 105681 explains this feature and the rest of the new procedure in great detail. For the purpose of this book, I'll show the Rebate functionality based on the original Rebate functionality.

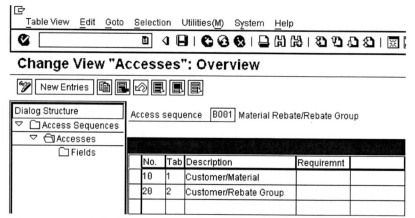

Figure 4.3.1.6: Rebate Access Sequence Detail

Rebate-related Condition Types are identified by Condition Class "C" (Expense Reimbursement). When a new Rebate Condition Type is created via IMG path *SPRO-> Sales and Distribution-> Billing-> Rebate Processing-> Condition Technique for Rebate Processing-> Define Condition Types,* make sure the Condition Class is changed to "C." You will realize that several fields that can usually be maintained in a regular pricing Condition Type will disappear or become unavailable. For example, you will not be able to use the settings for Condition Updates or Group Conditions. Instead, a configuration section ("Rebate") exclusively available for Rebate Condition Types is displayed in Figure 4.3.1.7.

Table View   Edit   Goto   Selection   Utilities(M)   System   Help

Change View "Conditions: Condition Types": Details

New Entries

Condit. type	B001	Group Rebate	Access seq.	B001	Material Rebate/Rebat
					Records for access

Control data 1

Cond. class	C	Expense reimbursement		Plus/minus	X	Negative
Calculat.type	A	Percentage				
Cond.category						
Rounding rule		Commercial				

Changes which can be made

| Manual entries | | No limitations |

Scales

Scale basis	B	Value scale		
Check value	A	Descending	Unit of meas.	
Scale type		can be maintained in con		

Rebate

| Rebate proc. | | Depend.on sales vol. | Provision Con | | Always corrected |

Control data 2

| | | | Exclusion | |
| | Qty conversion | | | |

Text determination

| TextDetPrc | | Text ID | |

Figure 4.3.1.7: Rebate Condition Type Configuration

If the "Rebate proc." field is blank, accruals will be posted on each applicable Invoice. Entering an "A" in that field will prevent the automatic generation of accruals on Invoices. The latter would make sense if you don't base your Rebate payment on actual sales but on the specific performance of the customer (such as a display in a store or an advertisement in the paper). These Rebates would be paid out as a lump sum and would require the creation of a Manual Accrual. For example, you want to give the customer a $5,000 Rebate if he displays your product at the entrance of his store. You would then create a one-time Manual Accrual of $5,000. Once you have proof of customer compliance, you can create a lump sum payment in that amount to reverse the accrual and pay the amount to the customer.

With the "Provision con." field, you determine if you want to reverse your accruals at time of partial payment (we will cover payments later). Leaving this field blank will reverse the accrual; a value of "A" will not reverse it.

After defining the Rebate Condition Types, they can be added to the regular Pricing Procedure via IMG path *SPRO-> Sales and Distribution-> Billing-> Rebate Processing-> Condition Technique for Rebate Processing-> Maintain Pricing Procedures*. Figure 4.3.1.8 shows that not all configuration fields are available for the Rebate conditions in the regular Rebate functionality. The columns for Alternate Condition Type "CalTy" and Alternate Condition Base Value "BasTy" will not allow any manipulations on how the Rebate is calculated. Also, it is not possible to do any manual changes to Rebate conditions. As with the exclusion indicator in the Rebate Access Sequence, turning on the "New Rebate Procedure" will make these fields available.

The pricing requirement "24" in column "Reqt" prevents the Rebate condition from being displayed on any document type but the Invoice. Simply take this requirement off if you want to have visibility of Rebates at Sales Order entry time as well.

A very important setting for the Rebate conditions in the Pricing Procedure is the "Account" keys. As I mentioned earlier, accruals are created at invoice time and posted to accounting to give you visibility on how much you owe your customers in the future. The posting of this accrual is done by accounts assigned to the "Account" key in column "Accrls" (Accruals), usually a sales deduction and an accrual account. The settlement document, in the form of a credit memo, uses the accounts assigned to the account key in column "ActKy" (Account Key) to reverse the accrued amounts and credit the customer.

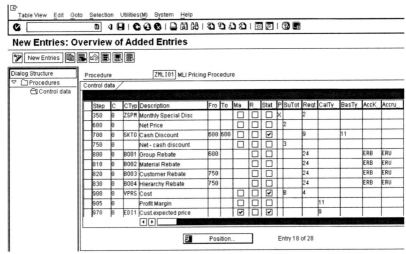

Figure 4.3.1.8: Rebate Condition Types in Pricing Procedure

It is also imperative that any subtotal line to which a Rebate condition refers is stored in one of the seven available "Subtotal" fields ("KZWI1" through "KZWI6" and "BONBA" in column "SuTot"). If you are using multiple Pricing Procedures, you want to keep the subtotal designations common (i.e. "1" for gross price, "2" for Net Price). In the Pricing Procedure in Figure 4.3.1.8, Rebate Condition Type "BO01" references the Net Price in line 600, stored in subtotal "2." Condition "BO03" references line 750, which is stored in subtotal "3" and which represents the value of the Net Price minus any applied cash discount amounts.

Just as with the previously discussed Sales Deals, the Rebate Agreement is based on the same principal, but much more powerful in its configuration. To maintain Rebate Agreement Types, use IMG path *SPRO-> Sales and Distribution-> Billing-> Rebate Processing-> Rebate Agreements-> Define Agreement types.* Click on the "New Entries" button to create a new Rebate Agreement Type, for which a sample type is shown in Figure 4.3.1.9.

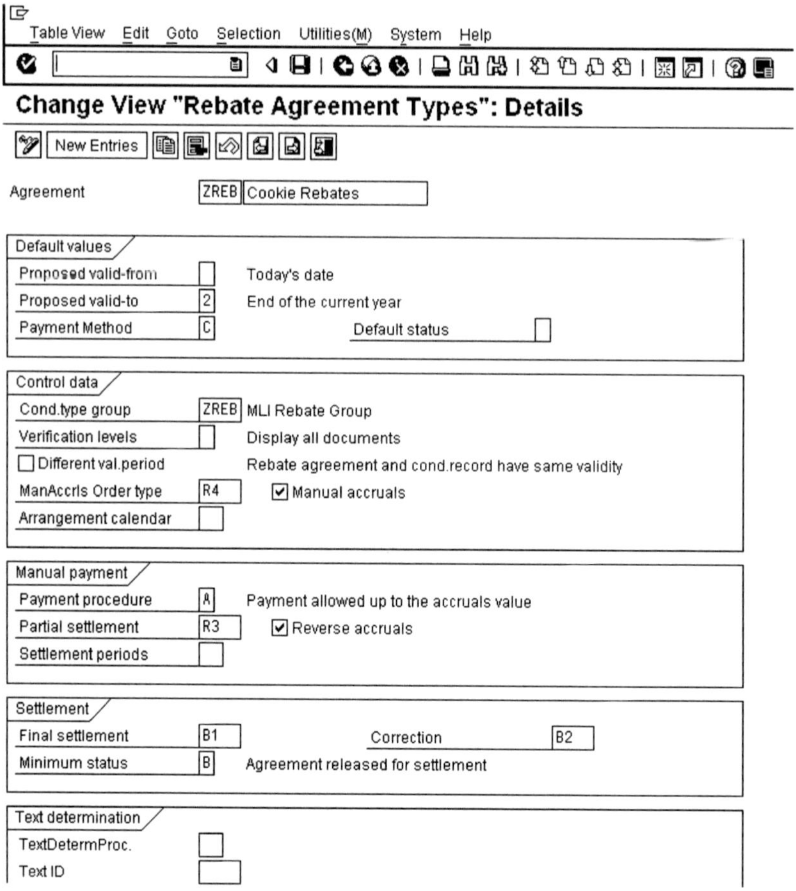

Figure 4.3.1.9: Rebate Agreement Configuration

The first section of the Rebate Agreement Type serves to define the defaults that apply for every Rebate Agreement of that type. You can define the default start and end date of the agreement. The default start date is important in regard to whether or not you want to allow retroactive Rebates. For example, if you set the start date of a Rebate Agreement to today's date, all Invoices from that moment on are eligible for the Rebate and will apply on the Invoice itself. However, if your default is the beginning of the current year, the system will calculate Rebates for all Invoices in the past, from the start date on, even if they did not apply on the past Invoices. These Rebates are called "retroactive."

The other default in this section allows you to set a payment method, which is freely definable to suit your individual situation. Every Rebate Settlement will create a credit memo request in SAP. If you set your payment method default to "C" for "Check," it will carry this flag forward to FI to later let you cut a check. Of course, all of these defaults can be overwritten during creation of the actual Rebate Agreement.

The Condition Type Group is linked to the Rebate Agreement Type in a different configuration transaction and is simply displayed here. The Condition Type Group defines which Rebate Condition Types are allowed for the Rebate Agreement Type.

The "Verification levels" field is also a default which defines the level of detail you see when you review applied Invoices within a Rebate Agreement. You can change this default while reviewing the verification level in the Rebate Agreement.

The "Different val. Period" option lets you define if the Rebate Condition Records created out of the Rebate Agreement can have Validity dates outside of the dates of the Agreement. I suggest you leave this field unchecked.

If Manual Accruals should be allowed, it is indicated and defined with the standard SAP Sales Order Type "R4" in field "ManAccrls Order type". The respective Billing Type for this scenario is "B4."

The same Rebate Agreement can be automatically created in regular intervals with the same data but different Validity dates. To turn on this feature, utilize the "Arrangement calendar" field. A standard or custom SAP calendar can be assigned here to schedule the automatic creation of Rebate Agreements. The full functionality of this feature is described in Chapter 4.4.

The "Manual Payment" section of the Rebate Agreement defines how much money can be paid out during a Partial Settlement. A Partial Settlement is used if, for example, the Rebate Agreement is defined for a full year, but the payouts are supposed to happen on a monthly, quarterly, or any custom-defined schedule.

You can choose if you want to limit any Partial Settlement to the amount of what was accrued up to the point of settlement. This is a good idea if you don't want to pay out more than what the customer is entitled to. However, you can also allow the payment of any amount if you choose to do so. As with Manual Accruals, you need to define the Partial Settlement Order Type in field "Partial Settlement" ("R3" in the standard SAP system). This results in a "B3" Billing Document. If you don't want to wait to reverse your accruals until the Final Settlement, you can do so by checking the "Reverse accruals" box to reverse the accruals on the Partial Settlement.

Just as with recurring Rebate Agreements, it is possible to schedule regular payments by entering the appropriate calendar in field "Settlement periods." This is described in Chapter 4.4.4 in greater detail.

The reversal of the accruals is independent from the payment amount of the Final Settlement. For example, if you accrued $10,000 over a given period, but the customer did not reach their sales goal, you might only want to pay half that amount or nothing at all. No matter what the payment amount is, the total remaining accrued amount for the agreement is reversed.

The "Settlement" section defines the Final Settlement Document Type ("B1" in standard SAP) and the minimum status that needs to be set in the Rebate Agreement before it can be finally settled.

The standard correction document type "B2" is needed if the statistical and actual accrual amounts in the system are getting out of sync. This is mostly the case for retroactive Rebates.

As with pricing conditions, text types can be assigned to the Rebate Agreement Type through standard SAP Text Determination, which will enable the attachment of comments. These comments can then be printed on a Rebate Agreement letter.

Earlier I mentioned the assigned Condition Type Group in the definition of the Rebate Agreement. With IMG menu path *SPRO-> Sales and Distribution-> Billing-> Rebate Processing-> Rebate Agreements-> Condition Type Groups->*

Define Condition Type Groups, you can freely define your Rebate Condition Type Group (see Figure 4.3.1.10). Make sure the “Cat.” (Category) field is left blank; this defines the Condition Type Group as relevant for Rebates. Sales Deals share this configuration transaction and would be identified with a category of “A.” Enter “ZREB” for our Condition Type Group.

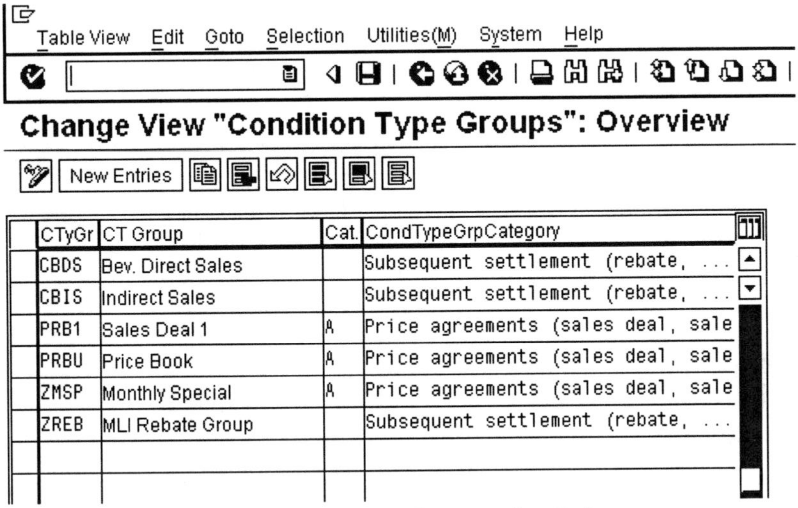

CTyGr	CT Group	Cat.	CondTypeGrpCategory
CBDS	Bev. Direct Sales		Subsequent settlement (rebate, ...
CBIS	Indirect Sales		Subsequent settlement (rebate, ...
PRB1	Sales Deal 1	A	Price agreements (sales deal, sale
PRBU	Price Book	A	Price agreements (sales deal, sale
ZMSP	Monthly Special	A	Price agreements (sales deal, sale
ZREB	MLI Rebate Group		Subsequent settlement (rebate, ...

Figure 4.3.1.10: Condition Type Groups for Rebates

Next, assign Rebate Condition Types and Condition Tables to the created Condition Type Group with IMG path *SPRO-> Sales and Distribution-> Billing-> Rebate Processing-> Rebate Agreements-> Condition Type Groups-> Assign Condition Types/Tables To Condition Type Groups*. Define which Condition Tables of which Rebate Condition Types should be allowed for a specific Condition Type Group, and in which order they should appear in the Rebate Agreement (see Figure 4.3.1.11). Since the standard SAP Rebate functionality does not allow exclusions in the Access Sequence, the order of Condition Tables can be freely defined here. You can assign multiple Condition Types with different Access Sequences. Enter the Condition Types and Condition Tables to Condition Type Group “ZREB” as shown in Figure 4.3.1.11.

Table View   Edit   Goto   Selection   Utilities(M)   System   Help

New Entries: Overview of Added Entries

CTyGr	Cond.type group	Cntr	CnTy	Condition type	No.	Table
ZREB	MLI Rebate Group	10	B001	Group Rebate	1	Customer/Material
ZREB	MLI Rebate Group	20	B001	Group Rebate	2	Customer/Rebate Group
ZREB	MLI Rebate Group	30	B003	Customer Rebate	3	Customer
ZREB	MLI Rebate Group	40	B002	Material Rebate	1	Customer/Material
			☑		☑	
			☑		☑	
			☑		☑	

Figure 4.3.1.11: Assign Rebate Condition Types and Tables to Condition Type Groups

Finally, you are able to link the Condition Type Group to the Rebate Agreement Type through the IMG menu path *SPRO-> Sales and Distributions-> Billing-> Rebate Processing-> Rebate Agreements-> Condition Type Groups-> Assign Condition Type Groups to Rebate Agreement Types* (see Figure 4.3.1.12).

Table View   Edit   Goto   Selection   Utilities(M)   System   Help

Change View "Allocation of Condition Type Group/Agr

AType	Agreement type	CTyGr	Cond.type group	
ZMSP	Monthly Special	ZMSP	Monthly Special	▲
ZREB	Cookie Rebates	ZREB	MLI Rebate Group	▼

Figure 4.3.1.12: Assign Condition Type Group to Rebate Agreement Type

4.3.2 Creating a Rebate Agreement

The Rebate Agreement is the central point for processing Rebates. Here are the main tasks that can be done out of this transaction:

- Define the payment method and Validity of the Rebate Agreement.
- Define the Condition Records with rates and Scales for which Rebates should apply. Be aware that you cannot create Rebate Condition Records with the regular pricing transactions "VK11" or "VK31" due to the Condition Class of "C" as indicated in the section about Condition Types.
- Review all applied Invoices to a specific Rebate Agreement.
- See which payments were already made and how much was accrued.
- Generate Partial and Final Settlements, as well as Manual Accruals. If you attempt to create any Rebate credit memo manually with "VA01", you will receive an error for the same reason as the Condition Records. To track all payments within the Rebate Agreement, they have to originate from that Rebate Agreement.

To create a Rebate Agreement, execute transaction "VBO1" or use menu path *Logistics-> Sales and Distribution-> Master Data-> Agreements-> Rebate Agreement-> Create*. In the screen shown in Figure 4.3.2.1, enter the Rebate Agreement Type and click on the "Organizational Data" ⬜ button. Enter the Sales Area in which the Rebate should be paid. It is important to understand that this Sales Area will be used to create the Rebate Settlements. The Condition Records that are created within this Rebate Agreement can be applicable for the same or for different Sales Areas. For example, Rebate payments are going to be made in Sales Area 3000,10,00. However, different Condition Records are set up for different rates in different Sales Areas (1% for 3000,10,02;

1.5% for 3000,20,01; etc.). Click on the "Copy" button to pro-
ceed.

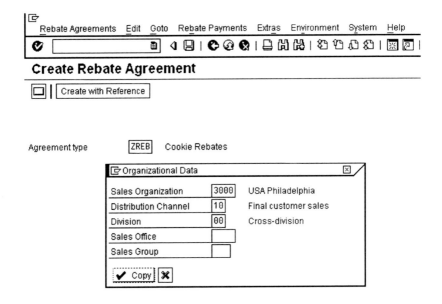

Figure 4.3.2.1: Creating a Rebate Agreement

On the next screen (see Figure 4.3.2.2), enter the description of the Rebate Agreement, the Rebate recipient, the currency in which the Rebate payments are going to be made, the payment method and the Validity Period of the agreement.

The Rebate recipient has to be a Payer partner. You must ensure that the Payer partner type (partner type "RG" in standard SAP) is linked to the account group that is used for the sold-to party ("0001" in standard SAP) because in the creation of Rebate Settlement credit memos, the Rebate recipient becomes the sold-to party.

The payment method defaults from the Rebate Agreement Type configuration setting and can be overwritten here. The same applies to the Validity Period. Originally the Valid-From date is defaulted to today's date (as set in the Agreement Type). If the agreement should be created for a time period prior to today, we need to back-date the Valid-From date to the first of the year, for example. For our purposes in this book, assume the Rebate Agreement is valid for the whole calendar year, but if a fiscal year is required you can adjust the dates as necessary. Once all this data is entered, click on the "Conditions" [Conditions] button to create Rebate Condition Records.

Agreement Edit Goto Rebate Payments Extras Environment System Help	

Create Cookie Rebates : Overview Agreement

Conditions | Pay | Accrue

Agreement		Agreement type	ZREB Cookie Rebates
Description	Customer Yearly Rebate		
Extended Bonus	☐ W/ VAKEY	☐ Ind. Settlement	☐ Periodic Settlement

Rebate Recipient

Rebate recipient	42	Scale Test Customer 01
Currency	USD	
Payment Method	C	Check
External description	YEARLY REBATE 2008	

Validity

Settlement periods	
Validity period	01 / 01 / 2008
To	12 / 31 / 2008

Control Data

Agreement Status	Open
Verification levels	Display all documents

Figure 4.3.2.2: Rebate Agreement Overview

The Condition Types and Condition Tables in Figure 4.3.2.3 represent the settings from the previously created Condition Type Group (see Figure 4.3.1.11). Double-click on the key combination for which Rebate Condition Records should be created. For the example Rebate Agreement, choose Condition Type "BO03" with the "Customer" key combination.

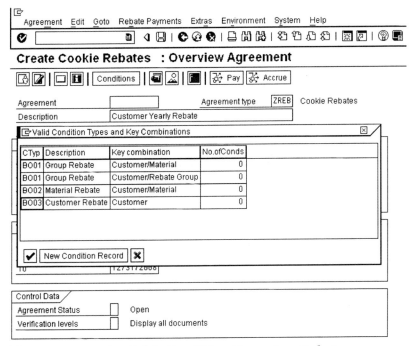

Figure 4.3.2.3: Available Condition Types in a Rebate

The Validity Period for the Condition Record defaults from the Validity Period of the Rebate Agreement. As defined in the Rebate Agreement Type, an attempt to change the Validity Period to one outside the agreement Validity Period would result in an error message. However, changing the Validity Period to one within the range of the Rebate Agreement Validity Period is possible. For example, if you set up the Rebate Agreement for the whole year and pay out on a monthly basis with different amounts, it makes sense to create multiple Condition Records with monthly Validity dates.

Enter Condition Records for three customers. This means the sales of these three customers apply on the Rebate that is paid out to the Rebate recipient. This is mostly used for the headquarters of several branch locations.

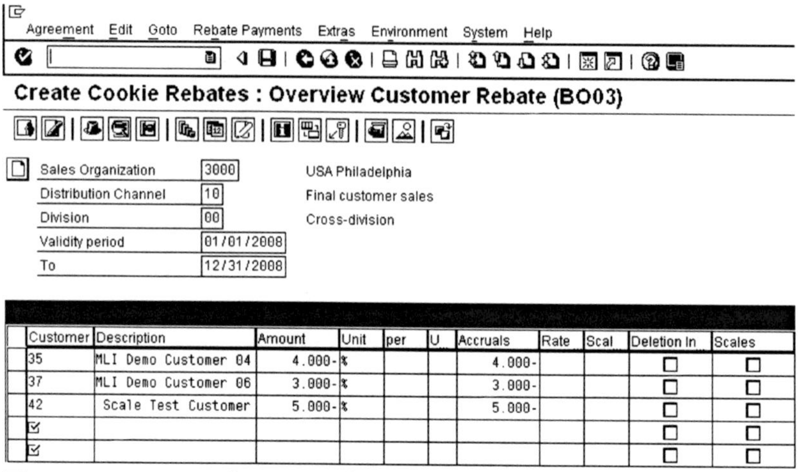

Figure 4.3.2.4: Rebate Condition Records

If you were to enter a rate in Figure 4.3.2.4 and press enter, the rate amount would also apply in the "Accruals" column. It is important to remember that the rate represents what is going to be paid to the customer, and the accrual is what gets accrued over time on Invoices. This becomes very clear when Scales are used. Although different rates based on different Scale levels of sales achievements are maintained in the Rebate Pricing Records, only one accrual rate can be maintained.

The accrual rate applies on each Invoice, at which time it is not known if a customer will reach the next Scale level over the length of the agreement. You might want to maintain an average accrual rate (for example, if there are Scale rates of 1%, 2% and 3%, your accrual rate might be the median of 2%). However, based on your accounting guidelines you also might either over- or under-accrue.

It is also possible to not accrue at all (e.g., in the case of a lump sum payment) by having no value in the accrual rate column. However, if in that case you are also trying to create Partial Settlements and have configured the Rebate Agreement to not allow higher payments than what was accrued, you will have to create Manual Accruals in order to do so.

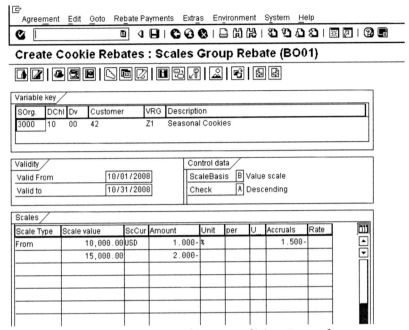

Figure 4.3.2.5: Scales in a Rebate Condition Record

Figure 4.3.2.5 displays the Scale setup for a Rebate with accruals.

We want to set a sales goal with Condition Type "BO01". The customer needs to buy $10,000 worth of seasonal cookies (represented by volume Rebate group "Z1" in the material master) in order to get a 1% Rebate. For sales over $15,000, however, 2% of net sales will be rebated back to the customer. The accrual will always be 1.5% on all applicable Invoices since we don't know at the beginning of the Rebate which sales goal the customer will reach. Once the Final Settlement is created, all applicable sales will be accumulated and compared with the Scale value. If the threshold is not met, nothing will be paid out, but all accrued values will still be reversed.

Select any Condition Record for the "BO03" Rebate Condition Type in Figure 4.3.2.4 next and click on the "Details" button.

At the bottom of the "Control Data" section of the "Details" screen (see Figure 4.3.2.6) you can see by the check in the "Subsequent Entry" field that the Condition Record was created retroactively. As a result, not only will Invoice line items apply from this day forward, but also the ones that were created from the Valid-From date of the Condition Record until today's date.

Since a Rebate Settlement in SAP is reflected as a credit memo request, a material number is needed to generate the credit. The material for this credit memo is stored in field "Matl. f. settl" (Material for settlement). Since the key combination we choose is by customer, we need to define a material of our choosing. Selecting a regular material might cause an issue with reporting, since the materials that are actually being accrued on cannot be easily tied to the material of the settlement. You will always have to choose a material for this field if the material number is not part of the selected Condition Table. In the latter case, the material number defaults as the settlement material. For our example, we create a dummy material to represent the Rebate material (see Figure 4.3.2.6).

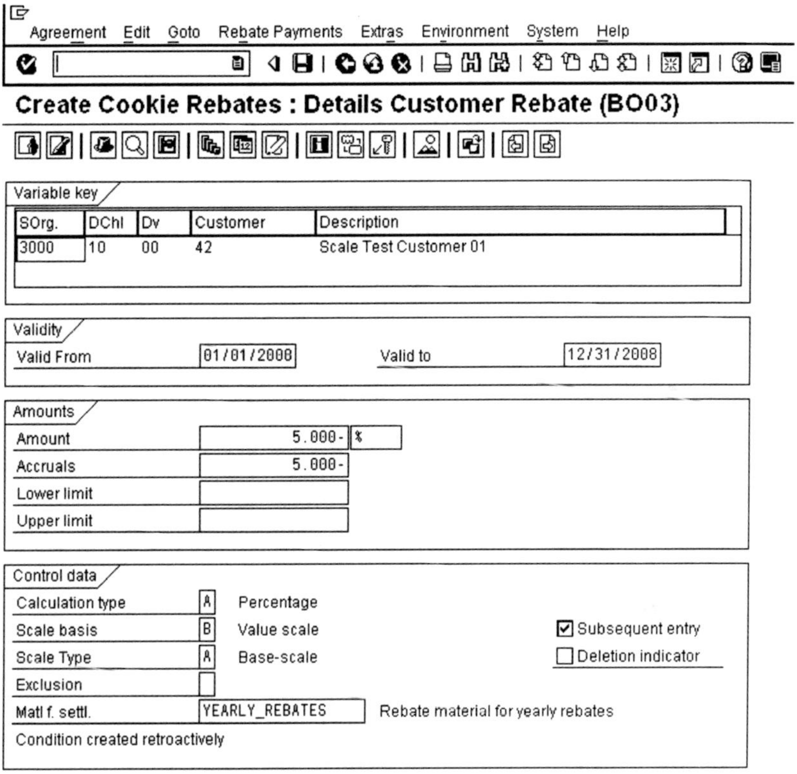

Figure 4.3.2.6: Rebate Material in Rebate Condition Record

If more Condition Records should be created, use the green back arrow to return to the "Valid Condition Type and Key Combinations" screen (see Figure 4.3.2.3). However, if you are done with all your Rebate pricing maintenance, you can now save the Rebate Agreement.

At this point, I would like to advise on the number of Condition Records that should be created per unique Rebate Agreement. Although three different Condition Types are allowed to be maintained within Rebate Agreement Type "ZREB", that does not mean they all have to be maintained in the same Rebate Agreement. It makes sense to distinguish multiple Rebate Agreements based on the type of Rebate you want to give. A material-specific Rebate might be maintained in one Rebate Agreement, whereas the customer's yearly Rebate is created in a separate agreement.

This way, if you want to see the status of one of your Rebate programs, you can look at it without having to dissect other Rebate Condition Records within a single Rebate Agreement. In addition, it improves system performance since not every Invoice line item has to be read every single time.

Another common mistake is that instead of creating new Rebate Agreements (for example, yearly renewals), the Validity end date of the agreement is just extended. The problem is that when you want to check which Invoice line items applied to the Rebate in real time, the system has to look back at two or more years' worth of data. (If you try it this way, you might as well just sit back and wait for the transaction to time out.) Instead of increasing the Validity Period, it takes as little time to create a new Rebate Agreement with reference by clicking the "Create with Reference" `Create with Reference` button in Figure 4.3.2.1. Or you can use the aforementioned automated Rebate Agreement renewal transaction "VB(D".

One more word about Rebate Agreements with Scales. The Scale levels are always only applicable to the Condition Record for which they were created. A scenario that would not be possible: if you buy $10,000 worth of item A, B and C combined, a Rebate is paid, where items A, B and C are not in some kind of grouping like the volume Rebate group in Figure 4.3.2.5.

However, starting with SAP release ECC 6.0, it is possible to group Condition Records together for Scale purposes, which I will explain later.

Also, since SAP R/3 release 4.5A, it is possible to use Graduated Interval Scales for Rebates.

After the Rebate Agreements are created we can check an Invoice that has these Rebate conditions applied. The Service Rendered Date, not the Pricing Date, of the Invoice line item is used to determine the Validity of a Rebate Condition Record. All Rebate conditions are line item conditions; therefore, go to the "Conditions" tab of an Invoice line item.

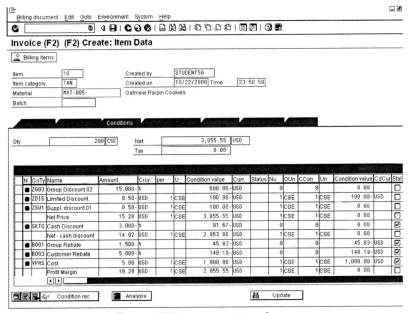

Figure 4.3.2.7: Rebate Pricing on an Invoice

Figure 4.3.2.7 shows that two Rebate conditions applied. "BO01" for the material promotion with a 1.5% allowance and the 5% of Condition Type "BO03" for everything the customer buys. It is possible the same Rebate Condition Type applies several times, unlike regular pricing conditions. You could, for example, have a headquarter Rebate that pays 3% of all sales of a payer. In addition, you have a Rebate Agreement that pays an additional 1% for a specific sold-to customer (for a new store promotion, for example). This would also be set up as a "BO03" Condition Record. You would see both "BO03" records on an Invoice line item, one with 3% and one with 1%.

Select Rebate Condition Type "BO03" and click on the "Details" button.

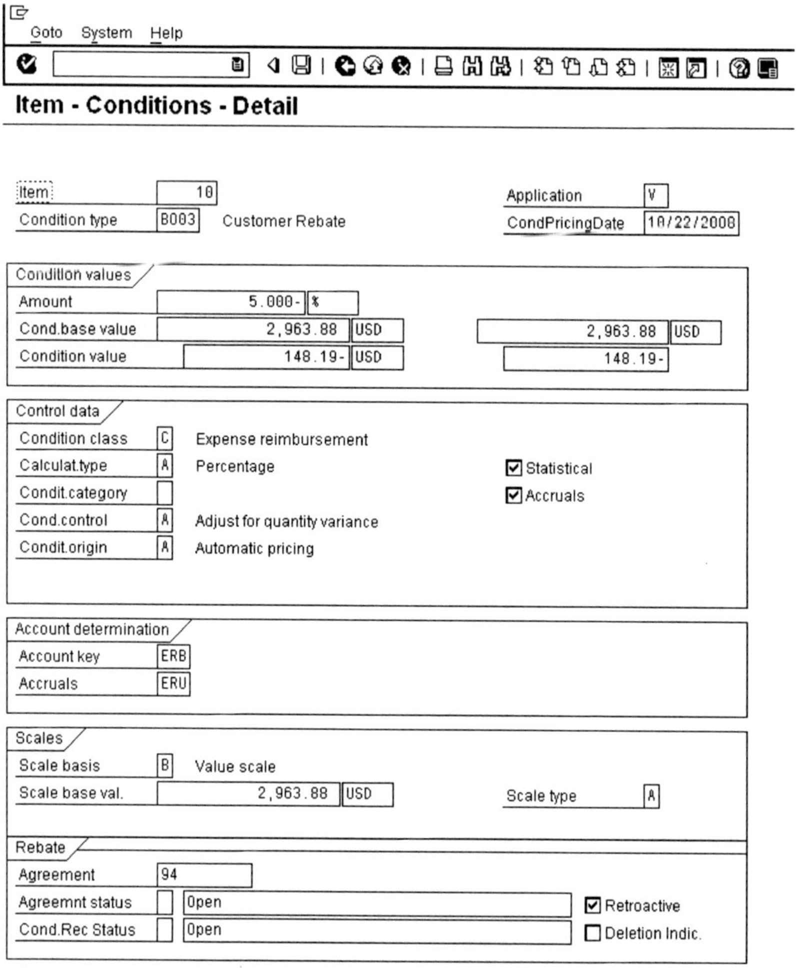

```
 ┌─
 │  Goto   System   Help
 ┌──────────────────────────────────────────────────────────────────────┐
 │ ✓ [           ]  🔲  ◁ 🖫 | 😊 😊 😊 | 🖦 🖬 🖬 | 🖫 🖫 🖫 🖫 | 🖳 🗐 | 😊 🖳 │
 └──────────────────────────────────────────────────────────────────────┘
```

Item - Conditions - Detail

Item	10		Application	V
Condition type	B003	Customer Rebate	CondPricingDate	10/22/2008

Condition values

Amount	5.000-	%		
Cond.base value	2,963.88	USD	2,963.88	USD
Condition value	148.19-	USD	148.19-	

Control data

Condition class	C	Expense reimbursement	
Calculat.type	A	Percentage	☑ Statistical
Condit.category			☑ Accruals
Cond.control	A	Adjust for quantity variance	
Condit.origin	A	Automatic pricing	

Account determination

Account key	ERB
Accruals	ERU

Scales

Scale basis	B	Value scale		
Scale base val.	2,963.88	USD	Scale type	A

Rebate

Agreement	94	
Agreemnt status	Open	☑ Retroactive
Cond.Rec Status	Open	☐ Deletion Indic.

Figure 4.3.2.8: Rebate Condition Detail on an Invoice

You can see by the check in field "Accruals" in Figure 4.3.2.8 that, although not specified explicitly in the Rebate Condition Type configuration, the Rebate condition is automatically an accrual. The Rebate Agreement number to which the Condition Record belongs is also shown in the "Rebates" section of this screen in field "Agreement." The check in field "Retroactive" indicates if the condition is retroactive or not.

4.3.3   Managing and Paying Rebates

After several Invoices were created, the Rebate Agreement can be accessed in either "Change" mode (Transaction "VBO2") or "Display" mode ("VBO3"). To see which Invoice line items applied, select the "Verification level" 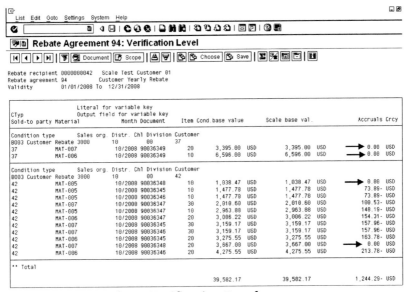 button shown in Figure 4.3.2.2.

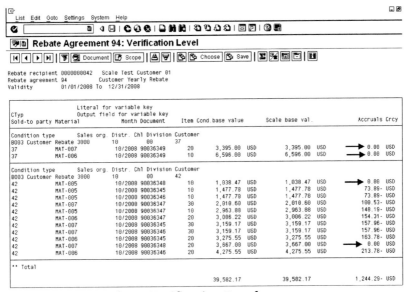

Figure 4.3.3.1: Rebate Verification Level

Items that show accrual values of "0" (indicated by the arrows in Figure 4.3.3.1) are Invoice line items that applied retroactively. Since the Rebate Agreement did not exist when they were created, no accruals could be made. Drill down to an individual Invoice by clicking the Invoice number once. To change the level of detail shown, select the "Verification Levels" [🖉 Scope] button shown in Figure 4.3.3.1 or select SAP menu *Settings-> Verification Levels*. Remember, the default verification level was set in customizing of the Agreement Type to "Open," meaning every line item is displayed. It might make sense to select verification level "D" if you have thousands of

Invoice line items and you would like to just see totals by customer. One thing to note is that the month displayed is always the calendar month, even if the Condition Records are set up by fiscal month. This can lead to misinterpretation of the data.

As mentioned above, the system may time out if you are trying to review the verification level online, due to the large number of applicable Invoice line items. In this case, use transaction "VB(8" to generate a verification report in the background.

4.3.4 Creating Partial Settlements

As mentioned before, Rebates can be settled automatically by periodic creation of Rebate payments. You need to decide if this option makes sense, based on the number and complexity of the Rebate Agreements you have. For example, it makes sense to schedule regular payments for Rebates where the customers get a certain percentage for everything they buy. However, Rebates that include Scales or that need other manual calculations or adjustments should be handled manually. This chapter explains how to create manual settlements.

Any kind of settlement has to be executed in "Change" mode (transaction "VBO2") of the Rebate Agreement. Clicking the "Create Manual Rebate Payment" button will open the "Partial Settlement" screen as seen in Figure 4.3.4.1. All Condition Records of this agreement are displayed. In the "Max amount" field, the amount accrued as of today is displayed, which, by our configuration setting, is the maximum amount that is allowed to be paid out in a Partial Settlement. If a higher amount were entered, an error message would be issued. Enter the amount that should be paid in the "Amt to be paid" field. The amount entered always defaults as a negative amount. Save the Rebate Agreement.

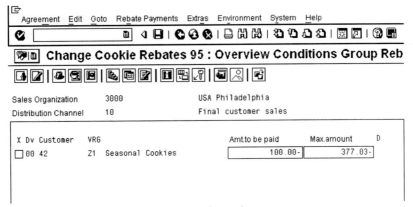

Figure 4.3.4.1: Creating a Partial Settlement

An information message with the credit memo request number is displayed, indicating a partial Rebate Settlement was created.

Be aware that you cannot create a Final Settlement until all open settlement credit memos are posted to accounting, since the actual payments are updated in the Rebate Agreement only when they are posted to accounting in order to determine what is left to pay. Additional Partial Settlements, however, can be created even if a previous Partial Settlement was not posted to accounting. The available amount left to be paid to the customer in the additional Partial Settlement is reduced by the previous Partial Settlement amount, even if the previous Partial Settlement did not post to accounting yet.

The created Partial Settlement credit memo request is processed with transaction "VA02". It was created with a billing block that needs to be released before the request can be invoiced. The block is set in order to establish another review point before the Rebate is paid to the customer. Looking at the line item pricing screen of the credit memo request (see Figure 4.3.4.2), you see that only the Rebate Condition Type is displayed, although the same Pricing Procedure is used for the Invoice. There are two entries: one is to actually credit the customer with the specified amount; the other is to reverse the accrual. Since the Partial Settlement was configured in the Rebate Agreement Type to always reverse the accrual (see Figure 4.3.1.9), the amounts are always the same in a Partial Settlement. Save the credit memo request and invoice it.

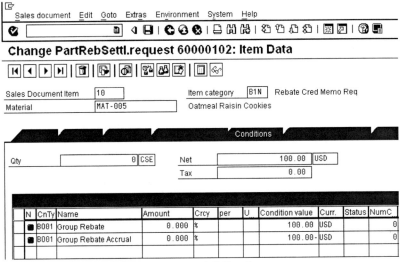

Figure 4.3.4.2: Pricing on a Partial Settlement

In case a mistake was made with the Partial Settlement and it is discovered before the credit memo Invoice is created, the credit memo request can be deleted with transaction "VA02", which will increase the available accrual amount in the Rebate Agreement again. If the settlement was already invoiced, the credit memo will need to be cancelled. Since the credit memo request cannot be deleted because a document link to the credit memo and cancellation already exists, all the line items on the credit memo request have to be rejected in that scenario.

Going back to the Rebate Agreement itself, the Partial Settlements that were already created for this Rebate Agreement can be displayed. Within transaction "VBO2" or "VBO3", select *Rebate Payments->Rebate Documents* and select the type of document you would like to see. Partial and Final Settlements can be accessed separately. Since we only created a Partial Settlement so far, this is the only option that is available. Select "Partial Settlement," click the check mark and you will see all Partial Settlements that were created for this Rebate Agreement (in our case, just one). Figure 4.3.4.3 shows the settlement amount that was credited to the customer and the reversed accrual amount. To branch into the actual credit memo, click on the Invoice number once. If you have a credit memo request that is not invoiced yet, you will see that credit memo request number here instead of the Billing Document number. This helps to determine if there are any open settlement documents for this Rebate Agreement.

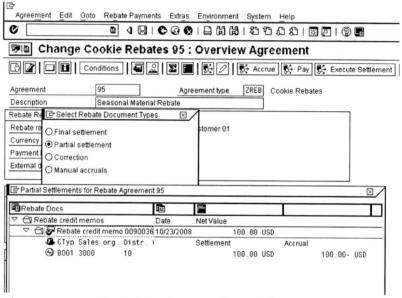

Figure 4.3.4.3: Partial Settlements for a Rebate Agreement

Another view of payment data can be accessed from within the Rebate Condition Record. In the recently accessed Rebate Agreement, go to the Condition Record for which the Partial Payment was issued and select *Goto->Payment data* from the menu. This view (see Figure 4.3.4.4) displays the total accrued dollars, how many accrual dollars were reversed and how much money was paid to the customer already. Indicated in the lower section of the screen is the amount of accrued money left to pay out.

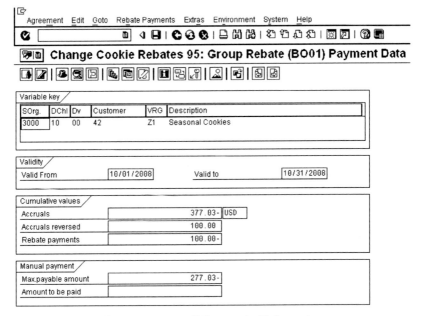

Figure 4.3.4.4: "Payment Data" Screen in Rebate Agreement

From this screen it is also possible to initiate a Partial Settlement by entering a payment amount in field "Amount to be paid." The same check for maximum accrued value occurs here.

4.3.5 Creating Manual Accruals

As mentioned before, sometimes Manual Accruals need to be made in order to increase the accrued amounts for a given Condition Record. The most likely scenario is when a Rebate Agreement is created in the middle of the year but set retroactively to be valid for the whole year. The system will take previous Invoices into consideration, but no accruals for these Invoices are accounted for since they did not exist when the Rebate Agreement was created. If Partial Settlements should be made, not enough accrued dollars are available to pay out as much as needed. The accrual amount needs to be increased by creating a Manual Accrual. In order to know how much needs to be accrued in addition, click the "Sales volume" Σ button on the "Agreement Overview" screen. The resulting screen (see Figure 4.3.5.1) shows the actual eligible Rebate amount (in our example, $599.72) and the accrued amount ($377.03). We need to create an accrual for the difference of $229.69.

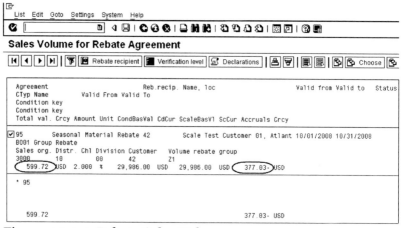

Figure 4.3.5.1: Rebate Sales Volume

This can be accomplished by clicking the "Create Manual Accrual" Accrue button on the "Rebate Agreement Overview" screen. In the resulting screen (see Figure 4.3.5.2) the Manual Accrual amount can be entered. A negative amount will increase the total accrual amount; a positive amount will decrease it. Save the document and a message will indicate that a Manual Accrual has been created. Invoice the credit memo request to post it to FI. Return to the Rebate Agreement afterward and check the Sales Volume again: the accrual amount now matches the eligible payout amount.

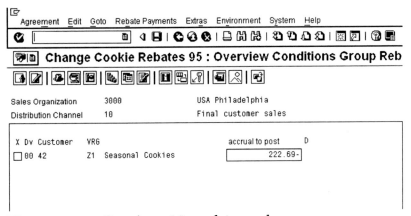

Figure 4.3.5.2: Creating a Manual Accrual

4.3.6   Create Rebate Correction Documents

Instead of trying to figure out the Manual Accrual difference, there is another way to correct the Rebate Agreement. When the Rebate Agreement includes retroactive documents, it's possible that Billing Documents and statistical data (the accrual amounts that are stored in SIS structure "S060") might be out of sync. To see these discrepancies, run report "RV15B002" with transaction "SA38" or via IMG path *SPRO-> Sales and Distribution-> Billing-> Rebate Processing-> Compare Rebate Basis And Correct Accruals*. Enter the Rebate Agreement number and execute. Figure 4.3.6.1 shows that Billing Documents applied to the Rebate Agreement in the amount of $377.03, but the statistics ("S060") show $449.80 accrued. Instead of doing a Manual Accrual, just click on the "Correct Backlogs" ⌷Correct backlogs⌷ button, which will automatically create an "R2" correction credit memo request.

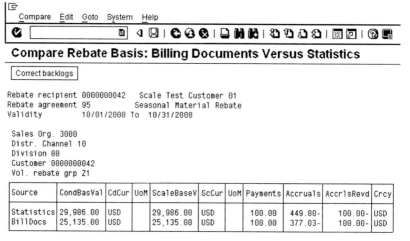

Figure 4.3.6.1: Rebate Basis Out of Sync

The pricing information in the resulting "R2" credit memo request in Figure 4.3.6.2 shows that only an accrual is booked, but no payment.

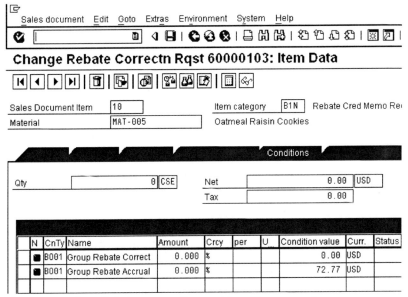

Figure 4.3.6.2: Pricing on a Correction Document

After invoicing this credit memo request, the Billing Document and statistic amounts are equal when accessing the "RV15B002" report again (see Figure 4.3.6.3).

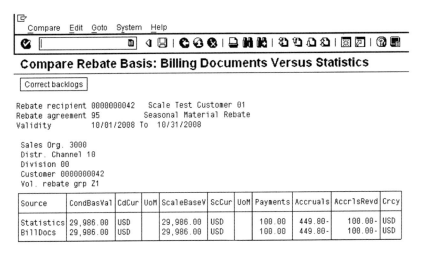

Figure 4.3.6.3: Rebate Basis After Correction

4.3.7   Create Final Rebate Settlements

At the Validity end of the Rebate Agreement, the Final Settlement is executed to close the Rebate Agreement. As defined in the Rebate Agreement Type, the "Agreement status" field needs to be set to "B" (Agreement released for settlement) on the "Change Rebate: Overview Agreement" screen. This is a manual check that prevents the accidental closing of the Rebate Agreement. Select the "Create Final Settlement via Payment Screen" 🔧 Execute Settlement button from the "Change Rebate: Overview Agreement" screen. Regardless of what was accrued, the Final Settlement payment screen shows what Rebate amount the customer is eligible for, including retroactive amounts (see Figure 4.3.7.1). At this point it is also possible to pay out more than the eligible amount, even if the amount exceeds the accrued value. Make any necessary adjustments and save the Rebate Agreement.

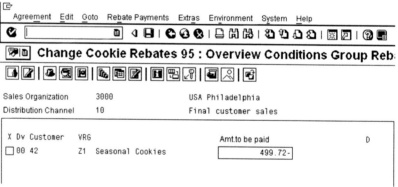

Figure 4.3.7.1: Creating a Final Settlement

Another way to create the Final Settlement is to use the "Create Final Settlement" 🔧 button from the "Rebate Agreement Overview" screen, which creates a credit memo request right away without giving the opportunity to manipulate the final payment amount.

After the credit memo request is created, the Rebate Agreement status is set to "C," which prevents the creation of any further settlements out of this Rebate Agreement.

The Final Settlement credit memo request uses the last day of the Rebate Agreement Validity Period as the billing date. It can be created manually as just shown or via the same batch job ("RV15C001") with which periodic Partial Settlements can be created.

Invoice the credit memo request. Looking at the pricing screen of the credit memo (see Figure 4.3.7.2), you see that the payment amount is higher than the accrual amount, since we can't reverse more than what was accrued. In a scenario in which nothing would be paid out (if certain sales goals were not met), only the accrual amount would be reversed in a Final Settlement. Once the credit memo is posted to FI, the Rebate Agreement status changes to "D." This effectively closes the Rebate Agreement.

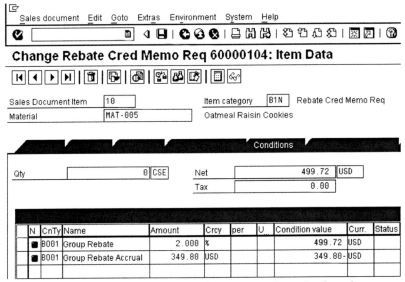

Figure 4.3.7.2: Pricing on Credit Memo for Final Rebate Settlement

After the Final Settlement is executed, no changes can be made to the Rebate Agreement anymore. It can be reviewed in "Display" mode only.

4.3.8 Create Rebates with Scale Grouping

As mentioned before, the Scales entered for SAP Rebates were always limited because they applied only to the Scale of that particular Condition Record. Starting with SAP release ECC 6.0, Scale Groups have been introduced to allow the grouping of several Condition Records for Scale purposes.

Example: A Rebate Agreement will pay a customer a 2.5% rebate for the combined sales of three materials. Each of these material-specific Condition Records can have their individual Scale levels. Material "MAT-001" will pay the 2.5% if sales are over $10,000, material "MAT-002" will pay the 2.5% if sales are over $5,000 and material "MAT-003" will pay the 2.5% if sales are over $15,000.

In order to group the sales of these three materials together, enter a common Scale Group in the "Scale Group" column in Figure 4.3.8.1, in our example "COOK".

Create Cookie Rebates : Overview Group Rebate (BO01)

Sales Organization	3000	USA Philadelphia
Distribution Channel	10	Final customer sales
Division	00	Cross-division
Customer	40	MLI Demo Customer 09
Validity period	10/01/2008	
To	10/31/2008	

Material	Description	Amount	Unit	per	U.	Accruals	Rate	Scale Group
MAT-001	Chocolate Chip Cookies	2.500-	%			2.500-		COOK
MAT-002	Peanut Butter Cookies	2.500-	%			2.500-		COOK
MAT-003	Sugar Cookies	2.500-	%			2.500-		COOK

Figure 4.3.8.1: Rebate Condition Record with Scale Grouping

289

After creating an Invoice for these three items for a total value of $8,350, of which no line item individually reached the established sales goal, the sales volume in Figure 4.3.8.2 shows that only a Rebate for material "MAT-002" will be paid out, since the Scale level in that Condition Record was reached.

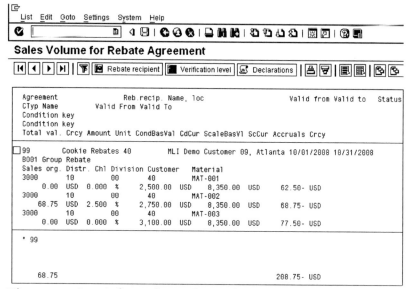

Figure 4.3.8.2: Sales Volume for Scale Group Records

Entering another Invoice for a net value of $4,087.50 now triggers the payment for material "MAT-001" as well, since the combined Invoice value now is $12,437.50, exceeding the Scale value of $10,000 for material "MAT-001" in Figure 4.3.8.3.

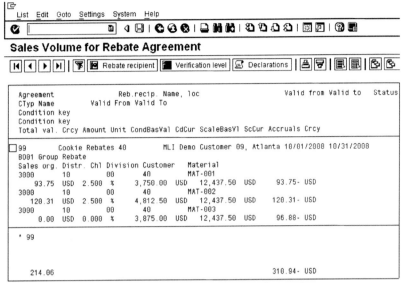

Figure 4.3.8.3: Sales Volume After Several Invoices

Additional Information Regarding Rebates

If a Rebate Agreement already has Invoices applied against it and you want to cancel the Rebate Agreement, select *Agreement->Delete* from the "Rebate Agreement Overview" screen. The Agreement will not be physically deleted but set to a status of "C" and will automatically create a Final Settlement credit memo request that will reverse all outstanding accruals. This can also be done if Partial Settlements were already processed for this Rebate Agreement.

If you mark a Payer customer to be relevant for Rebates after the Rebate Agreement was created, the billing index needs to be updated for the Invoice documents that were created since the start date of the Rebate Agreement. Run report "RV15B001" with transaction "SA38" or access it through IMG path *SPRO-> Sales and Distribution-> Billing-> Rebate Processing-> Create Billing Index.*

If changes are made to Rebate-relevant subtotals in the Pricing Procedure, these subtotals need to be recalculated with report "RV15B003" as accessed via IMG path *SPRO-> Sales and Distribution-> Billing-> Rebate Processing-> Recalculate Subtotals For Rebate Processing.*

A great OSS note to supplement the Rebate information in this book is 75778 (Consulting/troubleshooting for Rebate processing). It gives an overview over the most common problems in Rebate processing and explains in more detail why Rebates work in SAP the way they do. This OSS note is constantly updated with new information.

The "New Rebate Procedure"

By now, you might have noticed that several times throughout the Rebate chapters I mentioned the "New Rebate Procedure" that enhances the standard Rebate functionality. This new functionality is available since SAP R/3 release 4.5A. OSS Note 105681 explains in detail how this new procedure can be turned on. Basically, SIS structure "S136" will need to be activated for synchronous update. The following features will then be available: exclusion indicator in Rebate Access Sequences, field "Alternate Condition Type" and field "Alternate Condition Base Value" in Pricing Procedure.

Here are some examples of Rebate scenarios that cannot be handled by the standard SAP functionality:

- Apply a Rebate condition only if the Net Price of the item is under a certain amount.

- Calculate a Rebate for all materials in a material grouping (for example, by volume), *except* materials A and B. In this case, Rebate amounts would be over-accrued for all items within the volume Rebate group. Before the payment, run a report of sales for the two items that should be excluded, then deduct the applicable Rebate amount for these two items from your payment amount.

- Pay the customer the Rebate amount at the beginning of the year and track throughout the year if they met their sales goal. If they did not meet the goals, create a debit memo; otherwise, create additional settlements.

4.4   Manage Rebate Agreements Automatically

So far we discussed the manual creation and payments of Rebate Agreements, which is necessary if a decision process is required whether to pay a Rebate or not.

As mentioned several times before, Rebates can be automated if they do not require manipulation at the time of payout and are always created the same way. This chapter describes the automatic extension and payment of Rebate Agreements that do not require manual intervention.

Example: For our purposes in this book, we will offer to pay a customer $1,000 every month for the duration of a year. The customer does not have to buy anything, so it is not a performance-based Rebate tied to sales volume. We don't want to manually settle the Rebate every single month, so we will set up a base Rebate that will automatically extend itself and settle itself each month.

4.4.1   Configure Lump Sum Rebates

The fields "Arrangement Calendar" and "Settlement Periods" in the Rebate Agreement Type allow the attachment of calendars to the Rebate Agreement that define the days on which a Rebate Agreement should be extended or be paid out.

Before configuring or maintaining Rebate Agreements, an appropriate factory calendar needs to be created for our purposes. Use IMG menu path *SPRO-> General Settings-> Maintain Calendar*. Select the "Factory Calendar" option and click on the "Change" 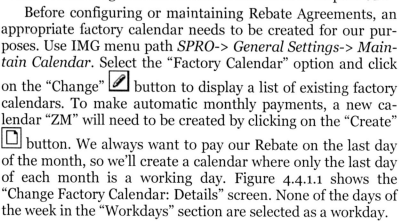 button to display a list of existing factory calendars. To make automatic monthly payments, a new calendar "ZM" will need to be created by clicking on the "Create" button. We always want to pay our Rebate on the last day of the month, so we'll create a calendar where only the last day of each month is a working day. Figure 4.4.1.1 shows the "Change Factory Calendar: Details" screen. None of the days of the week in the "Workdays" section are selected as a workday.

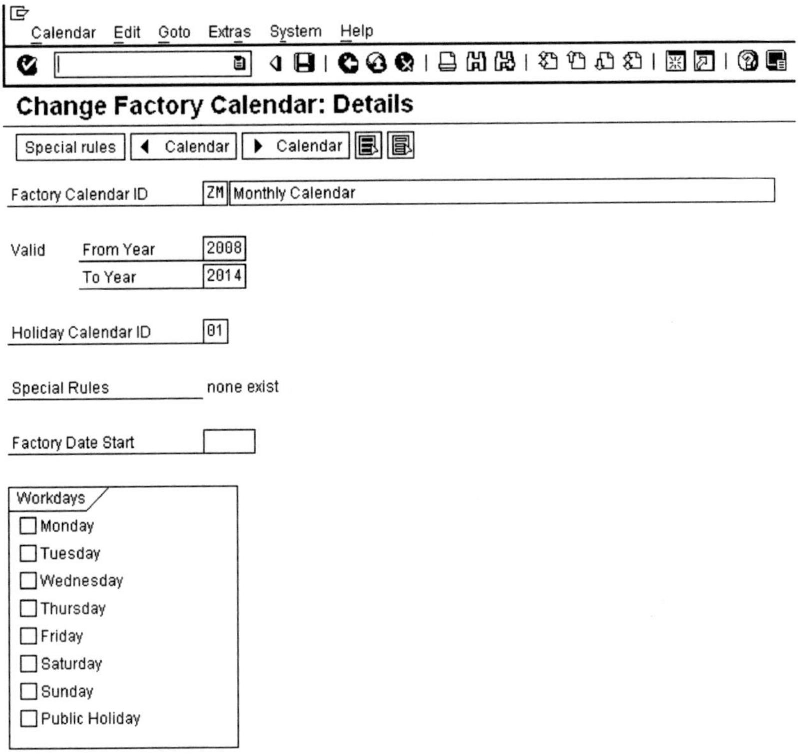

Calendar Edit Goto Extras System Help

Change Factory Calendar: Details

Special rules ◀ Calendar ▶ Calendar

Factory Calendar ID	ZM Monthly Calendar

Valid	From Year	2008
	To Year	2014

Holiday Calendar ID	01

Special Rules	none exist

Factory Date Start	

Workdays
- ☐ Monday
- ☐ Tuesday
- ☐ Wednesday
- ☐ Thursday
- ☐ Friday
- ☐ Saturday
- ☐ Sunday
- ☐ Public Holiday

Figure 4.4.1.1: Factory Calendar

For the payment schedule, only the payment dates will be defined as workdays. To do this, select the "Special Rules" Special rules button in Figure 4.4.1.1. Click the "Create" button on the "Change Factory Calendar: Special Rules" screen (see Figure 4.4.1.2) to enter a Valid-From and a Valid-To date, as well as a description. Make sure the field "Workday" is selected. Since only one day of the month should be a workday, the Valid-From and the Valid-To date is the same. Enter the last day of the calendar month (or fiscal month, if a company operates on a fiscal business year).

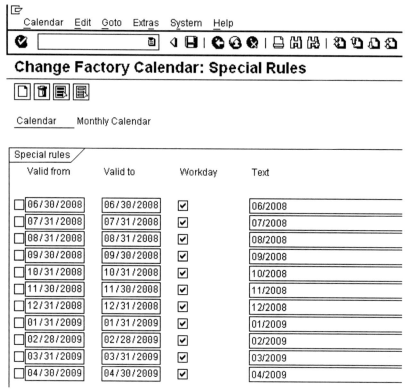

Figure 4.4.1.2: Define Workdays

We'll assume a calendar year as the business year for our example. Repeat the maintenance of workdays for each month of the years that are maintainable in the calendar configuration. This example explains the setup for a monthly calendar schedule. If Rebates should be automatically paid on a quarterly basis, a separate calendar needs to be created in which the special rules are defined as indicating that the last day of each calendar (or fiscal) quarter is a workday.

After defining all workdays, save the calendar by clicking "Save" 🖫. A message will indicate that calendar changes need to be manually transported, along with detailed instructions on how to do this.

To review the custom calendar that was just created, select the "Display Calendar" 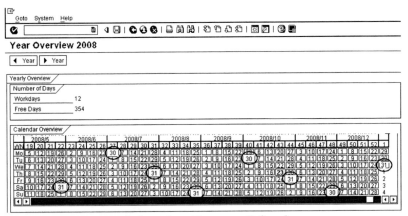 button from the "Change Factory Calendar: Overview" screen. From there, select the year to be reviewed. Figure 4.4.1.3 displays the workdays of that calendar. The workdays are circled and *not* highlighted.

Figure 4.4.1.3: Workdays in a Factory Calendar

Once all applicable calendars for our Rebate payment schedules are defined, it is time to configure the respective Rebate Agreement Types.

Figure 4.4.1.4 shows Rebate Agreement Type "ZLUM" which will allow the payment of lump sum payments to customers. Several settings in this Rebate Agreement Type are needed to accomplish this.

In the "Control Data" section, maintain the newly-created calendar in the "Arrangement Calendar" field. A list of calendars is available in the pull-down next to the field. The Arrangement Calendar is used when Rebate Agreements are automatically extended, meaning a new Rebate Agreement is created as a copy of an existing one, with a new Validity Period based on this Arrangement Calendar. The "Proposed Valid-To" date in the "Default values" section of the Rebate Agreement Type configuration should be set to "6" in order to set the Valid-To date based on the calendar attached to the Rebate Agreement Type.

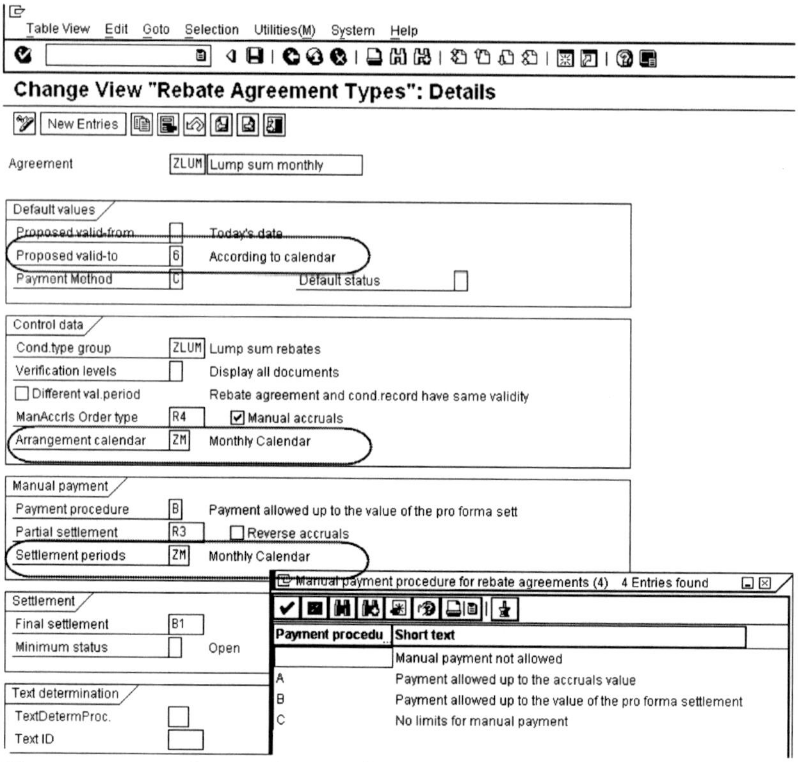

Figure 4.4.1.4: Lump Sum Rebate Agreement Type

This setting will always default the next calendar workday as the Valid-To date. For example, should a Rebate Agreement be entered on October 9, 2008, the default Valid-To date with a monthly calendar would be October 31st, 2008; or, with a quarterly calendar, December 31st, 2008. The settlement calendar maintained in field "Settlement periods" in the "Manual payment" section defines the days used by the automatic settlement program to determine when a Rebate should be settled. In our case, the calendar is the same. In the same configuration section, the payment procedure needs to be defined in field "Payment Procedure."

There are several things to be aware of when setting this value.

While setting up an auto-pay scenario, the initial goal would be to have a Rebate Agreement that would be valid for a year but would automatically pay out a lump sum each month to the same customer. To accomplish that, the Validity Periods in the Condition Records would be allowed to differ from those of the Rebate Agreement. Trying to maintain multiple monthly Condition Records for the same customer in the same Rebate Agreement would not be allowed by the system. An error message would be issued, reading: "The condition is being processed in the current session." This is a standard SAP feature that only allows one unique key combination within the time period of an agreement, such as a Rebate or Sales Deal.

Setting the value to "No limits for manual payment" for the payment procedure would allow the system to pay out the same lump sum amount as defined in the Rebate Agreement every period according to the settlement calendar. But when you try to execute the automatic settlement program to create a Partial Settlement, you would receive an error message stating that for auto-payments, the payment procedure must be either "B" or "C."

Since lump sum payments are not accrued, the payment procedure for lump sum Rebate Agreement Types needs to be "B" (Payment allowed up to the value of the pro forma settlement). This makes sense, as it prevents the system from paying settlements indefinitely, in case you forget to allow a Rebate Agreement to expire.

After all of the proper configuration settings are made, save the new Rebate Agreement Type.

Next, configure the Rebate Condition Type for the lump sum payment. Figure 4.4.1.5 displays the configuration of Condition Type "ZLUM". The Rebate Procedure setting in section "Rebates" is "A" for "Independent of sales volume," and the Accrual Correction Procedure in field "Provision Con" needs to be set to "A" for "never corrected." These settings establish that the Rebate can be paid out without having to accrue any amounts and, therefore, no accruals ever need to be corrected. Save the new Condition Type.

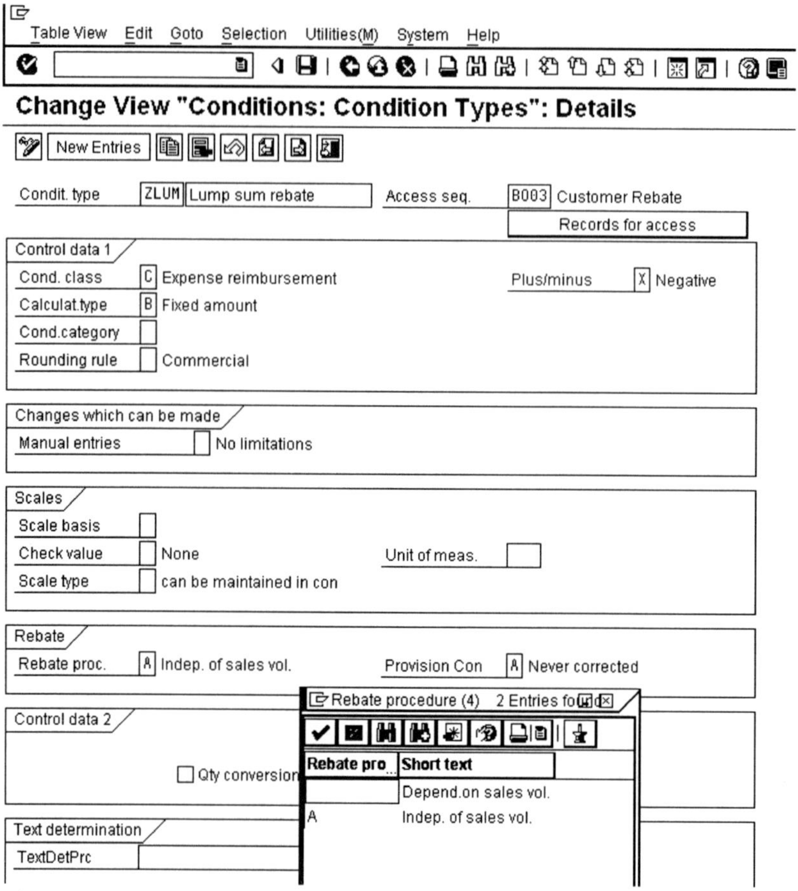

Table View   Edit   Goto   Selection   Utilities(M)   System   Help

Change View "Conditions: Condition Types": Details

New Entries

Condit. type   ZLUM Lump sum rebate   Access seq.   B003 Customer Rebate
                                                              Records for access

Control data 1
Cond. class   C Expense reimbursement   Plus/minus   X Negative
Calculat.type   B Fixed amount
Cond.category
Rounding rule   Commercial

Changes which can be made
Manual entries   No limitations

Scales
Scale basis
Check value   None   Unit of meas.
Scale type   can be maintained in con

Rebate
Rebate proc.   A Indep. of sales vol.   Provision Con   A Never corrected

Rebate procedure (4)   2 Entries fo

Control data 2

Rebate pro...	Short text
	Depend.on sales vol.
A	Indep. of sales vol.

Qty conversior

Text determination
TextDetPrc

Figure 4.4.1.5: Lump Sum Rebate Condition Type

4.4.2 Create a Lump Sum Rebate

Create the initial lump sum Rebate Agreement with transaction "VBO1". Figure 4.4.2.1 shows the Arrangement Calendar is already being proposed in the Rebate Agreement; the field is not changeable. The settlement calendar is also proposed in field "Settlement periods" based on the previous configuration step but can be changed if needed. For our example, leave the default calendar as is. As I mentioned before, the Valid-To date would default to 10/31/2008 based on the attached monthly Arrangement Calendar. However, for demonstration purposes, I manually changed that date to 12/31/2008 to show the system's reaction. The detailed message shown in Figure 4.4.2.1 warns that the Valid-To date is not the next possible workday according to the calendar attached to the Rebate Agreement. This is just a warning message in case the date is accidentally changed.

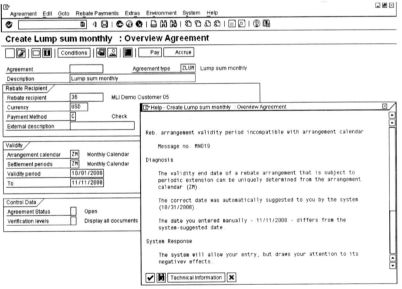

Figure 4.4.2.1: Incorrect Validity Date

A review of the condition maintenance for this Rebate, as per Figure 4.4.2.2, reveals that based on the Condition Type configuration setting in Figure 4.4.1.5, no accrual rates can be maintained for this Rebate condition. For our example, we are going to pay the customer $1,000 every month. This Rebate Agreement is just the baseline for the first month. All subsequent months will be created automatically in the next step.

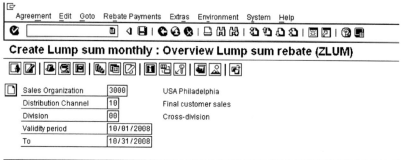

Figure 4.4.2.2: Lump Sum Condition Record

4.4.3 Extending Rebates

To automatically extend Rebate Agreements, execute transaction "VB(D" or use the SAP menu *Logistics-> Sales and Distribution-> Master Data-> Agreements-> Rebate arrangement-> Extend.* The resulting selection screen, shown in Figure 4.4.3.1, determines which Rebates are taken into account for the extensions. As you see from the selections in that figure, only Rebate Agreements with a monthly "ZM" arrangement calendar and which are valid up to the end of the month should be included. Select a specific Sales Area or leave these fields blank. In the "Rebate Settlement Status" section, define which Rebate statuses are to be taken into account for the extensions.

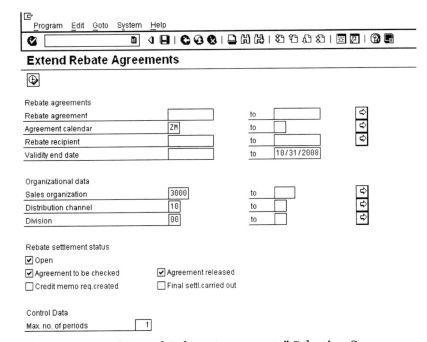

Figure 4.4.3.1: "Extend Rebate Agreements" Selection Screen

The "Max. no. of periods" field located at the bottom of Figure 4.4.3.1 is used to determine the number of periods in advance that the system reviews for extending the Rebate. If a job is scheduled on a monthly basis a few days before the month's end, this value can remain at "1" to do the following: Based on the Valid-To date of the last Rebate Agreement in a row of extended agreements (in our case it is 10/31/2008), the program checks if a Rebate Agreement for the next period (+"1") already exists. If there is none, it extends the Rebate. On the other hand, if a Rebate Agreement already exists for the next period (11/01/2008-11/30/2008), no new Rebate Agreement would be created and the message shown in Figure 4.4.3.2 would be displayed.

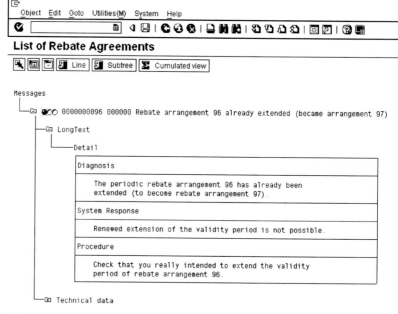

Figure 4.4.3.2: Repeated Extensions

The period in field "Max. no. of periods" would need to be "2" in order to extend the Rebate Agreement for two periods ahead.

After running this program successfully, the "List of Rebate Agreements" screen (Figure 4.4.3.3) displays all extended Rebate Agreements together, along with the extended Rebate Agreement number and corresponding Validity Period.

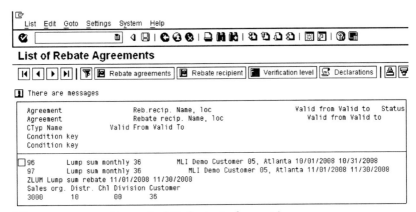

Figure 4.4.3.3: Extended Rebate Information

Agreement 96 with a Validity Period of 10/01/2008-10/31/2008 was extended to Rebate Agreement 97 with a Validity Period of 11/01/2008-11/30/2008. If this program were to run next month, it would extend Rebate Agreement 97 to a new Rebate Agreement with a Validity Period of 12/01/2008-12/31/2008, and so on.

To see the history of a Rebate Agreement and its extended documents, go into the original Rebate Agreement with transaction "VBO2" or "VBO3" and select menu *Extras->Extended agreements*, as illustrated in Figure 4.4.3.4.

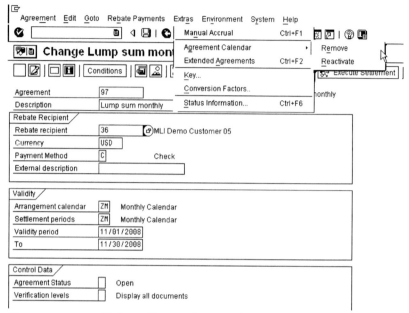

Figure 4.4.3.4: Rebate Extension Options

The screen shot in Figure 4.4.3.5 displays all the Rebate Agreements that were extended from the base Agreement created at the beginning. Each Rebate Agreement is displayed with its release status and its Validity Period.

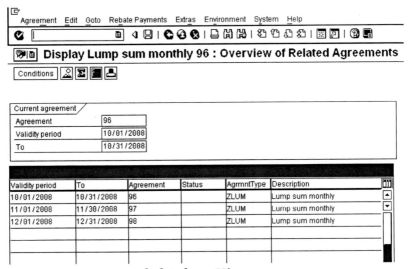

Figure 4.4.3.5: Extended Rebate History

Extending Rebates can be done indefinitely as long as calendars are maintained. But what happens if a certain Rebate Agreement should be expired? Earlier we discussed how the Agreement Calendar wasn't changeable or removable in the Rebate Agreement. The way to remove a Rebate Agreement from the extension schedule is to select *Extras-> Agreement calendar-> Remove* on the "Rebate Agreement Overview" screen, as shown in Figure 4.4.3.4. The result is that the field "Arrangement Calendar" is then not displayed or available for entry on the Rebate Agreement anymore. Therefore, this Rebate Agreement will not be extended the next time transaction "VB(D" is executed.

To schedule a recurring job, use program "RV15C005".

4.4.4 Automatic Payment of Lump Sum Rebates

Now that the automatic creation of Rebate Agreements is taken care of, let's focus on the automatic payments. SAP offers transaction "VB(7" or SAP menu *Logistics-> Sales and Distribution-> Billing-> Rebates-> Rebate Settlement* for this purpose. On the selection screen in Figure 4.4.4.1, select the "Validity End Date" to be the last day of the month. This will cover all monthly, quarterly or yearly payments.

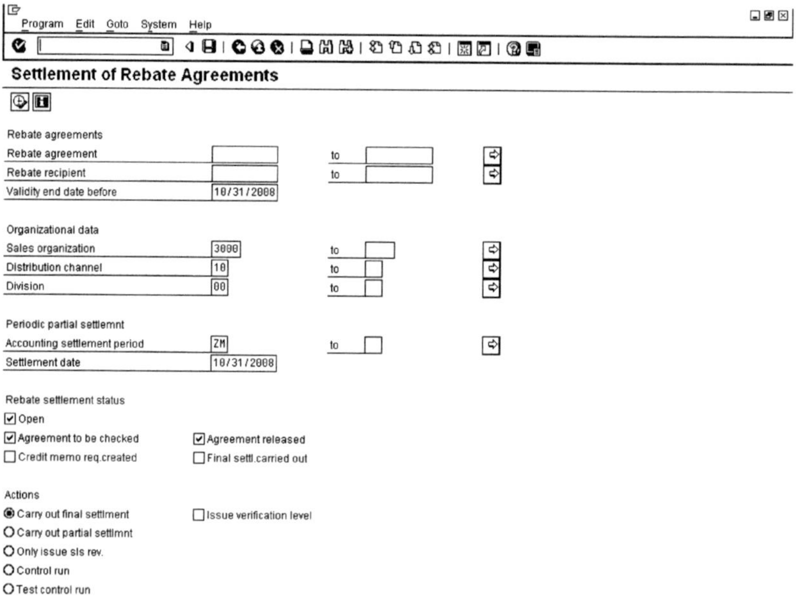

Figure 4.4.4.1: "Settlement of Rebate Agreement" Selection Screen

For the "Accounting Settlement Period" enter the settlement calendar (again in our case, "ZM") based on which schedule the payments should be made. The settlement date is also the last day of the month. This date is not as important for lump sum payments, since the total amount of the Rebate is paid out. But this date is important when dollars are accrued on a Rebate Agreement; for example, 5% off gross sales. In that instance, the system would only pay out as much as what was accrued up to that settlement date. In addition, in Partial Settlements, this settlement date becomes the service rendered date on the resulting credit memo request. In a Full Settlement, the credit memo request service rendered date is the creation date of the Sales Document.

Select the appropriate statuses. Since we are issuing a lump sum payment in the full amount of the Rebate, a Final Settlement will be carried out. After all selections are made, execute the program.

The screen shot in Figure 4.4.4.2 displays the amount of the payment that was made. Select the "Declarations" Declarations button in this screen to obtain the credit memo request number created as a result of the settlement.

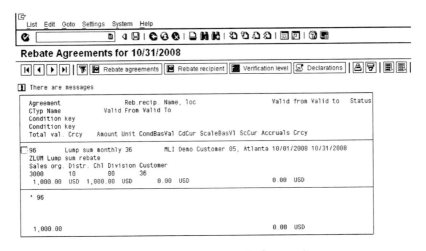

Figure 4.4.4.2: Lump Sum Payment Information

The condition screen of the Rebate credit memo request, as shown in Figure 4.4.4.3, confirms again that no accruals are reversed and the $1,000 was paid. Just remove the billing block from the credit memo request to create the Billing Document and send the payment to the customer.

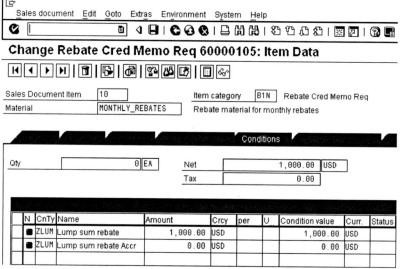

Figure 4.4.4.3: Pricing on Lump Sum Credit Memo

To schedule a recurring job, use program "RV15C001".

4.4.5 Comparison of Sales Deals and Promotions

As a conclusion of this chapter, I would like to point out the differences between Sales Deals and Rebates in Figure 4.4.5.1.

Sales Deal	Rebate
Off-Invoice allowances	Accruals (allowances are paid out later)
Offers different payment terms and value days to manipulate customer payments	No capability of different payment terms and value days
No retroactive application of Condition Records	Retroactive application of Condition Records
One Condition Type can only apply once on a document line item	One Condition Type can apply multiple times on a document line item
Very limited analysis capabilities	Verification level on Rebate Agreement and several standard reports allow tracking of applicable Invoice line items
Condition Records can be created outside a Sales Deal (and linked to one later)	Condition Records have to be created from within a Rebate Agreement
No need to maintain a settlement material in the Sales Deal agreement	Settlement material is mandatory in a Rebate Agreement

Figure 4.4.5.1: Comparison Between Sales Deal and Rebate

Chapter 5: Custom Modifications in Pricing

In Chapters 1-4 I tried to give you a thorough understanding of how pricing is set up and maintained, and how it applies in your business processes in the standard SAP system.

Several times throughout the book I referred to custom modifications that are possible in order to comply with your specific business requirements. These modifications are not covered with the standard SAP functionality, but I will explain them in this chapter.

5.1 Adding Fields to the Pricing Field Catalog

In Chapter 1.1 the pricing Field Catalog was explained. Most of the fields available in the standard customer, material and organizational tables are included in the standard Field Catalog. However, certain fields, like "Customer Group 1," are not included in the Field Catalog. To add it to the catalog, the field needs to first be added to the underlying pricing DDIC structures. For Header-related fields, the table is "KOMK" and for item-related fields, it is "KOMP".

SAP provides Include structures for each of these tables to which the new fields can be added. For the Header fields the Include table is "KOMKAZ"; for the line item fields it is "KOMPAZ".

For the example in this book, we will add the aforementioned "Customer Group 1" field to the pricing Header table.

Execute transaction "SE11", enter table "KOMKAZ" in field "Database Table" and click on the "Change" button. The DDIC table structure in Figure 5.1.1. is displayed.

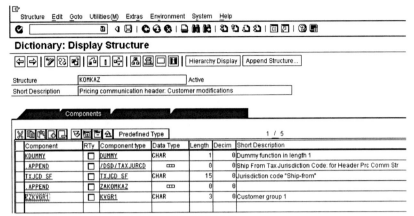

Figure 5.1.1: "KOMKAZ" DDIC Table

In the "Component" column you can see that the append structure "ZAKOMKAZ" allows the addition of new custom fields. Enter field "ZZKVGR1" in field "Component" and "KVGR1" in field "Component Type." Generate the DDIC structure.

Go back to the configuration of the Field Catalog and add the new field "ZZKVGR1" as instructed in Chapter 1.1

313

5.2   Populating Custom Fields in a Condition Table

Although we just added the new field to the pricing Field Catalog, pricing on Sales Documents or Invoices will not work for Condition Tables that include this new field unless the new field is populated properly.

Form "USEREXIT_PRICING_PREPARE_TKOMK" in program "MV45AFZZ" allows the population of this new field. Add the following code statement to populate the "Customer Group 1" field at Sales Order time:

```
KOMK-ZZKVGR1 = VBAK-KVGR1.
```

Form "USEREXIT_PRICING_PREPARE_TKOMP" in the same program is used to populate line item fields in DDIC table "TKOMP".

The same logic as for the Sales Order has to be executed at billing time, and the form to use for that is also "USE-REXIT_PRICING_PREPARE_TKOMP" in user exit program "RV60AFZZ". Since the "Customer Group 1" field is not available on the Invoice, the value has to be read from the customer master at billing time. The following code example accomplishes that:

```
SELECT SINGLE KVGR1
INTO TKOMP-ZZKVGR1
FROM KNVV
WHERE KUNNR EQ VBRK-KUNAG AND
      VKORG EQ VBRK-VKORG AND
      VTWEG EQ VBRK-VTWEG AND
      SPART EQ VBRK-SPART.
```

5.3   Creating a Pricing Requirement

Pricing requirements are used in Pricing Procedures (see Chapter 1.4) and Access Sequences (see Chapter 1.2) to control if a Condition Type applies on a document or not. Going to transaction "VOFM" via menu *Requirements->Pricing* displays all standard pricing requirements.

To create a new requirement, scroll to the end of the list and enter a new (not previously used) three-digit number between 600 and 999. If an existing requirement should be copied and modified, overwrite the existing requirement number with the new one. This will prompt the input of a development access key. Once this is done, the requirement can be modified.

As an example, restrict the use of a Condition Type if the price list type on the document is "90." If the existing requirement "002" was copied, the following code example would accomplish this requirement:

```
FORM KOBED_900.
  SY-SUBRC = 4.
  IF KOMP-KPOSN NE 0.
    CHECK: KOMP-PRSFD CA 'BX'.
    CHECK: KOMP-KZNEP = SPACE.
*** START OF CUSTOM CODE
    CHECK: KOMP-PLTYP NE '90'.
*** END OF CUSTOM CODE
  ENDIF.
  SY-SUBRC = 0.
ENDFORM.

* PRESTEP
FORM KOBEV_002.
  SY-SUBRC = 0.
ENDFORM.
```

In general, the return code ("SY-SUBRC") is originally set to "4" (unsuccessful). Only if the statements below are successful will the return code be set to "0" (successful) and the Condition Type can apply.

5.4 Creating an Alternate Condition Base Type

As discussed in Chapter 3.5, the Customer Expected Price logic is controlled by the Alternate Condition Base Type "8" or "9." In case the Customer Expected Price or value should be checked against a different value than the Net Price, copy Alternate Condition Base Type "8" and modify it accordingly. Execute transaction "VOFM" using menu *Formulas->Condition Value* and overwrite value "8" with a number between 600 and 999. Assuming that the Customer Expected Value should be compared against the value in subtotal "1," change the line:

DIFFERENCE = KOMP-NETWR – XKWERT.

to

DIFFERENCE = KOMP-NETWR – KZWI1.

5.5   Creating a Custom Scale Base Rule

Chapter 3.9 explained the use of Group Conditions and the potential issues of Scale Records causing pricing issues at billing time if a Sales Order is delivered differently than what was on the Sales Order.

The creation of a customer Scale Base Rule can avoid these issues.

First you will need to create a new custom field in tables "VBAK" and "KOMK" to store the Scale Basis (like total quantity, volume or weight) that is used to determine the Group Condition Scale. Then, this new field will be populated in user exit program "MV45AFZZ", using the following routine: "USEREXIT_PRICING_PREPARE_TKOMK". This has to be done because SAP does not store a total volume or weight in the Sales Order Header database table.

Although total volume and weight can be seen on the "Sales Order Header Shipping" screen, they are dynamically calculated and not stored at Sales Order save time.

To create the customer Scale Base Rule, go to menu *Formulas->Scale Base* in transaction "VOFM". Create a new Scale Base Formula in the customer reserved namespace (starting with number 500), similar to the pricing requirement in Chapter 5.3. To base the Scale value on the stored Scale base of the Sales Order, add the following code in the formula:

XKWERT = TKOMK-ZZWEIGHT

After saving the Scale Base Rule, attach it to the Condition Type in field "Scale Formula" (see Figure 1.3.6). The Scale Basis Formula will then use this stored field value at invoice time as the Scale Basis value, even if Scales are re-determined.

5.6 Modifying the Pricing Date in Sales Orders

In Chapter 3.1, the importance of the Pricing Date was explained in detail, as well as the standard default values that can be configured for the default of the Pricing Date.

If none of the standard options meets your business requirements, the available user exit to change the default is "FORM USEREXIT_MOVE_FIELD_TO_VBKD" in program "MV45AFZZ".

For example, if the purchase order date should be defaulted as the Pricing Date, add the following code statement:

VBKD-PRSDT = VBKD-BSTKD.

5.7 Modifying the Pricing Date in Billing Documents

As with the Pricing Date in the Sales Order, a user exit is available at billing time to change the Pricing Date to a different date than the standard SAP setting as explained in Chapter 3.10.

As an example, default the Actual Goods Issue Date from the Delivery as the Pricing Date on the Billing Document. Of course, this would only make sense if any kind of pricing is re-determined at billing time.

In "FORM USEREXIT_FILL_VBRK_VBRP" of program "RV60AFZC", add the following code statement:

```
VBRP-PRSDT = LIKP-WADAT_IST.
```

5.8 Creating a Default Pricing Rule

In Chapter 3.4 we discussed Pricing Rules. During the manual re-pricing of a document or document line item, a list of Pricing Rules is presented to the user. If the same Pricing Rule should always be used in these scenarios and you want to avoid an accidentally picked, incorrect Pricing Rule, form "USEREXIT_CHANGE_PRICING_RULE" in user exit program "LV69AFZZ" can be utilized. Assuming the Price Rule "C" should always be used, add the following source code in this user exit:

RV61A-KSTEU = "C".

5.9 Re-pricing Based on Changed Fields

In Chapter 3.4 we also discussed the automatic re-pricing of line items due to the change of particular fields. If you are interested in seeing which standard field changes trigger a re-pricing of a line item, please review standard SAP programs "FV45KFKD_VBKD_PRICING", form "VBKD_PRICING" for changes in fields of table "VBKD" as well as "FV45PFAP_VBAP_BEARBEITEN_ENDE", form routine "VBAP_BEARBEITEN_ENDE" for fields in table "VBAP".

To re-trigger pricing due to the change of fields that are not in these two programs, there are two user exits where additional code can be added.

First, in form "USEREXIT_NEW_PRICING_VBAP" in user exit "MV45AFZB", field changes of the Sales Order Header table "VBAK" and Sales Order line item table "VBAP" can be checked. An example would be the change of the plant on the line item. The following source code example describes the necessary changes:

```
IF VBAP-ROUTE NE *VBAP-ROUTE.
    NEW_PRICING = "H".   **Re-determines Freight
ENDIF.
```

Of course, any Pricing Rule can be defined here based on your business requirements.

Second, in form "USEREXIT_NEW_PRICING_VBKD" in user exit "MV45AFZB", field changes of the Sales Order Header table "VBAK" and Sales Order Business Data table "VBKD" can be checked. Here is another code example for the changing of the price list type:

```
IF VBKD-PLTYP NE *VBKD-PLTYP.
    NEW_PRICING = "B".   **Re-price everything
ENDIF.
```

5.10 Create Custom Report for Sales Deal Reporting

At the end of Chapter 4.2, I mentioned the limitation of Sales Deals not having a standard tool to identify the Sales Orders or Billing Documents on which a Sales Deal-related Condition Type applied. A custom report is needed, and this chapter gives guidance on how to approach this task.

If you (procedurally) made sure that only one Sales Deal will apply on a given Sales Order or Invoice line item, you can read the Sales Deal number ("VBAP/VBRP-KNUMA_AG") and/or Promotion number ("VBAP/VBRP-KNUMA_PI") directly from the respective Sales Order and Invoice line item tables.

Procedures are nice; however, there is no guarantee or configuration option to prevent multiple Sales Deals from applying on the same line item. If this were the case, the system would store the first Sales Deal number found for this line item in the Sales Order/Invoice table. This would make reporting results unreliable.

That's why we need to get into more detail to see where the unique Sales Deal number for a Condition Record is stored. To retrieve the applied Promotion or Sales Deal number, read the following tables:

- "VBAK-VBELN" with the Sales Order number to retrieve "VBAK-KNUMV" (document condition).
- "KONV-KNUMV" with "VBAK-KNUMV" to retrieve "KONV-KSCHL" (Condition Type) and "KONV-KNUMH" (Condition Record number).
- For each Condition Type, read "KONH-KNUMH" with "KONV-KNUMH" to get the Promotion number ("KONH-KNUMA_PI") and Sales Deal number ("KONH-KNUMA_AG").

With this approach, you will read a lot of data and unnecessarily use system resources without knowing if there is a Sales Deal in the Condition Record or not. That's why I would like to refer again to my previous comments in regard to defining unique Condition Types for Sales Deals. If you knew your

Sales Deal-specific Condition Records, you could look only for these Condition Types (in step two above), which would reduce your processing time significantly.

The best option, however, is to have all your document data flow to BW (or any other data warehouse system) and query your reports from there.

5.11 Creating a Custom Area Menu For Transaction "VK31"

Chapters 2.2.6 - 2.8 described the new "Pricing Maintenance" screens that are based on the Pricing Area Menu. In order to add custom Condition Types and Condition Tables to this Area Menu, the standard menu needs to be enhanced.

Execute transaction "SE43" to access the maintenance for Area Menus. The menu for pricing is called "COND_AV". Click on the "Display" button, shown in Figure 5.11.1, to see the standard Pricing Area Menu.

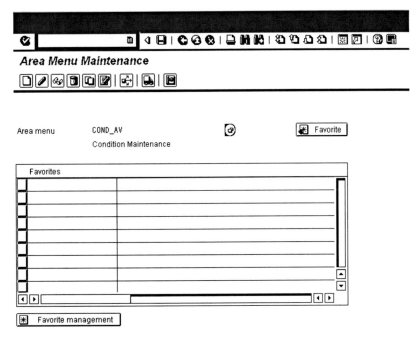

Figure 5.11.1: Area Menu Maintenance

As you can see, the menu in Figure 5.11.2 looks exactly like the one accessed with transactions "VK31" through "VK34".

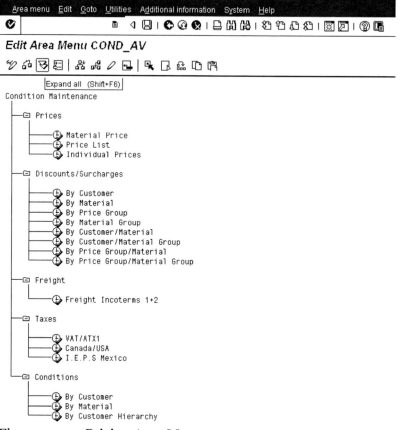

Figure 5.11.2: Pricing Area Menu

Go back to the initial screen (see Figure 5.11.1), click on the "Change" button and select "Extend" in the pop-up window (see Figure 5.11.3).

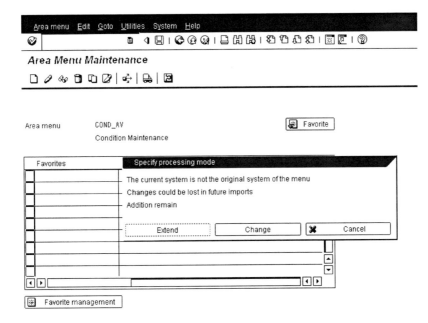

Figure 5.11.3: Adding Custom Objects to the Area Menu

Since we are adding a custom object, click on the "Create" button in Figure 5.11.4 to enter an enhancement ID and text. Remember to adhere to SAP naming conventions for custom objects. Save this ID.

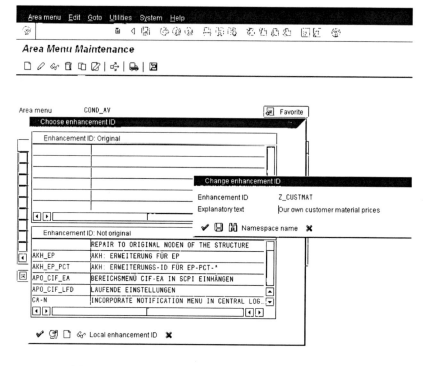

5.11.4: Adding a Custom Enhancement ID

Now double-click on the newly created enhancement ID ("Z_CUSTMAT"), as shown in Figure 5.11.5.

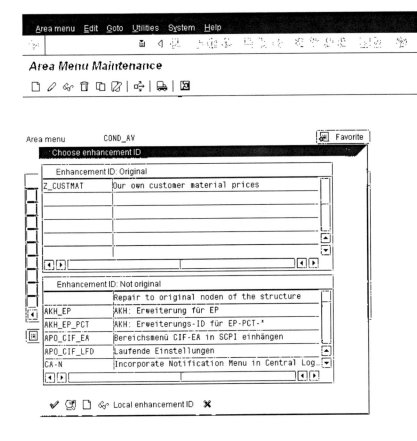

Figure 5.11.5: Available Enhancement IDs

The current Pricing Area Menu is displayed, to which we will add our custom node. Click on the "Add entry at the same level" button, shown in Figure 5.11.6.

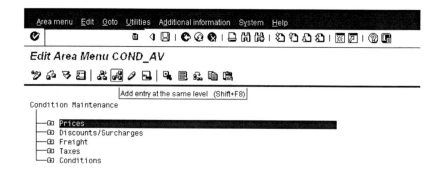

Figure 5.11.6: Standard Pricing Menu

In the "Edit Area Menu COND_AV" screen, shown in Figure 5.11.7, enter the name of the node being created. In our example, this is "Customer/Material Specific Prices." Click the check mark.

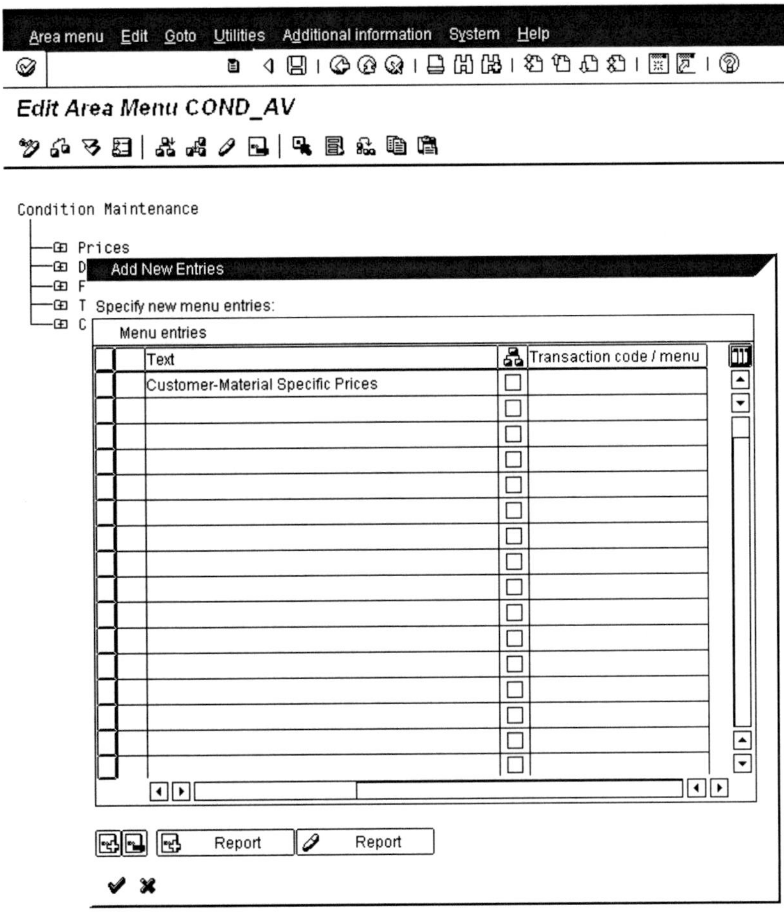

Figure 5.11.7: Adding a Node to the Pricing Menu

Our new node is now part of the Standard Pricing Menu and shows our enhancement ID next to it. You have the ability to change the position of the node if you wish. Now place your cursor on the newly created node, and click on the "Add entry as sub-node" button to attach our custom Pricing Report, created in Chapter 2.5, to the menu (see Figure 5.11.8).

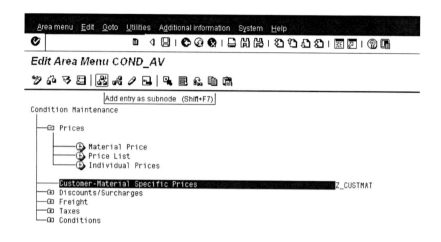

Figure 5.11.8: New Node in the Pricing Menu

Click on the "Add report" button shown in Figure 5.11.7. Enter the name of the Pricing Report that was created before. To get the full name of the report, execute the Pricing Report with SAP menu *Logistics-> Sales and Distribution-> Master Data-> Conditions-> List-> Pricing Report*. On the selection screen, select *System->Status* and copy the report name to the "Report" field, shown in Figure 5.11.9.

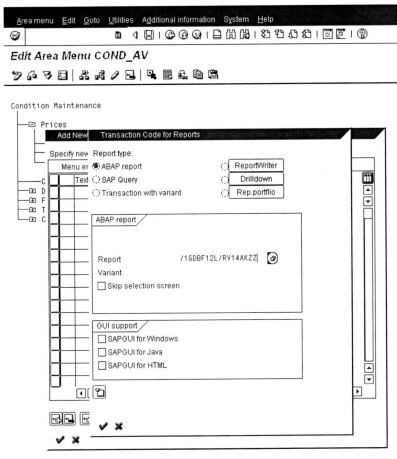

Figure 5.11.9: Adding a Report to a Menu Node

Our custom Pricing Report is now attached to our newly created node, as can be seen in Figure 5.11.10. Save all your changes. This concludes the setup to maintain our custom Condition Table via transactions "VK31" through "VK34".

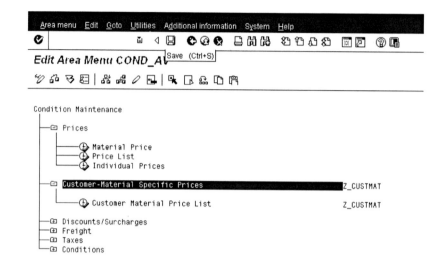

Figure 5.11.10: Pricing Report in the Pricing Menu

To see how these changes affected the pricing maintenance, execute transaction "VK32" and you'll discover that the Standard Pricing Menu now displays a node for customer/material specific prices (see Figure 5.11.12).

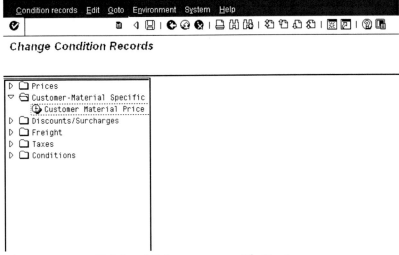

Figure 5.11.11: Pricing Maintenance with Custom
Key Combination

APPENDIX A: Pricing Data Dictionary Tables

KONH	Condition Record Header
KONP	Condition Record Item
KONH	Condition Record Scale information
KONM	Quantity Scale
KNOW	Value Scale
Axxx	Pricing Condition Table
	(xxx = Condition Table number)
KOTNxxx	Free Goods Condition Table
	(xxx = Condition Table number)
KOTExxx	Rebates Condition Table
	(xxx = Condition Table number)

APPENDIX B: Transaction Codes

Pricing Configuration

VOK0	Pricing Customization Menu
OV24	Pricing Field Catalogue
V/03	Create Condition Table
V/04	Change Condition Table
V/05	Display Condition Table
V/06	Maintain Condition Types
V/07	Maintain Access Sequences
V/08	Maintain Pricing Procedures
OVKP	Maintain Customer Pricing Procedure Indicator
OVKI	Maintain Document Pricing Procedure Indicator
OVKJ	Assign Document Pricing Procedure Indicator to Sales Document
OVTP	Assign Document Pricing Procedure Indicator to Billing Document
OVKK	Maintain Pricing Procedure Determination
OV31	Maintain Pricing Exclusion Group
OV32	Assign Condition Types to Exclusion Group
VOK8	Assign Exclusion Procedure to Pricing Procedure
VOFM	Configuration Menu for Requirements and Formulas
OVU0	Optimize Condition Access
OV23	Exclusion Indicator
VB(B	Copy Conditions – Copying Rules
VB(C	Copy Conditions – Copying Rules for Condition Types

Pricing Master Record Maintenance

VK11	Create Pricing Condition Records Using Condition Type
VK12	Change Pricing Condition Records Using Condition Type
VK13	Display Pricing Condition Records Using Condition Type

VK14	Create Pricing Condition Records with Reference Using Condition Type
VK31	Create Pricing Condition Records
VK32	Change Pricing Condition Records
VK33	Display Pricing Condition Records
VK34	Create Pricing Condition Records with Reference

Free Goods Configuration

V/N1	Free Goods Access Sequence
V/N2	Create Free Goods Condition Table
V/N3	Display Freed Goods Access Sequence
V/N4	Free Goods Condition Types
V/N5	Free Goods Pricing Procedure
V/N6	Free Goods Pricing Procedure Determination

Free Goods Master Data

VBN1	Create Free Goods Records
VBN2	Change Free Goods Records
VBN3	Display Free Goods Records

Promotions and Sales Deals

VB(A	Maintain Promotion Types
VB31	Create Promotion
VB32	Change Promotion
VB33	Display Promotion
VB35	List Promotions

VB(9	Maintain Sales Deal Types
VB21	Create Sales Deal
VB22	Change Sales Deal
VB23	Display Sales Deal
VB25	List Sales Deals

VB(3	Condition Type Groups (for Sales Deals and Rebates)
VB(4	Assign Condition Types/Table to Condition Type Group (for Sales Deals and Rebates)
VB(5	Allocation of Condition Type Group to Agreement (for Sales Deals and Rebates)
VB(6	Maintain Volume Rebate Group (for material master)

Rebates

VB(2	Rebate Agreement Types
VB(7	Settle Rebates
VB(8	List Rebates
VB(D	Extend Rebates
VBO1	Create Rebate Agreements
VBO2	Change Rebate Agreements
VBO3	Display Rebate Agreements
V/LD	Execute Pricing Report
V_NL	Net Price List

Other SD-related Transaction Codes

VA01	Create Sales Order
VA02	Change Sales Order
VA03	Display Sales Order
VA05	List Sales Orders
VF01	Create Billing Document
VF02	Change Billing Document
VF03	Display Billing Document
V.01	Incomplete Pricing Report
V.25	Customer Expected Price Report

About the Author Matthias Liebich and MLI Solutions, LLC

Matthias sincerely hopes you enjoyed the *Ultimate SAP Pricing Guide* and found it beneficial to your work. He strongly encourages you to try out several of the business scenarios described in the book, change different configuration settings and observe these effects on your pricing calculations.

If you have difficulties with any of the concepts explained in this book, or you need help with your specific pricing design, Matthias can provide consulting services through his company MLI Solutions to assist your needs. Reviewing your current pricing design to provide suggestions for improvements or complete re-designs of your pricing procedures are just a few of the things he could do for you.

Matthias has led projects where system performance was improved significantly by making a few simple changes in the pricing configuration. Other accomplishments included the reduction of pricing master data maintenance by over 50%, and the elimination of over 90% of pricing Condition Records while maintaining the same business information.

In addition to providing consulting services for pricing, MLI Solutions covers all SAP SD areas, with extensive experience in the consumer products and beverage industry.
Matthias has over 18 years of SAP SD consulting experience, acquired during numerous full life cycle implementations in the US and Germany, as well as hands-on experience in new implementations, upgrades, mergers, divestitures and bolt-on integrations. This gives him the necessary background to deliver results on time and on budget without sacrificing any requested functionality.

Matthias is known for his common sense approach to difficult subject matters, which is admired and respected by clients and peers alike. He also played a crucial role in the world's first implementation of load optimization software on the Sales Order level, saving millions in transportation costs.

A regular contributor of SAP SD related articles to the ERPtips journal, one of the leading SAP journals in the world, got him started writing about SAP-related content.

Matthias also has experience in testifying as an expert witness in lawsuits regarding the capabilities of SAP standard functionality.

In addition to consulting services, he also offers training in the SD area.

Readers' Feedback

Matthias would appreciate any feedback about the book. Please feel free to contact him at mliebich@mli-solutions.com or visit www.mli-solutions.com.

About the Editor Jon Reed and the Publisher JonERP.com

Jon Reed is an independent SAP analyst and SAP Mentor who blogs, Tweets, and podcasts on SAP market trends. Jon has been publishing SAP industry analysis for more than 15 years. As the driving force behind JonERP.com, Jon continues to issue frequent commentary on the SAP skills marketplace. Over the last 15 years, Jon has served as the editor on numerous SAP book projects. He was the founding editor of the ERPtips Journal in 2002, where he and Matthias first began their collaborations.

The Ultimate SAP Pricing Guide is the second JonERP.com SAP book title. The first, *The SAP Consultant Handbook*, has been the go-to SAP career guide since the late 1990s.

On JonERP.com, readers can find more information on the *Ultimate SAP Pricing Guide* and pose questions to Jon regarding SAP Pricing skills trends. Jon sees book publishing as a fluid event that should lead to additional author conversation and interaction, so he looks forward to hearing from readers on JonERP.com and facilitating those conversations.

The *Ultimate Pricing Guide* will be available in paperback, Amazon Kindle, and eBook editions. The eBook will be available through a number of SAP affiliate sites, including JonERP.com and MLI-Solutions.com, author Matthias Liebich's web site.

LaVergne, TN USA
21 March 2010
176664LV00006B/18/P